to be a pilgrim

a memoir of
ERNEST A. PAYNE

to be a pilgrim

a memoir of
ERNEST A. PAYNE

W. M. S. West

LUTTERWORTH PRESS
Guildford, Surrey

First published 1983

ISBN 0 7188 2559 4
Copyright © W. M. S. West

Printed in Great Britain by
Butler & Tanner Ltd, Frome and London

There's no discouragement
Shall make him once relent
His first avowed intent
   To be a pilgrim.

   John Bunyan, 1628-88

So shall God's Will on earth be done
New lamps be lit, new tasks begun,
And the whole Church at last be One.
   Alleluia.

   George K. A. Bell, 1883-1958

Contents

Preface

This book does not pretend to be a critical biography of Ernest
Payne. Rather is it a memoir which seeks to record the events
of his life from his childhood days in East London to his final
retirement years in Oxford. It attempts to trace what happened
to him through 77 very crowded years. Perhaps it may best be
likened to a series of transparencies which recall for his contemporaries and illustrate for posterity, some at least, of the
achievements of his life and of the adventures of his journey.

The publication of this book has been made possible through
the generous support of his friends, Horace Gale, Ernest Tim-
son and Edward Vinson, to whom, not only the author, but all
who were influenced by the life of this remarkable Christian
pilgrim will be always grateful.

Anyone setting out to write about Ernest Payne is faced with
an embarrassment of material. He has left a journal, written in
retirement, which runs to nearly 200,000 words. This is based
upon his own records and 27 travel diaries of his more significant overseas journeys. There is a collection of letters from his
friend John Barrett, written during their friendship of more
than 50 years. All this is apart from the Baptist Union material
of Reports and Minutes, and the record of events in the *Baptist
Times*. The danger of so much material is that the detail can so
easily obscure the man. Whilst I have always been aware of
this danger, I cannot claim to have wholly avoided it.

With all this material and with a life so crammed with
incident, there has had to be selection. I have been greatly
helped by the Rev. Alec Gilmore of Lutterworth Press and by
my colleague, the Rev. Harry Mowvley, but the responsibility
for the selection is mine alone. I express my appreciation for
the help given to me by Ernest Payne's family, particularly his

wife, Freda, and also by his other executors, Gordon Holmes and Colin Saunders. They all answered my questions patiently and then generously left me to it. To the secretaries at Bristol Baptist College, Eunicé Welch and Pearl Woolnough, I owe an immense debt of gratitude. With remarkable fortitude and infinite patience, they typed and re-typed the various recensions through which the manuscript passed. Without their help the book would not have seen the light of day.

For myself, this book is some attempt to repay the debt I owe to Ernest Payne, who gave me freely of his friendship and introduced me to the riches of theological thought, the excitement of ecumenical encounter and above all taught me the importance of trying to become a scholar evangelist for Christ.

W.M.S. West
Bristol, 1983

Prologue

On a murky Wednesday in February 1980 at the unpropitious hour of six o'clock in the evening, an ecumenical congregation of many hundreds gathered in Westminster Abbey. All had come to pay tribute to the memory of a somewhat shy Baptist Minister, Ernest Alexander Payne, who had died on 14th January. Within hours of the announcement of his death, the Dean of Westminster had asked whether a Service of Thanksgiving for Ernest Payne's life could be held in the Abbey. Such a request was tribute enough in itself. The tribute was startlingly enhanced by the congregation that came together. It was remarkable, not only for its numbers, but also for its composition. All Christian traditions were present. There were so many clergy in attendance that overflow arrangements had to be made for those who wished to robe and process. An archbishop and bishops mingled with Baptist ministers and other Free Churchmen. University lecturers sat in the congregation alongside office workers. The Secretary of the World Council of Churches travelled from Geneva to take part, together with the Secretary of the British Council of Churches; Methodist, United Reformed and Baptist representatives as well as the Dean of Westminster shared in the act of thanksgiving. As the service ended, the bells of the great Abbey were rung in triumphant peal.

This book is an attempt to give some indication as to why so many people, from so many churches, and from so many walks of life came to Westminster Abbey on that February evening to honour the memory of Ernest Alexander Payne...

1

Early Days

Family Background

Ernest Payne was a Londoner and he was glad of it; he had a family tree whose roots were nourished by a variety of soils and he was strengthened by it; he came of strong nonconformist stock and he was proud of it; he was born into a generous-hearted Baptist family and he never ceased to thank God for it.

He was born in 1902 at Clapton, a mile or two east of London's centre. His father's family, the Paynes, originated in Norfolk. His mother's family, the Griffiths, combined Welsh and Hampshire origins. Both families belonged to the Downs Baptist Chapel in Clapton. The Paynes had been members of the fellowship since its foundation in 1869; the Griffiths had joined later, in 1886, on their move to London from Southampton. His grandfather, William Payne, a textile merchant, was treasurer and senior deacon; his grandfather, Philip Griffiths, had retired from the Baptist Ministry – he had been trained in Stepney College long before – and had become a loyal member of the Downs. His parents, Alexander Payne and Catherine Griffiths, first met in the context of that fellowship. To understand Ernest Payne requires, first, a brief introduction to those parents.

His father, Alexander Payne, was born in London in 1862 just one year after the family had moved from Norfolk. He was the eldest of twelve children. He qualified as an accountant and entered practice, in partnership with his brother, Henry, with offices at Finsbury Pavement in the City. Alexander described himself as 'a Quaker by conviction' and never became formally a member of the Downs Chapel. That did not prevent him from singing in the choir, acting as superintendent of the

1

Sunday School, and, in an emergency, conducting a service. He was radical in politics also. The memory of his father's conviction and character disposed Ernest Payne more to the left in politics than to the right, and made him sympathetic of the more radical forms of religious dissent and suspicious of too great an emphasis on creeds and sacraments.

His mother, Catherine Griffiths, was born at Biggleswade in 1863 during her father's 22 year ministry there. She was a convinced Baptist, nurtured in loyalty to local Baptist Church life, but never a narrow denominationalist. Her home was hospitable. She shared her husband's political views, and was possessed of a remarkable strength upon which Ernest Payne came to rely.

After a long courtship, Alexander Payne and Catherine Griffiths were married in March 1900 at the Downs Chapel by the minister, James Mursell. Alexander was 37, Catherine a year younger. Their first home was 38 Ickburgh Road. At the turn of the century this was a quiet, pleasant road in a neighbourhood known as *Upper* Clapton. The local Great Eastern Railway station to Liverpool Street was conveniently situated at one end of it. The house still stands today, though the two small trees, which, in Ernest Payne's memory, graced the front garden, have now grown so large that they almost obscure the whole of the front of the house. At the turn of the century Upper Clapton was emphatically a middle class neighbourhood. It stood geographically, and in other ways as well, between the poverty of South Hackney and Bethnal Green and the relative affluence of Stamford Hill. The residents in Ickburgh Road were proud to be in *Upper* Clapton.

It was the very end of the Victorian Age. Open-topped, horse-drawn buses made their way up and down the High Road in Clapton. The sweep and the knife grinder were still familiar figures, as well as the muffin man. The baker's boy with a tray of loaves and buns on his head plied his trade. The lamp lighters came round on a winter's night at dusk, carrying the pole with which the lamps were lit.

This, then, was the context into which on 19th February 1902, Alexander and Catherine Payne's first child, a boy, Ernest Alexander Payne, was born. By that time, Alexander and Catherine had been joined in their home by Grandfather Philip Griffiths, who was then 78 years old and was to live with the family until his death at the age of 91 in 1913. He lived from the reign of George IV through the whole of the Victorian Era, the Edwardian Era, and to the beginning of the reign of George V. The young Ernest was fascinated by this grand old gentleman who always remained, for him, 'Grandpa Griffiths'. He wrote of him in the *Baptist Times* in February 1974, and there are also two delightfully irrelevant childhood memories of him. He recalls his grandfather's skill at swatting flies, and his generosity at dispensing acid drops! More importantly, Ernest Payne later discovered, with great pleasure, that Grandpa Griffiths had been entrusted with the taking of the minutes of more than one important meeting of the Baptist Union, and that he was respected as a stedfast and loyal supporter of the denomination.

Ernest Payne's other grandfather, William Payne, died when his grandson was six years old, but the childhood recollections of him remained vivid and were related particularly to the Downs Chapel. William sat at the table beneath the pulpit conducting the early part of the service. After the notices for the week had been given and the offering taken, William Payne would walk slowly down the aisle to join his large family in the back pew. He was regarded as a 'mighty man in Israel'. But his religious interests were not limited to the local church. In 1874, he had become a personal member of the Baptist Union and an elected member of the committee of the Baptist Missionary Society. In 1879, he became a manager of the Baptist Building Fund and was its treasurer from 1898 until his death in 1908. He was a subscriber to Regent's Park College before being elected, in 1894, a member of the committee. His interests were not limited to the Baptist denomination. His place of business was near the Bow Church in Cheapside and he became a well known and generous supporter of that church also.

These then are the forebears of Ernest Payne. It is evident that both sides of the family showed a deep, and long, tradition involved in Baptist Church life. Both grandfathers had had close connections with Regent's Park College and both men had goodwill towards Christians beyond the Baptist denomination.

3

Childhood and schooling

In 1903, a daughter, Margaret, was born to Catherine Payne, and, in 1905, another boy, Philip. All the evidence suggests that the childhood memories of Ickburgh Road were pleasant. Grandpa Griffiths was an accepted part of the household and William Payne a regular vistor. It was a good middle-class, nonconformist home of that era – sensibly strict in discipline, without being oppressive, quietly pious in family worship without being over religious, temperate in habit without being prohibitive. Alexander Payne travelled to his accountant's office for a long working day. He had built up a good practice and was a well-liked Christian business man, honoured by his business associates and respected by his children. At home, Catherine Payne created a deep bond of affection with all her children. Each of them was to make demands upon her in different ways, but she supported, encouraged and cared for them. She gave of her time and of her love unstintingly. The affectionate atmosphere and the secure stability of the home in those earliest years remained for Ernest Payne an abiding memory.

A further child, Catherine, was born in August 1908, but sadly died the same day. At this time also Grandpa Griffiths was growing weaker and more demanding of care. The result of this domestic situation, together probably with the fact that there was a desire to help two of the daughters of the then secretary of the Downs Chapel (the Misses Cox, who ran a small Preparatory Boarding School) meant that Ernest Payne was sent, in May 1909, to their school at St John's, Walmer in Kent. He had already been at school briefly at a kindergarten at Kenninghall Road, Clapton, run by a Miss Baker, but now he was faced with boarding school life. The advertisement for St John's, Walmer, described it as 'a high class Preparatory School for boys'. It went on to say, 'the Misses Cox receive a limited number of boys from four to fourteen, to prepare for the Public Schools. There is no over pressure, but the boys are thoroughly grounded and taught on modern methods, all the usual subjects, Mathematics, French, German, Latin and Educational Handwork. St John's is within five minutes walk of the sea. The water supply is good, the sanitary arrangements of the house are certified by a competent authority. A careful

4

attention is given to drilling, physical development and sports.'
The pupils are further promised 'home comforts' and are encouraged to take an interest in nature, and to think for themselves about all that they see.

The school was in a private house, and the number of boys just under 20. The drill that was promised took place in the small garden behind the house, and there was some informal attempt to play cricket and football in a field opposite. More startling was the way in which the young boys were taught to swim. In the summer they were taken out in a rowing boat in which they undressed. A piece of canvas was attached by a length of rope to a pole and was fastened around the chest of the unfortunate bathers. The boatman then ordered the boys to jump into the water. The sea was often rough as well as cold. However, the method worked for Ernest Payne who became a competent swimmer! To somebody as young and as sensitive as he was, Walmer was an ordeal. He missed his home desperately. He was unhappy a good deal of the time and spent many hours wondering whether, and if so, how, he could run away. But in spite of the difficulties of being away from home so young, he was given a good grounding in reading, writing and arithmetic. His experience of boarding school life ended in July 1911.

It was clear that it was never intended by his family that he should be prepared for Public School life, and in the autumn of 1911, Ernest Payne was sent to the Hackney Down Secondary School. It was a school founded by the Grocers Company in 1876 and taken over by the London County Council in 1905 following the Balfour Education Act. At a preliminary interview, Ernest Payne clearly failed to do himself justice, probably through shyness, and was placed in Form I. His parents protested, and within a few days he was catapulted up to Form 3B. He spent eight years at Hackney Secondary School. It would not be true to say that for him the school days were the happiest days of his life. Probably the reverse is true. He did not find either the boys or the masters very congenial. He was discovering already that, through what seems to have been an inherent shyness, particularly in a community like a school, he was all too often alone and lonely.

It had been the intention of Alexander Payne that when his son had been five years at the Grocers, he should be moved on to the City of London School where Alexander himself had been as a boy. Unfortunately, Ernest Payne became ill with German measles whilst sitting the entrance exam for the City of London School, but he had in any case failed to impress Dr Chilton, the headmaster, in an interview. Dr Chilton proved a somewhat severe person. He threw the confidence of Ernest Payne by sharply correcting his pronunciation of 'Tuesday'! The failure to gain entrance to the school, however, may not have been entirely a bad thing for the journey to the City of London School near Blackfriars Bridge would have become increasingly difficult in war-time, and in any case during the same years, the financial situation of Alexander Payne became difficult.

The First World War covered four years of his stay at the Grocers. It was a period of stringency and difficulty. Younger masters volunteered or were called up for active service. Mistresses took their places. The London County Council decreed that no form prizes should be given and in the last eighteen months of the war particularly, the growing casualty list contained the names of those who but a short while before had been monitors and prefects.

The boys at school in the latter part of the war were all put into a school battalion. This meant that they were regularly drilled with rifles of wood, either in the playground in front of the school, or on Hackney Downs. Ernest Payne showed little pleasure in this and initially little prowess at sport. The school playing field was in Lower Edmonton, which is a considerable distance away from Hackney Downs. The boys had to make the journey by train to Edmonton almost every week, and the only really cheerful memory of the required sporting activities that remained with young Ernest was that of being able to buy some sweets somewhat delightfully called 'callibonkers' from the tuckshop on the school field! On the annual sports day in the summer, the boys were paraded in the school battalion, commanded by the senior master, who was a survivor from the days of the Grocers Company control of the school, and who drilled the battalion dressed always in frock coat and top hat.

If he showed little prowess on the sports field, either at games or in the school battalion with the dummy rifle of wood, Ernest Payne certainly showed considerable promise in the classroom. He progressed up the school satisfactorily and would have won prizes had there been any. He remained grateful for the benefits of the education in those days. Not least of these was the requirement to learn English Grammar and the analysis of sentences to bring home proper sentence construction. The memory passages learnt at school remained with him throughout his life. He often echoed a quotation from Addison which he had to learn, and which for him the touch of life turned to truth: 'But for my own part, though I am always serious, I do not know what it is to be melancholy and can therefore take a view of nature in her deep and solemn scenes with the same joy as in her most gay and delightful ones.'

By February 1918 he was a monitor and second to the head boy. He was preparing for the London External Intermediate Arts Examination under the direction of one of the war-time mistresses, Miss Barbara Lowe. She was a fascinating and rather frightening figure, but clearly stimulated the class to which she was assigned, for they all achieved extremely well in the examination. When, early in 1919, the Senior History Master, Mr Trenchard, returned from active service in the war, he was immediately anxious, when he saw Ernest Payne's work, that he should sit for a scholarship to Cambridge. But this could not be. Even if he had been successful it is unlikely that the family resources would have been sufficient to support him at Cambridge. So the idea of Cambridge was quickly dropped and he began to look towards London University. Before we follow him on his university career, we must catch up upon events within his home and church during his schooldays.

In 1906 the family had moved from Ickburgh Road to nearby Thistlewaite Road and this remained the family home until 1924. Politically the first decade of the 20th century was one of Liberal dominance. Although there were two general elections in 1910, the Liberals managed to hang on to power. This was a cause of great satisfaction to the Payne household. The Liberal Candidate for Central Hackney was Sir Albert Spicer, who was a prominent Congregationalist and Alexander Payne was one of his leading supporters. Sir Albert visited the home at Thistlewaite Road more than once and the young Ernest found himself in the midst of all the political excitement of elections. This early involvement stimulated a keen political interest which remained throughout his life.

7

The Downs, Clapton

But if things were politically satisfactory in the Thistlewaite Road household, the situation in the Downs Chapel was not. In 1903, F. G. Benskin had succeeded James Mursell. Benskin's ministry at the Downs was extremely effective and drew to the chapel the largest congregations that it had ever known or that it was ever to know. Although the chapel seated more than 1,000 people, for the special Sunday evening popular services held each month, chairs had to be put in the aisles. Benskin was small in stature, but large in heart and voice and ability. But in 1908 he left the Downs Chapel for Broadmead, Bristol. Whether he left with a measure of relief in view of what happened later is difficult to tell. Certainly Benskin subsequently told Ernest Payne that he would not have been able to cope with the rest of the diaconate had it not been for William Payne. Perhaps it is not without significance, therefore, that Benskin left for Bristol a few months after William Payne died.

The church then entered upon a very sad period in its history. There was a long interregnum and the members found it difficult to agree upon whom to invite as the next minister. There were those attending the chapel who had been drawn into the Downs under the ministry and preaching of the first minister, Dr Tymms, who had served from 1869–1891, when he became principal of Rawdon College. Others had joined the church in the more recent years and felt that there was need for a change. Eventually however, in 1910, an invitation was sent to the minister of Westgate, Bradford, the Rev. David Lindsay. He had already begun to make a name for himself as a result of a small volume of sermons, *The Social Gospel*. As soon as he arrived at the Downs Chapel, he began to deal in his evening sermons with social problems. It was not long before some of the older members of the diaconate, survivors of the days of Dr Tymms, became concerned at some of the things mentioned from the pulpit, and judged that they were not really fit matters to be dealt with in sermons. A serious division developed within the fellowship. Lindsay offered his resignation, feeling perhaps that he had made a mistake in coming to the church. The prospect of another interregnum caused dismay and the officers of the church begged him to stay. Yet within a few months relationships had become so strained that the deacons told Lindsay that he had better leave. By that time, however, he had his own strong following among the members and the congregation. The dispute came to a head in 1913. After months of tension, the whole of the diaconate and their families began to absent themselves from Sunday services. This apparently was in an effort to force the minister's departure. Friendships were broken and families became divided. Within the Payne family there were frequent heated conversations concerning the difficulties at the church. Division developed between Alexander and Catherine Payne on the one hand and the several Payne sisters on the other. Ernest Payne's parents, though not approving of all that the minister said and did, were convinced that it would be wrong to leave the church. His aunts, however, supported the diaconate. With a number of others from the Downs Chapel, they began to attend the Clapton Park Congregational Church. Downs was never the same again, although Lindsay remained throughout the war and on until 1927. The immediate effect of the division, particularly on the children of the church, was to interrupt, and sometimes to end, friendships that had begun. The children suffered because of the disagreements of their parents. The particular outcome for Ernest Payne was that he lost a number of friends of his own age. The church became impoverished by this division, not only in numbers but most particularly in a sense of fellowship and in spirituality. Without doubt this experience helped to develop the strong sense that Ernest Payne always had of the necessity of speedy reconciliation before disputes went too far.

His spiritual development followed the traditional pattern set within the middle-class, nonconformist, chapel-going homes. He was at church twice on Sunday and at Sunday School. He was being nurtured for Christian commitment. But his parents did not put pressure on him. Every year or so a series of special services was held which lasted a week or ten days. They were intended to quicken and deepen the spiritual life of the members, to draw in outsiders and to bring young people to decision for baptism and church membership. Some of these services Ernest Payne found unattractive and even embarrassing. In 1915, however, the missioner was Dr A. C.

Dixon, an American, who was at that time minister at Spurgeon's Tabernacle. He held afternoon Bible studies which Ernest Payne attended after school. Dixon was a fundamentalist with an evangelical approach. Those afternoon Bible studies meant a lot to Ernest Payne and in retrospect he saw them as a stage in his adolescent development, both emotional and religious. They required him to face the issue of an open and individual response to Christ. He did not, however, make any public response, but by 1916, he was often, on a Tuesday evening, attending the Young Peoples' Meeting of which his mother was a joint leader, and sometimes went to the midweek service. In February 1917, on the eve of his 15th birthday he joined the church. He was given the right hand of fellowship at the evening Communion service in the Downs Chapel. Five months later he was baptised.

It is always difficult to analyse the reasons for decisions taken by other people. It meant much to him to join the church that he had always viewed as the church of his fathers; it was the natural thing for him to do. So much of his life and the life of his family was in the church. He was regular in worship there. The family had stayed loyal in the face of all the difficulties. Yet there are indications that the decision to join the church was a decision that followed a good deal of hesitation and there is more than a hint that persuasion, not from his family, but from members of the church, had a part in it. Of his baptism he wrote in later years: 'I have to confess – perhaps to my shame, and certainly to continued psychological perplexity on my part – that I remember far less about that occasion than I do of the occasion when I joined the church.'

Perhaps because of his shyness, he found that the gift of belonging in Christ within the fellowship of believers was more immediately relevant to his spiritual needs than was the necessity to rejoice constantly in his own personal salvation. Nevertheless, he recognised only too well the essential nature of an individual Christian response in faith to Jesus Christ. Throughout his life he was one who understood and shared something of Martin Luther's view that it is a great holding point in the Christian faith to be able to say with all the believers in Christ 'I am baptised'. But his own Christian experience is reflected in the emphasis within his theology upon the Church, its corporate worship, its mission and its unity.

The War

The world that he and all his contemporaries knew was to change drastically with the outbreak of war. On that August day in 1914, he ran upstairs to his father with the copy of the *Daily News* which carried on the front page in heavy type the announcement that Britain was at war. His father's reaction of dismay and apprehension cut short the excitement that Ernest Payne was expressing in his voice. To Alexander Payne, the Quaker, a man with strong peace convictions, the problem of attitude to the war was immense. But when Germany quickly invaded Belgium, it had the overwhelming effect of uniting those who might otherwise have been deeply divided in Britain. So far as the Free Churches were concerned, the reaction of Dr John Clifford of Westbourne Park was important. He had always been prominently connected with peace organisations. When he came out in favour of the war effort, many including Alexander and Catherine Payne, reluctantly, and with a deep distaste for the war hysteria which quickly developed, supported the action taken by the Liberal leaders, Asquith, Edward Grey, and the attitude of the Baptist John Clifford. Whilst this lead by Clifford was undoubtedly followed by many Free Church people, there were those even in the Downs, Clapton, who did not see things in that light. In the chapel there was one lady who dressed like an old fashioned Quaker, and throughout the war stuck to her pacifist principles.

In addition to the war, another shadow was cast upon the Payne family. Like her brother Margaret was clever and had been doing well at the Skinner's Company School at Stamford Hill. Unlike her brother, she related well to people and had an easy outgoing personality. Then suddenly she began to be afflicted by some kind of paralysis affecting her legs. Eventually the doctors diagnosed that she was suffering from a rare disease known as Friedreich's Ataxia. This disease is said to be hereditary and the origin of it not clearly understood. The prognosis was that Margaret was not likely to live to be more than 30 years old. The disease is a rare one but it is known that it sometimes affects several children in one family, and before long it became clear that her brother Philip also was suffering from the same fearful disease. Little or nothing could be done to delay its slow but relentless progress.

Margaret's growing weakness deprived Ernest Payne of the active companionship of his sister at the very time when in his teens he would have been most glad of it, not only because of her companionship, but because of the possibility of being introduced to the wider social circle that Margaret's personality would surely have encouraged had she been physically fit. For he had few social contacts with his school fellows, and although he was in the midst of the church life at the Downs, it was a divided fellowship, and in any case he found himself in a circle of young people, most of whose parents had a somewhat different social and intellectual background from his own. Unlike the situation of today, he was the only one of the group who ultimately went on from school to college. Within the young people there was, however, the usual chopping and changing of friendships between the girls and the boys, though of course the relationships were much more formal and diffident than they are today. He remained largely on the circumference of all this, partly through his natural shyness, even timidity, partly because of the demands of the home situation and partly because his mother was emphatically against early involvement in romantic attachments. Throughout his life Ernest Payne was perhaps almost over-selfconscious of his own diffidence and shyness in relationships. Whilst lack of opportunities for social contacts in his youth contributed to this sense of social inferiority, at root it was inherent.

This then was the background against which the question of his future career arose. There were those in the Downs Chapel who suggested that his gifts and abilities were such that he should become a doctor – perhaps a medical missionary. Certainly, he had a growing interest in the missionary enterprise. His grandfather, William, had been a keen supporter of the Baptist Missionary Society and had kindled a like enthusiasm within the Payne family. The visits of missionaries on furlough stimulated the interest still further. He knew he could not be a medical missionary – he shrank too easily from the sight of blood – but a missionary pastor was certainly a possibility. Indeed from the time he joined the church in 1917, he was challenged by the growing conviction that he should become either a minister at home or a missionary abroad. His parents, although certainly not unsympathetic to this sense of vocation, did not actively encourage it. His mother was a daughter of the manse and knew only too well the demands involved in following such a calling. With the family circumstances growing more difficult, they would probably have preferred to see their eldest child established quickly in a more secure profession. His father would have gladly seen him as an accountant or an actuary. He had spent one or two wartime school holidays doing odd jobs in the Finsbury Pavement office and had shown some ability for figures. But he had no desire to enter accountancy, and office life made no appeal to him. He knew his education must continue in the university so that he might be fitted in mind as well as in spirit for what he growingly believed would be full time Christian service.

Further education was going to be difficult financially. Problems had arisen for the Payne family because of the death of a partner in his father's accountancy business. The partnership agreement between Alexander Payne and Walter Rowe had run out during the war. They decided to leave the question of revision or renewal of the partnership deed until a more favourable time. When, however, Walter Rowe died unexpectedly, Alexander Payne had to pay out Rowe's widow under the old and at that time crippling arrangements. This meant that from moderate middle class comfort the Payne family passed to a period of considerable financial stringency. Nevertheless his father said that he would see Ernest Payne through college. It was against this background that the possibility of going to Cambridge was dropped and the decision taken to try for London University. University College with its liberal tradition would have been perhaps the natural place for him to go, even though at this point Ernest Payne did not know that that college had, as one of its founding fathers, a Baptist minister, Dr Cox. King's College in the Strand had the greater attraction for him, for it had a theological faculty. Whilst he did not want immediately to read theology he thought he would need eventually to do so for he had a growing sense that his calling would come to its fulfilment in Christian ministry. So it was that he insisted he went to King's College and in the end he had his way.

2

Further Education

King's College, London

In the early summer of 1919, Ernest Payne went, together with
his father, to meet the Dean of Arts at King's College situated
in London's Strand. Both his father and the Dean expressed
some surprise and probably mild disapproval when he insisted
that he did not want initially to take an honours degree, but
rather a pass degree in Latin, English, History and Philosophy.
At this stage he was unwilling to commit himself to one subject
but was determined that he would get a foundation of education in literature, language, history and most particularly
philosophy. He was then scarcely 18 years old and he had little
idea what philosophy was, but he knew that it had something
to do with the problems of meaning and existence. Already his
active mind was becoming increasingly occupied with these
questions. Indeed it was probable that he was becoming more
and more troubled with these questions. The answers that he
had thus far received from within the strong yet traditional
Baptist heritage were not wholly satisfactory to the sharpness
of his acute mind. And so it was that in October 1919 with very
great eagerness and anticipation he began three years as a
student of London University in King's College. As he had
already successfully passed the external intermediate examination at school, he required only two years for the final
examination for a pass degree. He hoped that in the third year
he might try for an honours degree in one or other of the
subjects.

A week or so after entering King's he had a remarkable
mystical experience. It occurred in the Strand and in later life
he rarely passed the spot without it coming to mind. The date
is pin-pointed – 16th October. The year 1919 was the year

when the Downs Chapel celebrated its Golden Jubilee. The evening of 16th October was to see the main celebratory meeting of the Downs Chapel. Sir Alfred Pearce-Gould was to be in the chair. Previous ministers, F. G. Benskin and James Mursell were to be present, and a message was to be read from the elderly Dr Tymms. On that evening as Ernest Payne walked along towards St Clement Danes from Charing Cross on his way to Clapton, he was reflecting upon what the Downs Chapel had meant to himself, to his parents and to his grandparents. He became conscious of a Figure behind him with his hand on his shoulder impelling him forward. He took this figure to be Christ. The impression did not last long, but it was very strong and vivid. Almost certainly it contributed to his subsequent decision to seek theological training with a view to service in India, and this experience, brief though it was, became a determinative influence on his life. Such experiences do not require, nor can they be given, any explanation, humanly speaking. In retrospect it can be seen as a further stage in God's dealing with Ernest Payne, calling him into particular service in the life of the Church.

Certainly it is significant that it should take place within his own reflections on the church fellowship which meant so much to him. His loyalty to the Baptist tradition, the tradition of his fathers, remained firm and secure and the foundation of all his subsequent activities. Possibly we may add with interest that it took place in the middle of the busy City. So many of the activities in which Ernest Payne was to share in his Christian service were in the midst of the busyness of the world. Whatever may be the explanation, this experience makes it very clear that the heart of his faith and his calling was not solely a decision of the intellect in any limited sense, but was based upon as clear a conviction of calling and of personal encounter as has been the experience of all faithful Christian disciples from the earliest days of the Christian faith until now. This experience, brief though it was, vivid as it certainly was, anchored him often in the storms that were to lie ahead.

He entered into the classes at King's College with all zest and enthusiasm. He was fortunate in those who taught him. The Professor of Philosophy was Dr Wilden Carr. Wilden Carr was an impressive figure to look upon with a fine head and beard and he always lectured in a morning coat. His style was in the grand manner, graceful and impressive and rose at times to real eloquence. He undoubtedly kindled in Ernest Payne a very deep interest in philosophy, as one of the roads to travel in search for truth. As he listened to Wilden Carr he recognised that the intellectual atmosphere in which the discussions were leading him was a rarified and exalted realm which left far behind the Christian faith which he had thus far encountered and particularly the form of the Christian faith in which he had been nurtured. The effect this had upon him was on the one hand dangerous but on the other hand liberating. It was dangerous because all too easily he could have lost all foothold in his developing Christian faith and have been captured in a bemused sort of way by what he heard in the lectures. It was liberating because it opened up to him the recognition that a full-orbed Christian faith must include and deal with the challenges that philosophy makes to the Christian faith.

The fact that he did not lose his foothold was due, undoubtedly, first to his home influence in which he saw always that whatever may be the intellectual merits of their Christianity, it was a faith that was real, active and effective in all the variety of experiences of human life. Secondly Wilden Carr's assistant was one Hilda Oakley. She taught Early Greek Philosophy and was a deeply Christian person with convictions which enabled her to interpret to the seeking students the way in which the philosophical search can be related to the search for truth that comes also through the Christian faith. The third influence, and perhaps the strongest at that point, was that of the Dean of King's College, Dr W. R. Matthews. In the Michaelmas Term of 1920, Matthews gave the Boyle Lectures, under the title 'Some Philosophical Presuppositions of Christianity'. These lectures sought to show quite clearly to the student that Athens and Jerusalem are not necessarily hostile to each other, but are in fact, and necessarily should be, allies in the search for truth which demands the best of mind and heart and soul. Ernest Payne heard these lectures at the right moment and remained always deeply grateful to them and to the lecturer, for this recognition that philosophy and Christianity could and should belong together was an essential part in the development of his Christian experience.

There were other experiences in the university scene which contributed to Ernest Payne's theological development. In

King's College he found two fellow Baptists, T.D. Robinson, and Alexander Hodge. Together they went to some of the early meetings of the London Intercollegiate Union, and of the Inter Varsity Fellowship. He went to one or two vacation conferences at which Dr F. B. Meyer, then an aged but distinguished Baptist, was among the speakers. The Christianity presented was basic, straightforward and biblical, but Ernest Payne never felt entirely at ease in this theological context. This was particularly true when the emotion that is natural to Christianity descended to emotionalism. One night in January 1922 after a very emotional appeal at a meeting of the London Intercollegiate Union, he walked along the Embankment wrestling with the question as to whether the kind of conversion and commitment demanded was the only way into the Christian faith. It seemed to him that it required the rejection and the denial of so much that he was learning and sharing in at college. It was a surrender he felt he could not make. He did not believe it was the religion of his parents or of his grandparents. 'Thou shalt love the Lord thy God with all thy mind . . .' became more and more demanding upon him as a command from God at this stage in his life. He read the books of H. E. Fosdick, T. R. Glover and Dean Inge. Once again he found himself wavering between the scepticism that was coming across from the philosophical teaching and the Christian faith that had been nurtured within him. It was only by honestly facing this particular challenge that he came through. Because of the frankness and intensity of his struggle, there was a valid victory. This enabled him, throughout the rest of his life, to know that his faith was a faith that was honest in its convictions because it was made up of the experiences of Christ that life had brought to him in a variety of contexts. So it was then, steeped in the Baptist tradition within the Downs Chapel in Clapton, aware of the reality of the Christian life in his own home, sensing a call of God within his own heart, experiencing some mystical encounter in the midst of the City, recognising that the Christian faith demanded the best that he could bring of his undoubted intellectual gifts, he became ever clearer that God had, for him, some marked out responsibility within the life of the Christian Church. How great a responsibility this was to be, and how wide an influence he was to have, could not have been within the widest vision that he had at that time.

Within the life of the college, he made few close friends. He played little part in college politics, nor in the social life of the college. He still remained shy and reserved and found plenty of interest in his work and in the library of the college. The outcome of his single-mindedness was that he passed easily enough the final examinations in 1921 and obtained his pass degree. He decided somewhat obstinately in the face of other people's advice and in the face of much questioning as to its possibility and to its value, to try for an honours philosophy degree in 1922. There were just four students taking that particular course in the session 1921-22. The concentration on philosophy brought them into closer contact with W. R. Matthews, who took a special class on Aristotle's Ethics for them, meeting in his room in an informal manner. When the final examination results came out Ernest Payne was placed in the second class in the honours degree list in philosophy, but was told by Wilden Carr that he had only just missed a first class degree. But by the time the results came out in the winter of 1922, Ernest Payne was already a student in Regent's Park College.

Regent's Park College

At the turn of the year 1921-22 he made a further decision concerning his future. He applied to Regent's Park College, then in London, as an intending missionary candidate. There is no evidence that this was the result of a further experience of any sort, but simply the natural development of the way in which his life had been leading. Throughout his life he always sympathised with the view that on really important issues, it is not that the individual should make the decision, but rather that the decision should be said to come – as it were already made – to the individual. This is an important distinction and helped to form the undoubted conviction that he had throughout his life of what might be called the Christian inevitability of the path along which he was being led.

On the application form to Regent's Park College he gave as one of the referees, the minister at the Downs Chapel, the Rev. D.L. Lindsay. We do not know much about the relationship which the young Ernest Payne had with his minister but such information as we have suggests that it was uneasy on both sides. He resented the scorn that Lindsay often poured upon politicians, and upon Anglicans. Ernest Payne believed deeply that the Christian had to be a political person, living as he did in the midst of society. Already, because of his contacts in King's College and because of his reading he was recognising that the true Christian experience went far beyond the fellowship of the Baptist community. One significant incident occurred between himself and Lindsay which certainly resulted in a temporary breach between them. The occasion was a church meeting during the war years at which there was to be discussion and decision relating to women deacons at the Downs Chapel. In an introductory devotional period, Lindsay read without comment some of the Pauline passages on women and their place in the church. In so doing it seemed to Ernest Payne that Lindsay was attempting to secure the ultimate rejection of the idea. After the church meeting he wrote a letter of protest to the minister which, whilst it might have been somewhat precocious was nevertheless, from his point of view, fully justifiable. Not surprisingly it took some little time for the relationship between the minister and his young church member to reach normality again. But certainly by 1922 Lindsay was prepared to support his application to Regent's Park.

It was in February 1922, when Ernest Payne was just twenty years old, that he was called by Dr Wheeler Robinson to an informal interview at the college. Wheeler Robinson looked at Ernest Payne and asked him 'Are you a convinced Baptist?' He hesitated before answering. In that question he was being challenged to express the very tensions in which he was to live all his days. For not only had he graduated through King's College, but he had read with eagerness and approval the book written by Dr J.H. Shakespeare, the then Secretary of the Baptist Union, entitled *The Churches at the Cross Roads* which argued in favour of Christian union – even to the extent of the Free Churches accepting episcopacy. Indeed, he had won a prize offered by the Baptist Union in 1920 for an essay on that book. During June of 1920, in the Downs Chapel, there had been a debate on the subject of Christian unity. Ernest Payne had seconded a resolution in favour of the concept. It was firmly opposed by influential members of the church and the resolution defeated. But his colours concerning Christian unity were nailed to the mast. He had followed very closely the discussions which had followed 'the Appeal to all Christian people' which had come from the Lambeth Conference in 1920. So he told Wheeler Robinson frankly that he believed in the movement for Christian union. After a pause, Wheeler Robinson said with characteristic deliberation, 'I think, Mr Payne, that when you give your mind to the matter of Baptist principles in the way you have given it to other things, you will find there is more to be said for our Baptist position than you perhaps at present recognise.' It was all Wheeler Robinson did say, but the careful, honest and yet understanding way in which it was said won Ernest Payne to him as a man of open mind and deep thought.

In June 1922 he appeared before the College Committee Meeting in the college buildings at Regent's Park. It was a formidable committee and a frightening occasion for anyone of his temperament. Next to Wheeler Robinson sat the college treasurer, Mr John Chown, at that time President of the Baptist Union. Mr Chown asked him, 'Suppose you were sent out of the room and told to come back in half an hour and preach to us, what would your text be?' After what seemed a long pause, Ernest Payne stammered 'The text I wrote a sermon upon yesterday in the entrance examination.' There was apparently a subdued sound of amusement from some members of the committee. John Chown leant forward and looked severely at the candidate and said, 'I meant a text to choose for yourself, not one given to you.' In the midst of an interview such as this the obvious is very often difficult to call to mind. Ernest Payne's mind went blank and he tried to remember a text that he could quote – any text would do. At last he blurted out, 'Jesus Christ is the same yesterday, today and for evermore.' 'You have got the quotation wrong,' snapped Mr Chown. 'Do you know your Bible well, Mr Payne?' By this time Ernest Payne typically having overcome the initial shyness and fright was turning to the counter-attack. 'Not as well as I should like,' he said. 'That is why I want to come to College.' There was again the sound of suppressed laughter in the committee. A somewhat quavering voice sounded from beside the principal; it was Professor S. W. Green who had been a member of the staff since 1878. He said, 'Mr Payne did quite a good paper for me on the Bible yesterday.' Mr Chown continued to question Ernest Payne about wanting to be a missionary and a missionary teacher but clearly the interview had now turned from being a somewhat difficult one to being quite the reverse. Later on Mr Chown sought out Ernest Payne and spoke encouragingly to him.

Before long the college secretary, the Rev. C. M. Hardy, informed him of his acceptance by the committee. Hardy went on to say, in confidence, that the committee hoped that perhaps when he had taken his B.D., he might be the first Regent's Park student in Cambridge. At that time plans were being discussed in the committee and within certain circles of the denomination for moving Regent's Park College to Cambridge combining it with Cheshunt College, the Congregational College there. Undoubtedly this had long been the dream of Dr Shakespeare, and a number of other Baptist leaders. The scheme collapsed, however, largely because it proved at that time impossible to dispose of the remainder of the lease of Regent's Park College. But in due course the college was to move from London but not to Cambridge, rather to Oxford, and Ernest Payne was to play a significant role in that move. The delay, however, meant that his three years as a student at Regent's were all to be spent in London.

Influences and experiences

Regent's Park College had originally been founded in 1810 in Stepney and bore the name of Stepney College until it moved in 1855 to Holford House in Regent's Park. This was five years after Ernest Payne's grandfather Philip Griffiths had left the College. His other grandfather, William Payne, had been for a number of years a member of the college committee. In the 1890s Alexander Payne had undertaken the first professional audit of the accounts and was still auditor whilst his son Ernest was a student at the college. Indeed, the firm continued through Philip Payne to audit the accounts for very many years subsequently.

Holford House was an imposing Georgian mansion on the outer circle of the Park. It was not finally demolished until it was seriously damaged by bombing in the Second World War.

The students of Regent's Park College shared classes with the Congregational students of New College and Hackney College. The co-operation in theological training between the Baptists and the Congregationalists proved mutually beneficial. When Dr P. T. Forsyth died in 1922 the two Congregational Colleges of Hackney and New College united with Dr A. E. Garvie recognised as principal of the joint institution. The name, New College, was transferred to the Hackney College property in the Finchley Road.

The two members of the joint staff who made the most impression on Ernest Payne were the two principals, Garvie and Wheeler Robinson. Garvie's influence upon Ernest Payne was not so much because of his undoubted theological learning but because of his involvement in the developing inter-church contacts which had already begun. Garvie had had a part in the discussions that followed the Lambeth Appeal of 1920 and he was deeply involved in 1924 as Chairman of the National Free Church Council in the Birmingham Conference on Politics, Economics and Citizenship about which the students in the colleges then had a number of study groups. In retrospect that Copec Conference is seen by many to be a high point in English church life. David Edwards describes it as 'the high water mark of the wartime and post-war reforming tide ... There were those who regarded Copec as a peak moment of English religion before disillusionment in society brought a return to ecclesiastical obsessions, and to doctrinal rigidity.'[1] In 1927 Garvie was elected Vice-Chairman of the Lausanne Conference on Faith and Order and in the years prior to Lausanne had been deeply involved in the preparations for this highly significant conference. Garvie was also engaged at this point in preparations for the Stockholm Life and Work Conference which was held in 1925. He never shirked action in the name of thought. Thus the young Ernest Payne admired a man whose own interest and commitments went far beyond his own denomination and whose Christian concern was firmly rooted in the relationships between church and society.

The influence of Wheeler Robinson was of a different kind and quality altogether and went far deeper. In the novel *Robert Elsmere* by Mrs Ward, Henry Grey is described as 'a man in whom the generation of spiritual force was so strong and continuous, that it overflowed of necessity into the poorer, barren lives around him, kindling and enriching'. This aptly described the effect Wheeler Robinson had upon those around him. Some found him austere. Certainly he was demanding. He worked his students, as he did himself, very hard indeed. But almost without exception, his students became almost literally spellbound by this extraordinary person. He was one who was ahead of almost everybody in facing every intellectual issue and indeed it sometimes seemed to his students also in reading every book! He was one who taught the true meaning of reverence, and in so doing he taught the necessity of having a deep respect, not only for the Baptist tradition to which Wheeler Robinson was unswervingly loyal and deeply devoted, but also for those things that others regarded as sacred. Virtually everybody who came under the influence of Wheeler Robinson recalls the communion services held on the Friday evenings. Each Friday he gave a brief address. From the most varied starting points in literature, history and current events, he led the students to the heart of the gospel of God's many-sided wisdom and unfailing grace. Most of the students viewed Friday as a special day. At the close of the service, the students went often in silence to their rooms, many of them to write down what they could remember of the address.

Wheeler Robinson was one of the most decisive influences on Ernest Payne's spiritual and intellectual development. He opened up a vision of God in trinitarian revelation expressed as Father, Son and Holy Spirit – a God, therefore, to be at one and the same time, worshipped, loved and experienced. To the service of such a God the Christian must offer back the very best of spirit, mind and body. There could be no casual nor slovenly attitude towards God either in daily worship or in daily work.

Before he entered Regent's Park College Ernest Payne had little preaching experience. Indeed, the first service he conducted was at East Street, Walworth, on the evening of 6th August 1922. Soon after he entered Regent's, however, he began to share in the preaching work at the chapels familiar to students of those days. These were at Park Street, St Albans, at Harefield, at Baughurst on the Hampshire border, and in his second year at college he was chosen to be student pastor of a church at Brimpton in Berkshire. During his time as student minister there he learned much from the kindness shown to him during the monthly visits and began to experience something of the responsibilities of pastoral ministry.

As so often happens to students in theological colleges, certain preaching 'adventures' befell him. Perhaps the most startling, at least to him, was a visit to Swaffham in Norfolk in 1924. On the Saturday morning, he received a letter from the church secretary, saying that it was hoped that he would be willing to take an Infant Dedication Service on the Sunday. Such services amongst Baptists were rare in the early 1920s and he had never been present at such a service. He turned for advice to Wheeler Robinson, who himself could give very little help, save apparently for the practical advice of telling him not to hold the child for too long! He borrowed a copy of an order of service which had once been used by a fellow student, and set off on the journey to Swaffham from Liverpool Street Station.

Over supper on the Saturday night, his hosts informed him that there would, in fact, be several babies to dedicate, not just one. In the event there proved to be no fewer than four, though even in the vestry before the service, it was unclear as to how many exactly might arrive! To add to the preacher's embarrassment, no fathers appeared with any of the babies! The church secretary arranged that after the child had been handed to the preacher he would then be given a scrap of paper with its name on, so that he knew whether it was a boy or a girl and indeed what its name was. It is not difficult to imagine the problems all of this posed to an inexperienced student. Indeed it is highly probable that until that day Ernest Payne had never held a baby in his arms at all. From all accounts there were no disasters of any sort.

A further visit was a memorable preaching engagement at Faversham in Kent. He was entertained for the day at the home of Mr and Mrs Vinson. The preacher was conveyed then from the morning service to the hosts in a chauffeur driven Rolls Royce! In somewhat stark contrast, in the evening the preacher went to worship on the pillion of the motor-bike belonging to the son of the household, Edward, a contemporary of Ernest Payne, who was later to become a close and generous friend, well known in the affairs of Regent's Park College and of the Baptist Union.

Throughout his time at Regent's Park College Ernest Payne

sat lightly to the various activities of the college concerned directly with the home ministry. This was a loss that he subsequently regretted. He was, however, at this time still hoping that he would find his way to India as a missionary, and certainly with the Baptist Missionary Society. For whilst the influences upon him in college days particularly from Garvie increased his convictions concerning the movement for Christian unity, so also and more so did his conviction that there really were no better people than the Baptists and it was there, firmly embedded in the denomination, the community of his fathers, that he must remain and serve in whatever way God called him. It should also be noted that from these college days emerges an early indication of his political allegiance. He had a growing sympathy with the Labour Party, particularly with leaders such as Arthur Henderson and Philip Snowdon. In 1923 at college there was a mock election to coincide with the general election. In that mock election Ernest Payne stood as Labour candidate – and lost!

Of his contemporaries at Regent's three in particular should be mentioned. The first is Robert Child. They first met in January 1922 when Child had come to take the services at the Downs Chapel. The acquaintance was renewed when Ernest Payne entered Regent's as a student. Robert Child was rather older than most of the students, older even than the men who had entered college after seeing active service in the First World War. He was nine years older than Ernest Payne and had been in Customs and Excise for ten years, and therefore exempt from war service. He had graduated as a B.D. in 1922, and was preparing to take B.D. Honours. During the college days Child was somewhat remote from his fellow students, including Ernest Payne, and it was not until some years later that the two became very closely acquainted, but the foundation of their subsequent collaboration and friendship was laid during the time that they spent together in the college at Halford House.

Ernest Payne's closest friend was Max Hancock. Although different in temperament, he and Ernest Payne quickly became friends and saw a great deal of one another. There had been links between them, or at least between their families. Hancock's family had quite recently been connected with the Devonshire Square Baptist Church in Stoke Newington which was geographically close to the Downs at Clapton. Indeed,

Hancock himself had for a short time been at the Hackney Downs School. He was designated for missionary service and when in 1925 he subsequently set out for San Salvador in Angola, he was greatly missed by Ernest Payne. Nevertheless, throughout their lives, so different in Christian service, they kept in contact as events will reveal.

The other student was very different indeed. His name was Herbert Petrick. He started at Regent's Park College on the same day as Ernest Payne in 1922. He was a protégé of Dr J. H. Rushbrooke, who was just beginning his service to the Baptist World Alliance. Petrick's father had served for some time as a missionary in India and was of Slavic origin. Petrick himself had been a medical student in Germany when war broke out in 1914. He had married a girl of Polish origin and although not fully qualified as a doctor he served with the German medical forces throughout the war. Rushbrooke had found him in Austria after the war. He was already the father of four small daughters. Rushbrooke discerned that here was a potential leader for the Baptist work on the Continent in years to come. Someone of so different a background and with such extraordinary experience as Petrick was bound to contribute much to the life of the college fellowship. Ernest Payne found him a stimulating companion and they spent much time together in discussing matters both theological and political. Petrick became more liberal both theologically and politically during his time in Regent's and this made his subsequent life in Germany very difficult. It was to him that Ernest Payne owed his first introduction to the continent of Europe and in particular to Germany.

He enabled Ernest Payne, together with Max Hancock and Keith Bryan, who later became a distinguished missionary in China, to visit Germany in August 1923. It was an extraordinary visit taking place at the time when the German mark was beginning seriously and quickly to depreciate in value. The students started with £20 in their pockets and their rucksacks on their backs. Their journey took in Berlin, Dresden, Prague, Vienna, Lausanne and Paris. They were away a month and returned home still with some of their £20 and a vast number of German marks. The visit had not only been enjoyable as a holiday but had given the students an opportunity of meeting ordinary folk and Baptists in several lands. For Ernest Payne it was a formative experience, quickening his interest in, and understanding of, the opportunities and problems of the Baptists in Europe and giving him a great urge to discover opportunities for making more contact with them.

Ecumenical beginnings in the Student Christian Movement

It was during his college days that Ernest Payne made his first contacts with the Student Christian Movement. The SCM was then in its heyday and had great influence upon theological and other students between the two wars. It is probably no exaggeration to say that the foundations of the modern ecumenical movement were in part laid by the experiences that many students had between the wars in the context of the World Student Christian Federation and the Student Christian Movement. In the same summer as his first visit to the Continent Ernest Payne had been to a summer conference at Swanwick organised by the SCM, and eighteen months later in January 1925 he was at the Quadrennial Conference of the Student Christian Federation in Manchester. The speakers at that conference were F. R. Barry and William Temple. Both of them in their own and separate ways were a great influence on the younger generation. It was not surprising that some forty years later Ernest Payne discovered that half a dozen of the Central Committee of the World Council of Churches were also present at Manchester in 1925.

Other leaders of the movement included Tissington Tatlow, a remarkable Irishman who had been Secretary of the Student Christian Movement since 1903. He still retained skill and attraction as a guide and friend of the younger generation. Tatlow was a man whose part in the breaking down of the barriers between the denominations has perhaps not always adequately been recognised. But there were others, of a younger generation, then beginning to lead amongst the students: George Cockin, later to become Bishop of Bristol; Robert Mackie, significant in the World Council of Churches; Eric Fenn, who was to lead the Bible Society; Hugh Martin, who was involved in the SCM Press. Contact with all these people moved Ernest Payne into circles far beyond Baptist denominational boundaries. Indeed, the movement led him into contacts wider even than those he had known at King's College. It is probable that but for the SCM, he would have found even Regent's Park College somewhat restricting. He shared the enthusiasm of many students of those days who were eager to hear from others of different experiences of Christ in different denominations and most particularly in different parts of the world. It was a day of great adventure in contact, friendship and learning from each other and of each other. In the SCM circles it was the era of the open mind and open heart.

In March 1925 Alexander and Catherine Payne celebrated their Silver Wedding. Although a time of rejoicing, it was also a time of deep concern. Margaret had had to give up her course in modern languages at the East London College and was becoming completely dependent upon others. To give her more healthy and attractive surroundings, the family had decided in 1924 to move from Clapton and finally fixed upon a newly built house in the Avenue, in Potters Bar. This was a pleasant setting in a growing community situated in the countryside adjacent to London. The house gave Margaret a delightful view from the garden and there were helpful and friendly neighbours.

In October 1925 the doctor's prognosis that Margaret would never walk again was confirmed by a specialist. He indicated that he did not think that she would live beyond the age of thirty. This situation presented Ernest Payne with difficult decisions. Not only was there the question of his responsibilities to the family with Margaret so ill and Philip also stricken with the same illness, but there was also the haunting question as to his own health and whether he would be able to face the rigours of life in India. In January 1925 he had taken medical advice on this matter and all the indications were that there was no reason why he should not physically stand life in India. On the other hand the doctor could not give any final guarantee that there might not be a breakdown in health similar to Margaret's collapse. Medical science was then so unclear as to the cause of Margaret's disease that there was very little about which they could be certain. So Ernest Payne took a second medical opinion from the BMS Medical Missionary, Dr Vincent Thomas. His advice was to go forward and not at present to worry about the medical side. He decided to postpone a final decision as long as possible and sought the advice of Wheeler Robinson. The principal suggested that for the moment he should consider going on from Regent's Park College to Mansfield College in Oxford. Financial problems made this a difficult decision but in the end Ernest Payne decided to try this way and to sit for the Pegg Scholarship. This meant an additional programme of work to his B.D. examination which he was completing in the summer of 1925, and further he was elected Senior Student of the college during his final session, 1924-5.

It was at the July Student Christian Movement Conference in 1925 that a chance meeting determined the main direction of his studies in Oxford and seemed clear confirmation that he was right in keeping open the possibility of going to India. At the Swanwick Conference, Dr J.M. Farquhar was amongst the speakers. He had been Literary Secretary of the Indian YMCA, and was the editor of several series of books on Indian religion. He had recently become Professor of Comparative Religion in Manchester University. Ernest Payne took the opportunity of talking with Dr Farquhar who showed an eager interest in this young student hoping to go to India. Farquhar urged him to begin to learn Sanskrit and suggested that he should study the Sakta Movement in Hinduism about which there was need for considerable research. It was therefore with this possibility in mind that Ernest Payne looked forward to his year in Oxford.

Oxford and Germany

He arrived at Mansfield College in October 1925. The College had quickly established itself as a centre of learning and made a notable contribution to the university as well as to the life of the Free Churches. It was a Congregational Foundation and had been established soon after the university was opened to nonconformists in the late 1880s. The staff at Mansfield in 1925 was a remarkable group of distinguished people of different generations. Dr Selbie had been principal since 1909. He was a great friend and supporter of Wheeler Robinson. Selbie was not an outstanding scholar but was a very good preacher, a good conversationalist and, beyond all, a wise counsellor. He was a little man, and often described by the students as a great little man, and nicknamed by them 'the inspired mouse'! Through all that Selbie did there shone goodness and refreshing common sense.

A more senior colleague as far as service was concerned was Dr J. V. Bartlett who had been on the staff since 1889, when the college buildings had been opened. He was a conscientious Church historian and a faithful friend and colleague of Selbie. At the other end of the scale was the brilliant and youthful C. H. Dodd, already beginning to make a name for himself in New Testament studies.

Selbie insisted that in addition to the B.Litt. degree for which Ernest Payne was working, he should also take a number of the Mansfield College courses. It quickly became clear that if he was successfully to complete his work for the B.Litt. degree then there would be a necessity to stay a further year in Oxford. To make this possible he had to sit for the Dr Williams' Scholarship and for the Anderson Pratten Prize, both of which involved formidable papers on a considerable syllabus and indeed the Anderson Pratten Prize then required Rabbinic as well as Classical Hebrew. It took remarkable application for all this work to be carried through successfully in the 1925–26 academic year at Oxford.

To Ernest Payne the stimulus of Oxford was immense and exciting. He became a member of the Oxford Union. There he enjoyed the weekly debates, though never had sufficient courage to participate. The officers of the Oxford Union were men who subsequently became well-known leaders – Dingle Foot, Richard Acland, Henry Brook and a young man, Evan Durbin, who was the son of a Baptist Union Area Superintendent. Evan Durbin subsequently rose quickly to a position of trust in the Labour Party and became MP for Edmonton in North London. Sadly he was drowned in 1948 in a bathing accident whilst on holiday in Cornwall, and the Labour Party was robbed of one who would undoubtedly have become one of its significant leaders.

In the spring of 1926 a General Strike was called. There was much activity in Oxford including the formation of a conciliation committee under the leadership of the then Master of Balliol, A. D. Lindsay. Ernest Payne attached himself to this committee and on the very day that the strike was called off, he was on the way by road to London with a message from the committee to Free Church leaders, notably Dr A. E. Garvie. During his time in Oxford, Ernest Payne was also partly responsible for re-establishing the Baptist Students' Society, the John Bunyan Society. The Society had been in existence prior to the First World War, but had lapsed. A number of Baptist students then in Oxford revived it with the help of R. W. Hobling, minister of the New Road Baptist Church. The members had a common concern for the Baptist denomination and the Society also provided a context in Oxford for a meeting of the sexes. In the mid-1920s social contacts between male and female undergraduates were few and carefully controlled. The John Bunyan Society was an accepted setting for such meetings. It was a lively Society and included Wheeler Robinson's daughter, Monica, Marjorie Reeves, who became a distinguished historian, Leslie Stradling, who was the son of a Baptist Minister, but who subsequently became the Anglican Bishop of Johannesburg, Leslie Wenger, of New College, who went as a missionary to India, Murray John, who became a successful town clerk in Swindon, and Evan Durbin.

The year 1926 saw another significant beginning in which Ernest Payne was involved. Contact between the Baptist colleges at that time was minimal at both staff and student level. There were considerable differences, some theological and some personal between staff and students. But within the colleges there were those who felt that things should be rather different. A meeting was held at Student Movement House on the 21st April 1926 concerning a proposed Baptist Students' Conference. It seems that the prime movers in this were almost certainly Ernest Payne of Regent's, J. O. Barrett of Rawdon and Eric Knight of Manchester. This occasion was the first contact Ernest Payne had with J. O. Barrett, a contact that was to develop into a close friendship and produce a remarkable correspondence between the two which was maintained for more than fifty years. The three students shared a deep concern not only for relationships between the Colleges themselves but more particularly for the positive effect such relationships might have in the future for the denomination in the developing of fellowship and friendship within the Baptist ministry. So they planned a Baptist Students' Fraternal. They wrote to a number of laymen who they thought might be sympathetic and collected a small fund which, it has to be said, came very largely from the pocket of one man, Thomas Penny, a distinguished Taunton layman.

The students secured the use of what was then the Council Chamber, now the Shakespeare room, at the Baptist Church House and arranged hospitality in London for those who needed it. The conference took place at the end of 1926 and every college including Dublin was represented. The students discovered that there existed amongst them a real desire to start something more permanent. So there came into existence the Baptist Theological Students' Union which continued with somewhat fluctuating fortunes until just after the Second World War when it was merged into the wider work amongst Baptist students and became one of the contributory streams to the Baptist Students' Federation. The initial enterprise of the Conference in 1927 was an appeal to the students of the Baptist colleges for their own contribution to the ministerial superannuation fund which was launched at the 1927 Assembly. The students contributed very nearly £100, which was then, of course, a considerable sum of money.

The summer of 1926 saw Ernest Payne involved in another event which turned out to be of the highest importance both for him and for the whole denomination. This was the securing of 55, St Giles, Oxford, by Regent's Park College. One afternoon in June 1926 Dr Selbie sent Ernest Payne to call on a Mr J. T. Dodd who was the owner of 55, St Giles and some of the nearby property. He was received most graciously by Mr Dodd who told him that he had lived in No. 55 all his life as indeed had his father before him. Now as an old man he was moving down to the south coast and although he was an Anglican he was somewhat concerned that so much of Oxford property was passing into the hands of the Roman Catholics – sometimes directly, often indirectly. Loyalty to his own convictions and to his father's memory required that he should try to see that this did not happen to 55, St Giles. He believed that if he sold it to the Baptists, then it would be quite certain that if it were to be resold it would not be to Roman Catholics!

That June afternoon Ernest Payne stood on the spot now occupied by the Helwys Hall but which in 1926 was the site of the old stables. It seemed that negotiations could be opened immediately. Ernest Payne went back excitedly to Mansfield

College and wrote a full account of the afternoon's visit to Wheeler Robinson. He then had to sit back and leave the matter to others. Negotiations were carried on successfully with Mr Dodd by Mr H. H. Collier, a generous benefactor to Regent's Park College and a member of the college committee. The remainder of the Regent's Park College lease in London which was due to expire in 1932 was sold and the last College Reunion Dinner was held in the old buildings in the spring of 1927, at which Ernest Payne sang the College song! Later in 1927 he helped to unpack Wheeler Robinson's books when he moved in to 55, St Giles.

Earlier in 1927 Ernest Payne was offered a Proctor travelling scholarship by the Mansfield College authorities. Robert Child had had it the previous year and there were again no Congregational applicants. The Dr Williams' Trustees were prepared for Ernest Payne to use part of their grant for a further year's study in Germany. This made it possible for him to spend at least one semester – until February 1928 – in Germany. His brother, Philip Payne, and others were somewhat sceptical about this enterprise. Surely he had been in college long enough now and it was time that he did something which was more usually regarded as 'work'. He was not daunted by this initial discouragement and in fact before long his brother changed his mind and encouraged him to try to go to Marburg University. For part of the summer of 1927 he travelled again in Germany through the good offices of his friend Petrick. It was Petrick who warmly received him into his home for much of September and the early part of October 1927 and he was again the Petricks' guest for Christmas of that year. Petrick had by this time become the secretary of the German Baptist Young Peoples' Union but it was not an easy time for him because his developing religious and political outlook was rather more liberal than that of most German Baptists.

Marburg was a university of great historical importance. It was in the castle of Marburg that there was held the famous colloquy between Zwingli and Luther in 1529. Karl Barth had spent three semesters there as a student listening to the lectures of Hermann whom Barth regarded as *the* theological tutor of his student days. In 1927–28 every German university was in ferment over the teaching of Barth who by this time was professor in Münster. In Marburg, however, the New Testament scholar, Professor Bultmann was at the height of his fame. Bultmann was generally regarded as a supporter of Barth theologically but it was always something of a puzzle to his students as to how he was able to combine the dogmatism of Karl Barth concerning the scriptures and the incarnation of our Lord with his own extreme scepticism as to the extent of any reliable historical elements in the Gospel. Ernest Payne shared in that puzzlement. He attended Bultmann's lectures though did not find himself in great sympathy with his position. In fact, he found Bultmann's views distinctly unsatisfactory. It was possible for him to understand that the radical views that Bultmann held were a reaction from the liberal theology which seemed to have lost its credibility during the First World War, but to replace the historical Jesus sought by liberal theology with the colourless abstract Christ of the existential theology, a Christ who was at most an elusive figure, seemed not only unsatisfactory but seemed also to contain a paradox. He could not comprehend how anyone could believe that the almost ghost-like figure of the demythologised Christ was the divinely appointed means of forgiveness to be proclaimed for our generation – forgiveness to be received by faith. Also in Marburg at that time was Professor Heiler who lectured on comparative religion and who is perhaps best known for his book, *Prayer*. Heiler was of particular help to Ernest Payne in his work and interest in the Indian religions. Both Heiler and the Professor of Church History, Hermelink, had been present at the Lausanne Conference on Faith and Order in the summer of 1927 and there was a stimulation of interest in church relationships amongst their students as they reported on their experiences in Faith and Order.

Ernest Payne returned to England in March 1928 and soon after his return attended a memorial service in the City Temple to J. H. Shakespeare the recently retired Secretary of the Baptist Union. Ernest Payne came back, recognising that all thoughts of India had now to be set aside. The family situation was such that it would have been quite wrong in his judgment to go abroad. It was a decision that brought him deep disappointment but he accepted it in the confidence that God must have other plans for him. So he sent his name to the general superintendents with a view to introduction to vacant Baptist pastorates. Inevitably this would take time, and so he returned to Oxford for the summer term of 1928. It was during this term that he made contact with the first group of Regent's Park College students who had arrived in Oxford the previous autumn. He was also encouraged by Wheeler Robinson, somewhat surprisingly, to apply for the vacant Old Testament lectureship at Selly Oak Colleges. Rather hesitantly, he sent in his application supported by testimonials from both Wheeler Robinson and W. R. Matthews. That he was not appointed brought to him neither surprise nor any real sense of disappointment for he did not see himself as one cut out for Old Testament scholarship. During this term he also met Dr Albert Schweitzer. Dr Schweitzer preferred to converse in German, and consequently Dr Selbie invited to his lodgings any who could share in a conversation. By this time Ernest Payne was relatively fluent in German. He found Dr Schweitzer a fascinating and somewhat unconventional person. When Schweitzer was asked his opinion of Karl Barth, he paused and then said, 'I am not sure that I understand exactly what it is that Dr Barth is saying to us, but I am sure it is important.'

During the early part of July Ernest Payne was again at Swanwick for the first of the SCM's General Conferences. For him the outstanding feature of this Conference was the presence of C. F. Andrews who had had considerable contact and service in India. He talked with Ernest Payne about his contacts with both Gandhi and Tagore. To have met both Schweitzer and C. F. Andrews in the course of two or three months was a great experience for the young Ernest Payne. He was constantly open to new ideas and sought eagerly every opportunity to talk with and to question great thinkers and scholars.

Ministerial settlement

It was while he was at Swanwick that Ernest Payne received a letter asking him to preach at the village of Bugbrooke in Northamptonshire. His name had reached the church secretary at Bugbrooke, not through the superintendents, but through two Regent's Park students who knew that Ernest Payne was seeking a pastorate. He visited Bugbrooke on the last weekend in July 1928. He went with some apprehension, for truth to tell, he had not really contemplated the home ministry and did not feel at that point adequately prepared for it. His first weekend in Bugbrooke, however, proved memorable and decisive. He stayed at a large house called The Grange, the home of Mr and Mrs W.J. Adams. W.J. Adams was the church secretary and a prosperous farmer, then in his mid-sixties. The two men, the older and the younger, struck up an immediate rapport. They talked late on the Saturday evening, between the two services on Sunday, and again late into Sunday night. It was a rare experience for Ernest Payne to find himself so quickly and so completely at home with an older person and indeed one whose background and circumstances were so different from his own. Adams undoubtedly had a real and genuine interest in people whoever they were and whatever they were doing. He was a man of very great discernment both of people and of situations. He was the person in the village to whom all turned for advice and help.

On the Monday morning Adams asked Ernest Payne if he would come and preach again, giving the church two Sundays so that it would be possible to visit the village of Lower Heyford, where there was another chapel, which the Bugbrooke minister served on two Sundays a month, as well as one weekday evening. Adams made it very clear that he should not come again unless he was prepared to consider an invitation to the pastorate. Ernest Payne was faced with a difficult decision. Although he always felt that he would accept the first invitation that came, he had not really expected that it would come from a church in a rural setting. He was a Londoner. He had spent nine years in three different universities. He knew virtually nothing of rural life. But he had felt at home with the Bugbrooke people and he had only one other preaching engagement in prospect and that was at Golcar in Yorkshire on the last Sunday in September. In the end he agreed to go to Bugbrooke, encouraged by the knowledge that Wheeler Robinson thought that he would be right so to do. He preached in Bugbrooke and Lower Heyford on the first two Sundays of September in 1928. Ten days later he received an invitation to the pastorate and this he accepted, being offered a stipend of £200 per annum.

3

Gaining Experience

Pastor and husband

Bugbrooke in 1928 had about 700 inhabitants. Most of the male population worked on the farms, though there were a few railwaymen in Railway Cottages, and one or two others who travelled to Northampton each day to work. The village had no main drainage and no street lighting. It was an interesting challenge, to say the least, for one who had been nurtured in a city. The Baptist chapel was the only Free Church in the village. For a small community the morning congregation at Bugbrooke was unusually large and varied. Several farmers drove in from as far as three miles away, sometimes using gigs – cars were then still something of a novelty and a luxury. There were three families and four homes that dominated the chapel. There was the home of Mr and Mrs Will Adams at The Grange. Miss Jane and Miss Gertrude Adams still lived in Merriefield, the original home of the Adams, and one from which all the family had gone except the two unmarried daughters. The home at Merriefield was a remarkable house which reflected all the splendour and homeliness of village life. The third home was The Homestead, which was the home of Mr and Mrs John Campion. He was chairman of the Northampton Bench of Magistrates and a much respected schoolmaster. The fourth home was that of Mr Oliver Adams a brother of W. J. Adams and who had a farmhouse known as Whitehall.

Ernest Payne's ordination was on Tuesday, 23rd October 1928. There were two services, one in the afternoon and one in the evening with Greetings in between. The laying on of hands was shared in by Dr Wheeler Robinson, Dr Selbie and Mr Will Adams.

During the first few weeks at Bugbrooke the young minister

spent the time as a guest at The Grange whilst repairs were undertaken at the manse including, incidentally, the installation for the first time of an indoor pump to take water up to the bathroom. Ernest Payne needed someone to look after him and eventually a young man together with his wife and small son came and occupied half the house with the wife providing the minister with his meals.

He found himself fully occupied. Every Monday evening there was a prayer meeting at Bugbrooke. On Tuesday after lunch there was the cycle journey to Heyford to spend the afternoon visiting, with a children's service after tea and the mid-week service after that. The Band of Hope met in Bugbrooke on Wednesday evenings and on Thursday there was a midweek service. He soon arranged for a Friday evening games evening with table tennis, draughts and chess for some of the young men of the village for whom there was virtually no provision made for relaxation. When the Rector of Bugbrooke discovered, however, that a number of 'church boys' were coming, he declared that for any of his young people to set foot on chapel property was 'an insult to God'.

It is interesting to reflect that the attitude of the rector towards the Baptist Church was not untypical of the attitudes of 1928. There was another example of this in Bugbrooke which arose in connection with Armistice Sunday. There was a strong branch of the British Legion in the village and its members insisted upon a united service each year. The parish church was the only building large enough to accommodate the congregation. The rector, however, did not feel able to allow a Baptist minister to take part in the service there. Consequently it had to be held each year in the open air. Each minister led prayer and each gave a short address. The weather in November is not always propitious and certainly does not encourage open air gatherings of any length. On one particular occasion when the weather in the first part of November was extremely bad, the question arose as to whether the service might not be held in the church building after all. But the rector was adamant in refusing to allow the Baptist minister to participate. The Legion, however, refused to go to the church unless the Baptist minister took part. The rector, of course, refused to come to the chapel which was in any case too small a building for the congregation. On the Friday the rector called at the manse to assure Ernest Payne that his difficulties were ecclesiastical and theological and in no way personal and suggested confidently that their united prayers would resolve the situation. Sure enough on the Sunday at mid-day the rain stopped and the service took place on the Sunday afternoon in the dry, though somewhat uncomfortably because the field beside the church was extremely wet. In fact, most of the congregation stayed some distance off in the roadway!

The village of Heyford was a couple of miles from Bugbrooke, but different again. It was more truly rural and even less sophisticated. Of the people who made up the Baptist fellowship, one family, the Carringtons, played a large part. Mrs Carrington was a cousin of Dr Henry Townsend, principal of the Baptist College in Manchester. She and Mr Carrington had seven children, who formed later the basis of a young people's class.

The reflection of the situation between church and chapel in Heyford is illustrated by the fact that the rector and the Baptist minister scarcely ever met except occasionally on the Northampton bus. Ernest Payne discovered that after he had been at Heyford about a year, during his Tuesday afternoon visiting, he was involved in calling on more people who went to the Anglican church than in fact went to the chapel. He expressed his concern to Mrs Carrington, and she arranged for him to meet informally the churchwarden and his wife. They spoke most appreciatively of his visits and urged him to continue them. The churchwarden's wife commented that really they could not expect the rector to visit the likes of them for 'he's a gentleman'. No doubt this was really intended as a compliment both to the rector and to the Baptist minister!

It was not long before Ernest Payne persuaded a group of young people from Bugbrooke and Heyford to meet together on a Wednesday evening. It was called the Young People's Class or more often Mr Payne's class. It provided a steady procession of candidates for baptism and for church membership. Amongst them was one of the Carrington children, John, and a young lady named Norah Flemming who subsequently married John Carrington. These two were set eventually to become distinguished missionaries with the Baptist Missionary Society.

In January 1930 Will Adams died suddenly after a heart

attack. The whole village was stunned by the news for so much of its life had had this one individual at its centre. Not long before his death, Will Adams had agreed to take into his home and on to his farm his young nephew Griff Davies. Griff was the son of Mr Adams' sister Emily, who had died of cancer in 1921. Her husband, Norman Davies had married again and was living in Bracknell. On the death of Will Adams, Griff's sister, Freda, was sent for to help her aunt in the sudden and devastating shock she had sustained. So Freda Davies moved into the Grange and became an effective member of that household. It was not long before a friendship developed between Ernest Payne and Freda Davies which blossomed into romance. They became engaged and on 28th October 1930, they were married in the Baptist Chapel in Wokingham by the minister of College Street Baptist Chapel, Northampton, the Rev. E. Murray Page. Thus began a happy companionship in marriage which lasted for nearly fifty years.

There was a Fraternal of Ministers in West Northants which met sporadically and included ministers of most denominations. Papers were read which indicated the standing and the viewpoint of each person. As a result of these papers, each member grew more and more aware of how little they knew of each other's beliefs and practices. It was recognised that this lack of knowledge was at the root of many misconceptions, and consequently of misunderstandings. This again emphasised to Ernest Payne the importance of what are now known as ecumenical contacts.

The following year, the area superintendent sounded Ernest Payne about moving to Welwyn Garden City where a group of Baptists had determined to break away from the so-called Free Church in the Garden City, which was basically a Presbyterian Church, and to start a cause of their own. Ernest Payne knew something of the situation at Welwyn Garden City and knew that amongst those in the Presbyterian Church, and in responsible positions, were Baptists who were convinced of the rightness of one Free Church in the newly developing Garden City. He was quite unwilling, therefore, to become involved in a separatist move of the kind that was then projected. In addition he had no desire at all to leave Bugbrooke. Then quite unexpectedly there came another approach – this time from the Baptist Missionary Society. It had been decided

40

to appoint a Young People's Secretary to relieve Mr H. L. Hemmens of some of the varied work he had done for so long and so successfully. Ernest Payne was invited to consider the position. He had little hesitation in refusing. It was now the summer of 1931. There was a world wide trade depression and mounting unemployment. Missionary societies, like many other organisations, found themselves in a difficult situation and some retrenchment became necessary. The Baptist Missionary Society called a special meeting of its General Committee in Coventry, to discuss the situation. Amongst the matters discussed was Ernest Payne's refusal to accept the invitation to serve the society. The outcome of the discussion was that he received a renewal of the invitation but this time with even greater emphasis. In view of this and in the light of the challenging circumstances facing the Baptist Missionary Society he reconsidered the matter. He had hoped, of course, to serve the Baptist Missionary Society abroad, and now the society was asking for his help at home. But there were many things against such a move. He had been married for not much more than a year and they were settling happily in the Bugbrooke situation. There was promising developments in the churches at Bugbrooke and Lower Heyford. He had been elected secretary of the Northamptonshire Association with a place on the Baptist Union Council and he was increasingly committed to the work of the Association and to its development.

After several days of uncertainty, he decided to go to Oxford to seek Wheeler Robinson's advice, who, far from urging him to decline the invitation, left him with a clear impression that he thought that this service might well be the right line for him. Wheeler Robinson was frank in his assessment of Ernest Payne's potential and was quite emphatic that whilst he doubted whether he would ever be much good as a secretary responsible for raising money, such as might be the responsibility for a Home Secretary, he certainly could be of some use amongst young people and hopefully in helping with publications. In the end Ernest Payne decided that he must accept the invitation. He felt almost as though again the decision had been made for him. All his advisors pointed him in this direction. His friend John Barrett confirmed him in this view, pointing out that it was significant that the Baptist Missionary

Society had persisted in its invitation in the face of such adverse financial conditions. So at the end of March 1932 he concluded his ministry in Bugbrooke. At least, he had the satisfaction of knowing that neither the people in Bugbrooke nor in Lower Heyford wanted him to leave.

The first question that faced Freda and Ernest Payne was that of accommodation. A house was needed, if possible within easy reach of Potters Bar, for Margaret was becoming increasingly helpless and her parents were close on seventy years old. In the end the Paynes fixed on No. 4, Temple Avenue in Whetstone. This was a semi-detached house not far from a station on the line from Kings Cross to Potters Bar. The house served the family well for more than seven years in which not only they, but also the denomination and indeed the whole nation faced crisis and change.

The Baptist Mission House to which he went, somewhat nervously, in April 1932 was situated in Furnival Street, Holborn. It was a typically solid Victorian Building, and had been the headquarters of the Society since 1870. Until the opening of the Baptist Church House in Southampton Row in 1905 it had also contained the somewhat restricted offices of the Baptist Union. It still had beside it, in premises spreading round into Cursitor Street, the offices of the Psalms and Hymns Trust. The Senior Secretaries in 1932 were the Rev. C. E. Wilson (Foreign), the Rev. B. Grey Griffith (Home), Dr R. Fletcher Mooreshead (Medical), and Miss Eleanor Bowser (Women). Dr W. Y. Fullerton, former Home Secretary, was still coming into the house regularly as a consultant. Grey Griffith was assisted by H. L. Hemmens, who had served the Society for many years and had combined many duties including that of Editor, and had begun to develop the work among young people. It was to assist H. L. Hemmens that Ernest Payne came into the service of the Society.

The correspondence and discussions concerning his appointment had all been with Grey Griffith, but the first person he met on arrival was C. E. Wilson and from him he received words of welcome and encouragement. These he needed, because shortly afterwards, he discovered that no thought had been given at all as to where he should be located in the house. He followed Grey Griffith around as the Home Secretary tried to find somewhere to put him. Finally he was placed in a tiny attic room over the Cursitor Street property which was furnished simply with one table and one chair. In this somewhat unsatisfactory room Ernest Payne spent the first few days of his service to the Baptist Missionary Society finding time to read at least F. A. Cox's *History of the Baptist Mission* prepared for the Jubilee of the society in 1842. Eventually something better lay ahead. In June, H. L. Hemmens suggested that Ernest Payne should use his room whilst he was on holiday. This particular office was adjacent to that which Dr Fullerton was using when he visited London. This meant that Ernest Payne had some contact with Fullerton, an Irishman, who was a striking figure, big in body, mind and heart. He had had a link with C. H. Spurgeon whose later sermons he had put into shape for the printer. He was an outstanding evangelist, and a Baptist leader with a reputation and influence far beyond the boundaries of the denomination. During that summer, Ernest Payne memorably spent three or four weeks in daily contact with him. Sadly in August 1932 Fullerton died quite unexpectedly. But this contact with so giant a figure from the past, was always memorable to the new Young People's Secretary.

For the four years that Ernest Payne served as Young People's Secretary, his main administrative concern was developing the Society's Summer Schools, then largely centred at Seascale, Bexhill, and Felixstowe. He further had to develop and strengthen links with other organisations notable the Girls' Auxiliary which was then a considerable and well run organisation, related to the Baptist Missionary Society and serving it with great usefulness. He helped also with the Baptist Young Men's Movement, which was formed in 1927, and although small in number it played its part in inspiring the continuation and the development of the Baptist Men's Movement. There was also the monthly Missionary Conference Meeting on a Tuesday evening in the library of the Mission House, which drew a large company from the London churches. Its Chairman was Arnold Clark who had not yet been drawn into the service of the Baptist Union. Ernest Payne was given further opportunity and responsibility by representing the society on the United Council for Missionary Education which was a publishing venture in which the main societies co-operated under the sponsorship of the Conference of the British Missionary Societies. He also developed the contacts between the Baptist Missionary Society and the local churches, through young people's fellowships, Christian Endeavour societies, and Sunday schools. This involved him in a good deal of travel for Sunday services and mid-week meetings. The Baptist Missionary Society children's organisation, 'The League of Ropeholders,' was then active in a number of places, and although it had an honorary secretary, its activities fell under Ernest Payne's care. Before long he was serving also on the British Lessons Council, responsible for Sunday school lessons. Living in London, as he did, he shared in the formation and development of the John Clifford Society for the Baptist Students who were studying in London. All in all Ernest Payne wondered who was doing all the work he did before he was called to join the Society's ranks!

Of the staff at the Baptist Missionary Society at this point, H. L. Hemmens proved a most helpful guide and friend. Most particularly, however, it was Grey Griffith who kept an encouraging and watchful eye on Ernest Payne, as he did on all the staff. Grey Griffith was a truly remarkable person, full of energy and zeal, truly a Christian warrior, formidable in his commitment, and often in the expression of his commitment, but one with great kindness of heart, and always a great encourager of the younger person.

One other name that should be mentioned amongst the particular encouragers is one that is too easily forgotten, that of W. E. Cule. Cule was BMS Editor and it was he who encouraged Ernest Payne to write. He was a retiring and sensitive Welshman, and he had under his care the Society's magazines, the *Missionary Herald* and *Wonderlands*, which was his special creation for children. In addition Cule had recently launched *Quest*, a magazine for young people. Before long, Ernest Payne was contributing regularly to the *Herald* a number of biographical sketches of missionaries which Cule encouraged him to publish as a collection entitled *The First Generation*. This was published in 1936, to add to his 1933 book, *Freedom in Jamaica* written in connection with the centenary of the emancipation of the slaves, and his thesis, *The Saktas*, published in 1933.

His visits to Edinburgh House for the UCME Committees brought him into contact with a number of younger members of various headquarters staffs, including R. R. Williams who subsequently became Bishop of Leicester, Basil Matthews, the writer, and John Whale, who was before long to be Principal of Cheshunt College, Cambridge. Edinburgh House, where the meetings were held, was then the focal point in London of ecumenical developments. This was in the days before the British Council of Churches. In Edinburgh House, Ernest Payne had glimpses of the influential ecumenical figures William Paton and J. H. Oldham.

By 1939 Ernest Payne had become Chairman of the UCME and found himself during the first year of its existence on the Commission of the Churches for International Friendship and Social Responsibility which was one of the main contributory streams to the British Council of Churches. The chairman of that Commission was William Temple, then Archbishop of York.

During his time with the Baptist Missionary Society, quite unexpectedly his contact with Regent's Park College developed. In November 1933, the Rev. C. M. Hardy, who had been secretary of Regent's Park College since 1909, died suddenly. After consultation with Grey Griffith, Wheeler Robinson asked Ernest Payne whether he would undertake the work as Secretary of the College as a spare time occupation! He was assured that it would not involve him in a great deal of extra work and that a member of the clerical staff in the Mission House, Miss Winifred Knight, would help him with the correspondence. He was eager to help Wheeler Robinson, and accepted this responsibility.

The mastering of the job as Secretary of the College he had to do the hard way. On collecting the minute books and papers he found to his dismay that a record of the council meeting held months earlier had not yet been written up. From this experience he developed the disciplined habit of trying, if at all possible, to prepare Minutes within a few hours or, at the most, a few days of any meeting. Although the College Council met only two or three times a year, the House and Finance committee met much more frequently. This particular body was chaired by the college Treasurer, Herbert Marnham of Hampstead, a much respected denominational figure, who was also Treasurer of the Baptist Union. The committee was an impressive group of Baptist laymen, including Cecil Rooke, the Baptist Union solicitor, H. H. Collier, an estate agent, C. T.

LeQuesne, a barrister and from 1937 a member of the Continuation Committee of Faith and Order, Seymour J. Price, an insurance broker, and Herbert Chown, a stock broker. It was in the company of this distinguished committee that Ernest Payne served his apprenticeship as Secretary of Regent's Park College.

Care and precision were Herbert Marnham's watchwords. He insisted upon examining the counterfoils of every cheque drawn between meetings, and every cheque had to have on it the signatures of two members of the committee. The secretary was responsible for the paying of the Oxford staff and also the monthly bursaries to the 16 Regent's Park College students who were still studying in London. It wasn't long before he became caught up in the preparations for launching a building fund appeal in order to develop the Pusey Street site.

During the Furnival Street years his family responsibilities were increasing. To the great delight of parents and grandparents, a daughter, Elizabeth Ann, was born to Freda Payne on 10th March 1933. But the burden of responsibility for the Potter's Bar household was resting increasingly upon Ernest Payne. His father was finding the accountancy business more and more difficult; Philip Payne was continuing with great bravery and with great difficulty to work in the family business; and his sister, Margaret, was clearly in need of an increasing amount of assistance. To add to this his aunts Norah and Ethel, sisters of his father, both suffered serious breakdowns. In the mid 1930s it sometimes seemed as though one emergency followed another, and the pressures were extremely great. Grey Griffith was a tower of strength to Ernest Payne in these days and other new friends began to appear on the horizon, one of whom was Ronald Bell who lived at New Barnet and attended the North Finchley Church. He held a position of growing responsibility in the Temperance Building Society and frequently drove Ernest Payne to the City. Bell's abilities were already apparent. He was becoming influential in denominational affairs. Although outwardly somewhat severe, he was nevertheless a man of considerable sympathy and Ernest Payne became firm friends with him and growingly dependent upon him for advice.

An added concern was that the doctors made it clear to Freda and Ernest Payne that, in their opinion, the family history on the Payne side made it extremely unwise for them to have any more children. This was a matter of great disappointment. In 1937, however, a further responsibility came their way which they accepted willingly and which proved of great benefit to their family and another. C. E. Wilson, the BMS Foreign Secretary, had become very friendly with the Paynes, and they had come to know the four daughters of the Wilsons. The youngest of them, Norah, had married Dr Raymond Holmes, who was a missionary doctor in Yakusu. In 1937, the Holmes family was back in England with their baby boy, Gordon. Tragically, Norah was terminally ill. Freda and Ernest Payne had told Dr Holmes that if there was anything at all they could do to help him in the circumstances they would gladly try to do so. It was only later that they discovered that Norah, knowing that she was dying, had told her husband that she hoped he would be able to find some home, like that of the Paynes, where the boy could be cared for whilst he continued his missionary service. The outcome of that conversation and the Paynes' letter of sympathy, when Norah died, was that, in September, 1937, Raymond Holmes and his son joined the Payne household. Dr Holmes remained with them until his return to the Congo mission field some months later. Gordon Holmes was to remain for more than ten years with the Paynes, and to establish a close and permanent relationship of mutual affection.

Scarcely had the arrangements been made with Raymond Holmes, when Max Hancock and his wife on furlough from Portugese Congo asked the Paynes whether they would look after their daughter Betty, who was starting at Walthamstow Hall, a school for missionaries' children. After some hesitation the Paynes decided that they could not refuse. So it came about that, from 1937 onwards and throughout the Second World War, the Paynes had three children to look after.

Baptist World Alliance and Joint Headquarters

But all this is to anticipate. Ernest Payne gained his first experience of the work of the Baptist World Alliance in 1934 at the Fifth Baptist World Congress held in Berlin. Dr Rushbrooke invited him to speak on the subject, 'Anti-God Propaganda,' with special reference to what was happening in Russia. Grey Griffith encouraged him to accept this somewhat difficult assignment. So it was that he found himself returning to Germany at a critical moment in its history. He reached Berlin on Friday 3rd August 1934, the day that the aged President Hindenburg died. What was to happen next in Germany nobody quite knew. Hitler had become Chancellor in 1933. The German Baptist leaders were clearly on edge, but assured the executive of the Baptist World Alliance that the Baptist Congress would have adequate freedom of expression. Undoubtedly most Germans realised that a chapter had ended with the death of Hindenburg, and that the next chapter held many dangers and uncertainties for them. The funeral service for Hindenburg was on Tuesday 7th August and the Germans responsible for the Congress wanted the funeral proceedings together with the oration by Hitler broadcast to the congress session. This was refused, but as a compromise it was agreed that the congress should stand adjourned at the time of the funeral ceremony. When that moment came, before anyone could leave, the Germans occupied the platform, and placed on it an enormous wreath.

It was evident that all too few of the Germans present at that moment could see beyond the grief for the death of one who had become known as 'Father Hindenburg'. But there were exceptions. The wife of one of the leading Baptist ministers, a woman who was of Czech origin, and one whom Ernest Payne had known when he was a student in 1928, took him aside, led him to a secluded place behind the platform and spoke to him with concern and apprehension about the dangers that were now facing the Christians and indeed the whole German people. There was also a young German Baptist who was so concerned to make sure that Ernest Payne was aware of the dangers inherent in the German political situation that he took him to a restaurant at the airport and, lest it should be thought they were talking treasonable secrets, led him not to a side table, but a table right in the centre of the restaurant where he expressed to Ernest Payne his own opposition to Hitler's policies, and warned him of the events that he judged were about to happen. History proved this young man all too correct.

Ernest Payne's paper on anti-God propaganda[2] attracted a

good deal of attention. Both J. H. Rushbrooke and C. E. Wilson told J. H. Oldham about it. Oldham had just begun preparations for the 1937 Oxford Conference on Church, Community and State, and he sent Ernest Payne one of the preliminary pamphlets asking for comments and inviting him to meet and discuss it. This meeting was significant in stimulating Ernest Payne's growing interest in the infant ecumenical movement.

It is also probable that because of the attention gained by his address to the congress he was co-opted back on to the Baptist Union Council as one who had much to contribute in the future. When he returned to the council he found there had been considerable changes. There was a small group of younger people, who gradually became drawn to each other, not only because of age but because of similarity of outlook. This group met on the evening prior to the council to talk over denominational affairs in general and the major topics on the agenda. In due course the group became known as 'Focus'. The members in addition to Ernest Payne were J. O. Barrett, Ronald Bell, Frank Buffard, Frank Bryan, Robert Child, Charles Jewson, Ingli James, Guy Ramsay, J. B. Middlebrook, J. C. Rendle, and later they were joined by Gordon Wylie and Eric Knight. The group was often critical of the official line and did not hesitate to express its opinions. Not surprisingly the group was subject to some criticism by other members of Council as it appeared to be a critical pressure group yet without clearly defined alternative policies. Nevertheless it was rightly recognised as containing younger members of the denomination from whom much might be expected when they had the opportunity to move from the opposition to the responsibility of government within the denomination.

By this time also he was deeply involved in the work of the Baptist Historical Society. He had been a member of its committee since April, 1932, and had already contributed some dozen articles to the society's Journal, the *Baptist Quarterly*. He was to serve the society as editor, as a vice president and finally as its president. He believed in the society and the vital importance of its work. His concern and interest is reflected not only in his constant advocacy of the society's cause but also in the fact that in total he contributed more than 70 articles to the *Baptist Quarterly*.

One of the major denominational issues of the years just prior to the Second World War was the question of joint headquarters for the Baptist Union and the Baptist Missionary Society. The matter was brought into the open by C. E. Wilson and B. Grey Griffith when they learned that the Government had plans for enlarging the Patent Office which had premises in Furnival Street, adjacent to the Mission House. After sixty years the old Mission House was becoming somewhat old fashioned in appearance and atmosphere. In 1903, the Baptist Union had moved to the newly constructed Baptist Church House in Southampton Row and over three decades had developed into a substantial organisation. A growing number of laymen who supported both the Baptist Union and the Baptist Missionary Society wanted to see the two main denominational organisations again under one roof. A joint committee was set up consisting of twelve from each of the two houses. Ernest Payne was appointed as one of the representatives of the Baptist Missionary Society. Apparently his place on that committee was due to the advocacy of Miss Eleanor Bowser who argued that there ought to be someone on the committee who was at least likely to live and work in any new headquarters for a considerable period. Whatever may have been the reason, Ernest Payne was totally committed to the concept of joint headquarters from then until his dying day. In 1938, the discussions began in confident and hopeful mood.

It was at once recognised that there could and should be closer co-operation on a number of points. Complete integration had been twice previously suggested in 1874 and in 1904. The Joint Committee set up sub-committees to consider how the Carey Press, the Kingsgate Press, the Women's Departments and the Young People's Departments, might be brought closer together. But from the beginning, it was agreed that what must be provided was a new building, with separate suites of offices for the senior administrative executives of the two bodies, with a council chamber, committee rooms, and other facilities which either party could use. Most people believed that once the two bodies were under one roof, then there would be speedy progress, towards a more complete integration. Mr R. Wilson Black was instructed to seek a site and prepare plans.

The initiative came mainly from the side of the Baptist Missionary Society. On the Baptist Union side there was considerable reluctance to leave Southampton Row, and this was understandable. The site was a freehold site. The building was then only some thirty years old and was much admired. Mr Wilson Black produced a scheme which provided for a new headquarters on the north side of Russell Square, on a leasehold site, which was nevertheless offered on a lease of 200 years and might be argued by some as being as good as freehold. But the fact of it being leasehold at all was the cause of considerable hesitation on the part of many. M. E. Aubrey, then Secretary of the Baptist Union, was himself against the move. He sympathised with the idea of a joint headquarters but had very real hesitation not only about the leasehold question but also as to how it could be possible for there to be the two bodies within the one building, both seeking to administer the same building.

Looking back now, it is possible perhaps to see that the difference of approach and outlook was bound to cause division when the matter came for final decision at the assembly. But at the meeting of the Baptist Union Council on 8th March 1938, the scheme was accepted by a majority of 64–28. Not only, however, did M. E. Aubrey have hesitations about the scheme, but so did the newly appointed Baptist Union Treasurer, Arnold Clark. Following the council meeting, M. E. Aubrey published an article in the *Baptist Times* published on 17th March, in which he stated frankly that he had been opposed to the scheme, and that when it became clear that the council was going to accept the scheme, he was faced with a very difficult decision. He was advised that if he resigned it would make for a very difficult denominational situation. So he recognised that his duty was to accept the verdict of the majority and to work whole-heartedly to bring the scheme to fruition. Just as seriously, however, on the BMS side, the treasurer, Mr H. L. Taylor of Bristol, felt quite unable to support the scheme. His objections were that the site was leasehold and that he had some hesitation about the speculative elements within the scheme, in that some of the accommodation would have to be let for profit. Nevertheless at its meeting in April 1938, the General Committee of the Baptist Missionary Society voted overwhelmingly in favour of the scheme, whereupon Mr Taylor offered his resignation as treasurer.

All these events did not augur well for the debate at the

assembly. It was the afternoon of 25th April 1938, that the matter came for discussion. From the outset Ernest Payne had been wholly in favour of the scheme and believed that Mr Wilson Black's suggestion was the best that was likely to be possible in the circumstances. The proposals were submitted to the assembly by Mr Wilson Black who set out the scheme clearly and competently arguing carefully the financial merits of it. The resolution was formally seconded. There was an amendment on the agenda in the name of Mr Richard Jewson of Norwich to the effect that general authority be given to the council to provide a building on freehold property. Somewhat unusually the amendment went on with a negative, expressing disapproval of the scheme for a proposal to develop on lease-hold property. The amendment was seconded by the Rev. Gilbert Laws of Norwich.

Dr Whitley, the Baptist historian, argued that full support should be given to the proposal of the Council. Ernest Brown MP who was at that time a member of the National Government, doubted the wisdom of the scheme, and queried the speculative nature of it. Dr J. C. Carlisle then suggested that the Treasurers of the Baptist Union and the Baptist Missionary Society should be given an opportunity of stating their views. Whether Carlisle was aware that H. L. Taylor had resigned on the issue is uncertain, but is probable. He must certainly have known that Arnold Clark was opposed. Arnold Clark read a carefully prepared statement in which he spoke openly and honestly about his opposition to the scheme, but said that when it was passed by the council he felt that he must carry his opposition no further, but, like M. E. Aubrey, work whole-heartedly to make the scheme a great success. On reflection, however, he felt now that he must at this point speak openly. H. L. Taylor followed Arnold Clark and made it clear that he could not accept the proposal, indicating that he had voted against the scheme in the BMS General Committee.

As a member of the Joint Committee that had developed the possibility of the joint headquarters, Ernest Payne was a strong supporter of the resolution. In the assembly, however, he said nothing. His personal record of the assembly says this:

I felt an almost irresistable impulse to stand up and say that the assembly was being misled; that it had not really understood the scheme and the reason for it, or the unfortunate consequences that would follow its rejection. I have often wondered whether I ought to have done so, though I do not think the result would have been substantially different if I had.

In his history of the Baptist Union he makes this comment on the debate:

Within 17 months of the rejection of the Russell Square Scheme, the Second World War began. Was the denomination saved from a project which could not have succeeded in the changed financial situation? Was it saved from a plan which would have caused continuous embarrassment, because the vital matter of unified control was left on one side? Or was a great opportunity lost, and the cause of denominational unity and progress set back for many years?[3]

These are questions which can never be answered for certain. But the joint headquarters question was to be faced many times in the next 40 years, always without result, and it was to occupy many weary and worrying days in Ernest Payne's life.

It is difficult to escape the conclusion that for him the whole 1938 experience was one of disillusionment and caused him considerable personal distress. It coloured his attitudes towards denominational plans and undoubtedly made things no easier for him when he finally came to succeed M. E. Aubrey.

Whilst all this was going on, his own position in the Mission House had changed. In 1936 W. E. Cule had retired, and Ernest Payne was asked to succeed him as BMS Editor. This gave to him not only a further insight into the problems of meeting deadlines for publishing dates, but brought him also into more frequent and closer contact with the foreign side of the Society's administration and with the missionaries. It also developed his contacts further with Edinburgh House. He had already begun to see the possibility of a useful life's work in the service of the Baptist Missionary Society opening out before him. Already he had in mind the need for a new history of the Society. Within the Young People's work, he had tried to forge contacts and initiated joint actions with Dr Dunning at the Baptist Union. Into the Baptist Missionary Society there came Walter Bottoms, as Young People's Secretary, and Gwenyth Hubble as personal assistant to Eleanor Bowser. These two were nearer to him in age than many of the other members of the staff, and their presence seemed to confirm the brightness of the future in the Society.

The Sixth Congress of the Baptist World Alliance was planned for Georgia in July 1939. Dr Rushbrooke invited Ernest Payne to write a pageant for this Congress, and this he did together with Kathleen Shuttleworth of the Girls' Auxiliary. It was entitled *A Pageant of Baptist History* and was later published in 1942 under the title *Missionaries All*. It was impressively produced at Atlanta in the open air before an audience estimated to number some 60,000 people. He had also been invited to speak at a sectional meeting on youth. He was given 15 minutes to speak on 'Youth and Baptist Values'. This address gives an early example of his masterly ability to summarise arguments.[4] The five points of the Baptist faith which he judged to be perpetually relevant were the necessity of individual faith and conviction, the practice of believer's baptism, the understanding of the church as a spiritual fellowship made up of converted men and women, the missionary impetus and personal evangelism, and a passion for liberty. In a remarkable two or three paragraphs he illustrates what these may be said to have to do with youth. He indicates how these essential elements in the Gospel were discovered and rediscovered by young men and women. Thomas Helwys was not much more than 30 years old when he founded the first Baptist Church in England. Roger Williams was probably a year or two younger when he established the Rhode Island Colony. Carey was 34 when he reached India. Tom Comber was 24 when he went to Africa, and Gerhard Oncken, the father of German Baptists, was under 30 when he came to become a Baptist. C. H. Spurgeon's world famous ministry of preaching began in his 20's.

The party from Atlanta returned in the late August of 1939. Freda Payne and the children had been spending a month in Bugbrooke and on Friday, 1st September, Ernest Payne travelled down there. He was due to preach at Bugbrooke on Sunday 3rd September. His suggestion that the service at the chapel should be put back on the Sunday morning in order that folk might know what had happened about the expiry of the British ultimatum to Hitler at 11 a.m. was emphatically rejected by the Bugbrooke secretary. The Church's concern was with eternal and not with temporal matters! But war

54

came, and it was evident that it was safer for Freda Payne and the children to remain at Bugbrooke.

In the event of war, the Baptist Missionary Society had arranged to move its headquarters to the premises of Union Church, High Wycombe. This removal had begun at the end of August, and Ernest Payne found himself, together with other members of the staff staying locally. He was fortunate enough to be able to enjoy the hospitality of his friend Murray Page at Amersham-on-the-Hill. With considerable foresight, Ernest Payne moved the Baptist Missionary Society file of the *Freeman* and the *Baptist Times* to a basement room in the newly-built Regent's Park College together with several letter books of the Carey period and a number of cases of missionary letters and documents. In view of the subsequent destruction of the Mission House, this was a most fortunate action.

Regent's Park College again

During the last years before the war, the affairs of Regent's Park College had taken up a good deal of Ernest Payne's time and energy. On 21st July 1938, there had been a stone laying ceremony attended by most of the distinguished Baptist leaders of the day. The raising of the funds for the building at Regent's Park had been spear-headed by Wheeler Robinson and Ernest Payne. This had involved various lunches in different parts of the country and a considerable amount of planning and travelling. The first part of the building, that of the construction of the Helwys Hall, the library, the Collier lecture room, common rooms and kitchens was complete. In the summer of 1939 the College Council had had to face the crucial question as to whether to venture on the erection of the 16 study bedrooms on the north side of the site. There was virtually no money in hand for this – all of it had been expended on the first part of the building. Nor was there much sign of money in sight. Wheeler Robinson made it clear that the responsibility for the continuation or not must rest with the college council. Boldness won the day. The builders were directed to go straight on with the additional construction. This was completed in the summer of 1940 just as the Government found it necessary to prohibit virtually all private building.

There were changes in the offing on the staff at Regent's. Wheeler Robinson would be 70 years old in 1942. His heir-apparent was Robert Child. There were those who thought it would be wise if Child joined the staff immediately but there was a hesitation at this stage to promise Child the principal-ship. Not surprisingly in these circumstances, Robert Child stayed to continue his ministry at Broadmead, Bristol, which involved him facing up to and carrying through the life of the downtown Baptist church in the difficult and dangerous days of the German air raids. Leonard Brockington had been assistant in Old Testament teaching at Regent's since 1932. He was a young man, a capable scholar, but had had no pastoral experience, and was little known in the denomination. Wheeler Robinson thought perhaps the appointment should be of another young man who would make historical doctrine his main subject. The college council, however, and the committee charged with dealing with staffing matters, wanted someone who was already known in the denomination. There seems to have been something approaching deadlock on the nominating committee between the principal and those who thought like him, and the rest, which was probably the majority of the committee.

The BMS had largely returned to Furnival Street during the Autumn of 1939 and one afternoon, late in that year, Wheeler Robinson appeared in Ernest Payne's office, and made to him what was a quite startling suggestion, namely that he should join the staff at Regent's Park College. Ernest Payne's immediate reaction was that it was quite impossible. He had committed himself to the service of the Baptist Missionary Society and judged that this was to be his life's work. He had been out of college for some twelve years. He had not kept up his reading, particularly in the field of historical theology, which in any case was an area to which he was not particularly drawn. The fact that Freda and the children were still in Bugbrooke had meant that Ernest Payne could sometimes spend the night at Potters Bar and help his mother with the growing difficulty of caring for Margaret and also for his father who, by this time, was extremely frail, and sadly was largely unaware of all that was going on around him. To go to Oxford would mean moving further away from Potters Bar, and the responsibilities at Oxford would mean less freedom to act in emergencies.

Wheeler Robinson persisted with his plan. He was in a difficulty, and Ernest Payne knew that he needed help. Wheeler Robinson was now 68 years old and had been carrying almost single handed the burden of the move to Oxford, the erection of the new building, and a substantial teaching load.

The invitation produced much anxiety and perplexity in his mind. As so often when faced with these decisions, Ernest Payne depended very much upon the advice of others. He had always a deep loyalty to the work that he was doing at a particular time and the people with whom he was working. To move to a new situation was difficult for him, for it broke that loyalty. The situation was not made easier by the fact that his closest colleagues in the Mission House urged him to stay. But more influential members of the Mission House staff took a broader view. Eleanor Bowser felt he should go to Oxford. Dr H. R. Williamson, who had succeeded C. E. Wilson in 1938 as Foreign Secretary, doubted whether as Editor of the Baptist Missionary Society, Ernest Payne would ever have adequate scope for his many gifts. There was little likelihood in wartime conditions of any major changes in structure or personnel. Grey Griffith commented in his gruff but friendly way that the decision must be Ernest Payne's and obviously was one of high significance for his future. Philip Payne, who was always frank with his brother, and who was a shrewd judge of the situation, said that sooner or later he was bound to leave the Baptist Missionary Society and even at this moment there was not total pressure from the more influential people for him to stay. His mother and sister said that their situation must not influence him. These and other arguments meant that yet again he felt the decision was being made for him. It was right that he should accept, and to Oxford he must go. After much difficulty a house was discovered to rent at 151, Woodstock Road, and in July 1940 Ernest Payne and his family moved in.

A few weeks after the move to Oxford, he was preaching at the Baptist Church at High Road, Tottenham. It was 1st September 1940. He had decided to take the opportunity to visit his sister Margaret, who had temporarily gone into a nursing home in Winchmore Hill for treatment for anaemia. That September Sunday was one that was marked by daylight air raids. The morning service had scarcely begun before the air raid warning sounded and the church secretary urged everyone to go home. Some refused to leave and Ernest Payne conducted a short service for them in one of the classrooms. Afterwards, when the All Clear had sounded, he made his way to the nursing home at Winchmore Hill. His sister was very low, but was eager to hear about Oxford, and the move.

When the evening service was over, he returned to Potters Bar and was sitting with his mother at the supper table, when the phone rang with the message from Winchmore Hill that Margaret was unconscious. Later that same evening, very peacefully, she died. She had lived many years longer than the doctors had at first anticipated. She was uncomplaining in the face of an increasingly distressing helplessness.

After Margaret's funeral, the family were in the sitting room at Potters Bar. Outside the garden was bathed in warm September sunshine. Suddenly a butterfly stirred in the room and flew out of the open window into the sunlight. To the family it appeared a symbol of the freedom which had at last come to Margaret's long imprisoned spirit.

That beautiful September weather in 1940 issued in nights of fear for those who lived in London and other industrial centres. The air raids continued at night throughout the winter months and on 29th December a severe fire bomb attack on the City of London destroyed the offices of Payne, Stone and Fraser. The fire was so intense that the safes were melted by the heat, and all the books and papers belonging to the firm were destroyed, including the Payne family papers and many documents relating to Regent's Park College. The challenge to replace the records and documents as far as possible was undertaken with the greatest of courage and remarkable competence by Philip Payne.

There was yet more to be borne. On the morning of 23rd January 1941, Ernest Payne's father died. He had been all too little aware of events in the last year or so of his life. He had not appeared even to notice his daughter Margaret's death. The passing of Margaret and Alexander Payne meant that within four months two sadnesses had come to Catherine Payne, yet at the same time two heavy burdens which had rested upon her and which she had borne so courageously had been lifted. She picked up the threads of her life in Potters Bar and most particularly in the church.

Writer and scholar

For Ernest Payne the eleven years that he was to serve on the staff of Regent's Park College were busy, but they were also full of satisfaction and joy. If it is possible to categorise the years in other peoples' lives, it is probably true to say that the Oxford days were the happiest days of Ernest Payne's life. He greatly enjoyed the contact with the students and the subsequent friendships which resulted from them. He enjoyed the stimulus of teaching and of discussion. He created time within the Oxford scene for writing. He continued his involvement in denominational affairs, particularly the Baptist Missionary Society. During these years he had his introduction to the ecumenical movement in Faith and Order and then in the World Council Assembly at Amsterdam in 1948. The family was together in a city in which they found friendship within the university and within the local Baptist church in Woodstock Road. The College which he loved so well was now firmly established in Oxford, and when at last in 1945 the war was over and student numbers increased again, it seemed surely that there was to be a long season of clear shining after rain. He hoped that he had found at last the place and the context where he would serve all his days.

One of the immediate results of his move to Oxford was to stimulate further his desire for writing. He edited a book of essays which was presented to Wheeler Robinson on 6th February 1942 – Wheeler's 70th birthday – and published subsequently under the title *Studies in History and Religion* by the Lutterworth Press. In addition, Ernest Payne had been working for some time with the encouragement of the United Council for Missionary Education on an outline of the modern missionary movement. His manuscript was accepted by the Edinburgh House Press and appeared in February 1942 as *The Church Awakes*. The book was warmly received and widely taken up by other denominations. He then turned his attention to the writing of a book entitled *The Free Church Tradition in the Life of England*. He did this partly as an exercise for himself in order that he could clear his own mind and satisfy himself that there did remain an adequate case for continuing to train men for the Free Church ministry. But the other reason for writing was to set very clearly before the churches, the contribution that the Free Church tradition had made and was making in England. He believed that the book would assist the discussion on church relationships that was then beginning to take shape.

In the preface to this book he wrote: 'My deepest obligations are, first to a family tradition of nonconformity, stretching back to the opening of the 18th century, and perhaps earlier, and secondly, to a personal experience within the Free Churches which makes me increasingly sure that they are truly a part of the One Holy Catholic and Apostolic Church.'[5] Within this quotation are contained the two principles upon which he based his life of service to the Church. They were, first his denominational loyalty and secondly his ecumenical commitment. Both grew out of his basic Christian experience and he lived in the creative tension of these two principles all his life. The book itself was published by the SCM Press in its Religious Book Club series. It saw the light of day finally in September 1944 and was dedicated to his brother, Philip.

Whilst he was involved in the preparation of this book, Dr Dakin, the Principal of Bristol Baptist College, had prepared a small book which the Kingsgate Press was intending to publish under the title *The Baptist View of the Church and Ministry*. This book, to be published on behalf of the college principals, though not necessarily endorsed by them, had a prefatory note by M. E. Aubrey. A proof copy found its way to Ernest Payne. He read it with growing dismay, for it was, in his judgment, a one-sided and even inaccurate description of the Baptist tradition on the church and ministry. Dr Dakin argued that only a person appointed and acting as the pastor of a local Baptist church, had any right to the title of Baptist minister. To Ernest Payne there seemed little or no recognition of the fact that current Baptist practices and difficulties were the product of the individualism of the 19th century, and of a reaction against the Oxford Movement. What might be called 'classical Baptist thought' had some rather different emphases. These included the variety of functions that was open to those who sought to serve in the Baptist ministry, as well as the recognition by the wider Baptist fellowship of a man's particular ministry. Ernest Payne felt that Dakin's account of things would need to be challenged – and quickly.

Working under considerable pressure both of time and, one

suspects, of emotion, he wrote a criticism of Dakin's book, showed it to J. O. Barrett, and also to Wheeler Robinson. Wheeler Robinson gave him a covering letter to send with the typescript to M. E. Aubrey. The suggestion was that what he had written should be published as soon as possible by the Kingsgate Press and should have as much, or as little, backing from the Baptist Union as Dakin's publication was to have. Only so, could it be made clear that the Baptist tradition in regard to the church and ministry was rather more varied and complex than Dr Dakin suggested.

What that manuscript said in detail we shall be unlikely ever to know, for it never saw the light of day. There is some evidence that M E. Aubrey sympathised with much that Ernest Payne was saying, but there could really be no question of publishing this kind of controversial attack on the views of Dr Dakin who had been nominated in 1944 as Vice-President of the Baptist Union! Nevertheless, the Kingsgate Press was prepared to consider a book on the same, or a similar subject, provided it was not so obviously slanted against what Dakin had written. Under these circumstances, Ernest Payne wrote the book *The Fellowship of Believers: Baptist Thought and Practice Yesterday and Today*. The title was suggested by Dr P. W. Evans, the then Principal of Spurgeon's College with whom Ernest Payne had begun to develop a deepening friendship. This book like the one on the Free Church tradition, had considerable success and remains still in demand today.

As a postscript to these events, it is interesting to discover that late in 1943 at least two Associations, the Oxford and East Gloucestershire, and the Northants Association, nominated Ernest Payne for election for vice-presidency of the Baptist Union in 1944! When he discovered that Dr Dakin was also nominated and standing he decided that his name should not be allowed to go forward.

The background to these writing activities was the Second World War. More than once Ernest Payne reflected that had he had no family ties, he would seriously have considered offering for chaplaincy service, even though by 1942 he was 40 years old. Although he had sympathies with the pacifist position, he was not himself a pacifist and he seems to have been troubled by the fact that whilst he was too young for active service by the end of World War I, he was now escaping World

War II by being too old. It appears that he consciously accepted preaching engagements in dangerous situations both in London and on the South Coast whenever it was possible.

Catherine Payne died in September 1943. She was very nearly 80 years old and her final illness had not been a long one. Over the years she had been active in the Potters Bar church and was still the leader of the Women's Meeting in that church at her death. In the three years since Margaret's death, she had lived quietly and since her husband's death, her one anxiety had been Philip's precarious health. She was a remarkable woman. She was very close to her elder son. It was not that she dominated him, but that she proved a constant and consistent point of strength and reference for him. He recognised always how much he owed to her, and although he spoke little about her death, he clearly felt it very deeply.

Wheeler Robinson had retired in 1942 and was succeeded as principal by Robert Child. Ernest Payne and Robert Child had known each other for 20 years. They were at Regent's Park College together as students, though Robert Child was, in those days, somewhat remote from his colleagues. However, at Oxford as colleagues and friends in the college they had an excellent relationship which undoubtedly was mutually beneficial. Robert Child had no easy task. He had to succeed a principal of the highest intellectual calibre, and of considerable scholarly reputation. He was faced also with the fact that, like Ernest Payne, he had not taken the Oxford School of Theology examination for which most of the students had to be prepared. In February 1944, therefore, the University conferred the MA degree on both Robert Child and Ernest Payne, and admitted them to the membership of the Faculty of Theology. Robert Child was not an outstanding lecturer, nor, truth to tell, a great scholar. His real ability was in the one to one relationship which showed a deep personal concern for his students. He was a compassionate man but his compassion was exercised mainly in times of crisis. Most of his students look back with gratitude upon their experiences of him, recognising that they only really benefitted from his very many gifts when they acknowledged their own need of his counsel and help.

In 1943 Joyce Booth came to Regent's Park College. Originally she had served with the Girls' Auxiliary, but the war conditions made the work more difficult. Secretarial help was needed in Oxford and Ernest Payne had been asked to compile a bibliography which would be useful when the Baptist Missionary Society came to commission the writing of its history. Thus it was agreed that Joyce Booth should come to Oxford and give the college half her time, with the other half being employed in helping with the missionary bibliography. When that particular task was completed, the college offered her a full time appointment which she accepted, and served there until 1959.

The Second World War ended in Europe officially on 8th May 1945. The next six years in Oxford were probably the happiest of all the happy years that the Paynes spent in Oxford. Soon after the war the family had to move from 151, Woodstock Road which the owner wished to sell. They found a house in Lathbury Road which ran between the Woodstock and Banbury Roads. The house was admirably suited in location, and indeed in character, to be a tutor's residence. They moved into 27, Lathbury Road at Christmas, 1945 and there they stayed for the remainder of their time at Oxford. Ann was, by this time, at Oxford High School. Gordon Holmes was at a local private school, but looking forward to going to Eltham College, a school for the sons of missionaries, whilst Betty Hancock was at Walthamstow Hall. The Hancock family had, however, recently returned on furlough from Angola and made arrangements for Betty's future care to be in the charge of her uncle, which would bring her in closer contact with her grandmother and other members of the family.

Demobilisation brought ex-servicemen into the theological colleges in considerable numbers, and Regent's Park College filled up with an interesting company of mature men who had seen active service in many parts of the world. These were great days in Oxford. The Bunyan Society flourished and grew in numbers with Ernest Payne as Senior Friend. There he met a large number of Baptist students and established relationships and friendships which were to stand him and them in good stead in all the years that lay ahead. He was also given a title by the university of Lecturer in Comparative Religions and the History of Modern Missions. True this was an unpaid lectureship, but it gave him a status and he took the opportunity to give courses of lectures on the relationship of the historic religions. More than one student who came under his teaching at this point became in different ways well known in this field. It was Ernest Payne who started Trevor Ling on the study of comparative religion, and he acted also as supervisor to an Indian student, Russell Chandran, who came to Oxford to do research. Trevor Ling ultimately became Professor of Comparative Religion at the University of Manchester and Russell Chandran became Principal of the Theological College in Bangalore, and subsequently played a significant part in the World Council of Churches. A constant stream of students from many colleges came to Ernest Payne seeking advice on subjects related to the study of religions.

His main teaching work consisted of tutorials and lectures. He was not outstanding in the lecture room, but his classes were appreciated by those who attended and lasted the course! He obeyed Wheeler Robinson's desire that he should lecture first in historical theology which many of the students found a difficult and not particularly attractive subject. It was, however, as a tutor that he was most effective. He taught students from Regent's Park College and from other colleges, in a number of subjects, notably ecclesiastical history. His skill as a tutor was that he made his students think through issues involved. He was not one who would allow a student to accept the *status quo*, the normally recognised theory, nor the majority opinion without question. What he required of the student in his essay, was an assessment of the evidence, the consideration of the possibilities, and then a constructive point of view set down by the student himself. This would have to be defended in the tutorial against the incisive questioning of the tutor. Ernest Payne preferred the student to finish up with an original point of view in ruins rather than an uncritical statement of other people's ideas! The result of all this tutorial work was that he taught the students to become constructive critics. His concern was not just to transmit information but to educate in the fullest and finest sense of the word.

His students viewed him with a mixture of proper respect and considerable affection. He belonged so obviously to the place. Punctually each morning at 8.45, he would cycle down Pusey Street and in through the college gateway, a small figure perched on an enormous bicycle, his trouser turn-ups precisely enfolded within large cycle clips. His obvious enjoyment of the college, the university, the work, and the Christian faith was infectious. When a student preached at the Baptist chapel in Woodstock Road, at which he was a member, he would offer always an appreciative and encouraging word. His sense of humour too was acute. He enjoyed a joke – not least against himself. At the farewell Christmas Concert to him in 1952 before he left for service with the Baptist Union, the students produced their own version of *Alice in Wonderland* entitled *Ernice in B(L)Underland.* The Mad Hatter's tea party scene contained this rhyme:

> Twinkle, twinkle, E.A.P.,
> How we wonder if you'll be
> Under piles and piles of files
> Drinking tea with O. D. Wiles.

His enjoyment was such that he demanded a script!

Soon after the war, denominational office was pressed upon Ernest Payne. In 1945 he had agreed to become chairman of the West Indies Committee of the Baptist Missionary Society and in the same year there was further pressure to put his name forward again for the Baptist Union vice-presidency for 1946. He would not allow such a nomination, not simply because at this time he had no desire for it, but also because he felt there were a number of senior people in the denomination whom he judged to be more eligible for such a high office. Nevertheless in 1946 he was elected Vice-Chairman of the Baptist Missionary Society General Committee. This confidence in him was a source of great satisfaction. He was one of the youngest people ever to occupy that responsible position, being only 44 years of age at the time. As it turned out, his term of office was extended beyond the normal twelve months because ill health prevented his friend Murray Page acting as chairman for part of 1946–47 as had been anticipated.

During his time in office there was an attempt to re-open the question of joint headquarters for the Baptist Union and the Baptist Missionary Society. A sub-committee of five from each side met in November 1947 to consider the desirability of investigating the early establishment of joint headquarters. He was one of the five BMS representatives, but the discussions at that point were abortive.

He continued to write. He had published a memoir of Wheeler Robinson in 1946, which was well received, although he was somewhat disappointed with the deletions made by the Robinson family. It was in 1946 too that he began his great interest in the radical Anabaptist Movement, and he published a brief but significant statement on the *Baptist Movement in the Reformation and Onwards*. In 1946 also he began to translate Karl Barth's work on baptism, which made it clear that although Karl Barth was a resolute opponent of re-baptism, he had become convinced that the writers of the New Testament taught that baptism involved a personal confession of faith by the candidate. His translation, entitled *The Teaching of the Church Regarding Baptism* appeared finally in the Spring of 1948.

During the years from 1946–48 his experience of and influence in church affairs outside England became growingly significant. The Baptist World Alliance was to have a Congress in Copenhagen in 1947. In retrospect the Copenhagen Congress in 1947 was important in the Baptist World Alliance history for several reasons. The first was that it was this Congress that made the decision to establish a headquarters in Washington. This marked a significant shift in leadership of the Baptist World Alliance from Europe, particularly Britain, to the United States. Secondly there was a discussion about the attitude of Baptists in the World Alliance to the prospect of the World Council of Churches which was then in the process of formation.

It had been intended, just before the Second World War to form such a council and now after the delay of the war years it was planned to bring it into being at an assembly in Amsterdam in 1948. There were those within the Baptist World Alliance who tried to move a resolution critical in tone of the proposed world council and designed to remit decision as to any Baptist membership of a world council to the Executive Committee of the Baptist World Alliance. This move originated from representatives of the Southern Convention and it was known that on the Executive Committee, the Southern Baptist Convention had a dominant voice. Ernest Payne intervened in the discussion, having with him, in fact in his pocket, copies of the Constitution of both the Baptist World Alliance and the proposed World Council of Churches. He argued that the Baptist World Alliance Constitution made it clear that there could be no interference with the policies and decisions of individual unions and conventions. The World Council of Churches, he argued, was to be a council of Churches with which confessional organisations, such as the Baptist World Alliance, would have only a fraternal relationship. In the debate he challenged on a point of order, the validity of the motion that was being submitted. Ernest Payne's contention was accepted by the chairman. His intervention at this point not only avoided a bitter and divisive debate but also left it free for various members of the Alliance, without any pressure from others, to make up their minds concerning whether or not to affiliate to the forthcoming World Council of Churches. After this Congress Ernest Payne found himself elected on to the new Baptist World Alliance Executive in place of Grey Griffith who had retired believing that room should be made for younger members.

Wider horizons

It was in the same summer of 1947 that Ernest Payne had his introduction to the Faith and Order movement. This movement had been born at Lausanne at a world conference in 1927 and had been continued in a further conference in Edinburgh in 1937. The Edinburgh Conference had set up a continuation committee and this committee was to have its first post-war meeting in 1947. Both Hugh Martin and M. E. Aubrey were members of the continuation committee but neither of them felt able to continue active membership and requested that Ernest Payne should go to the meeting at Clarens as a proxy. It was at this meeting that Ernest Payne met some of the more distinguished Continental figures, Bishop Dibelius of Berlin and Dr Visser't Hooft, with whom subsequently he was to work in very close co-operation in the World Council of Churches.

Faith and Order was preparing for a Third World Faith and Order Conference to be held in Sweden. The 1937 Edinburgh Conference had agreed various theological commissions and these had to be reconstituted. They were three in number, the Nature of the Church, Worship, and Intercommunion. He found himself on the commission relating to intercommunion. At the end of the meeting at Clarens, he was made a full member of the continuation committee. It had been agreed that if the proposed World Council of Churches came into existence in 1948 then the continuation committee would be transformed into a constituent commission of the World Council – the Faith and Order Commission. This meant that he was being linked with the exciting ecumenical developments which were being proposed.

When he came home in September, he discovered that it was not only in wider fields that new and exciting vistas were opening up in church relationships in which he could be involved, but also in England. On 3rd November 1946, the then Archbishop of Canterbury, Geoffrey Fisher, had preached a sermon in Cambridge suggesting that consideration should be given by the Free Churches to taking episcopacy into their systems. The outcome was that talks were proposed between representatives of the Church of England and of the various Free Churches. The Baptist Union Council had agreed that Baptists should be involved in this follow-up. It was in this context that in January 1947 Ernest Payne had paid his first visit to Lambeth Palace for an informal meeting with representatives of Anglicans and Free Churches. Eventually it was agreed that there should be conversations between sixteen Anglicans and sixteen Free Church representatives. There were three Baptists amongst the Free Church representatives. Those elected by a ballot at the Baptist Union Council were Dr Percy Evans, the Principal of Spurgeon's College, the Reverend J. Ingli James, General Superintendent of South Wales, and Ernest Payne.

This ecumenical experience led Percy Evans into fields with which he was at that time unfamiliar, and although the acknowledged and effective leader of the Baptist group, he relied considerably upon Ernest Payne whom he used sometimes to call his 'armour bearer'.[6] It was also of considerable help to the Baptist delegation that Ernest Payne knew personally, through Oxford contacts, a number of the other representatives, notably Leonard Hodgson, an Anglican who was the Regius Professor of Theology in the university, and Nathaniel Micklem who was the Principal of Mansfield College and a distinguished Congregationalist. Apart from those he knew already, he met personally some of the Anglicans with whom he would have very close dealings in later years. Notable amongst these was Michael Ramsey who was later to become Archbishop of Canterbury, but who in 1947 was teaching in Cambridge.

At one stage in the proceedings Leonard Hodgson and Ernest Payne were asked to prepare complementary papers on episcopacy. Hodgson was to say what it meant to Anglicans and Ernest Payne was to deal with Free Church objections. It was published subsequently in June 1951 in *Theology* and again by the Carey Kingsgate Press as a pamphlet. It appears also in a collection of his essays *Free Churchmen Unrepentant and Repentant*. The essay raised points that are germane to the present day discussion on episcopacy. He argues that Free Churches have biblical, theological and historical difficulties with the concept of episcopacy as presented by the Church of England. But his main conclusion is the difficulty in discovering exactly what sort of episcopacy the Free Churches are being asked to accept. His essay concludes with two questions:

What exactly is the nature of the episcopacy which it is suggested the Free Churches should 'take into their own system'?[7]

Does it avoid the difficulties that Free-churchmen have felt and still feel regarding most of the episcopal systems they have known?

In the final report *Church Relations in England* published in 1950, which tried to indicate what would be involved in following up the Archbishop's suggestions, Ernest Payne was responsible for the first draft of the crucial chapter on the ministry. The report made clear that any further discussion would have to be on bilateral basis. By the time the Baptist attitude to the report was decided, Ernest Payne was in office in the Baptist Union.

During 1948 it became evident that he needed an operation for hernia and this he underwent in the Radcliffe Infirmary in Oxford. Perhaps it is significant in view of subsequent events that at the time of that operation the doctors reported a measure of uncertainty as to how his heart would react to a general anaesthetic. In the event all went well and he was able, after recuperation, to return to his work in Oxford during the summer term. Soon after that he was under pressure to accept a position of service with the British and Foreign Bible Society but at this point he felt he could not consider leaving Oxford.

The summer of 1948 saw the first Assembly of the World Council of Churches in Amsterdam. The Baptist Union had been allocated four delegates and these were elected by ballot at the Baptist Union Council. It is indicative of the growing confidence that the Union felt in him in that Ernest Payne was elected as one of the four, gaining more votes than other nominees of an older generation with rather more distinguished service. His fellow delegates were M. E. Aubrey, Percy Evans and C. T. LeQuesne.

The Amsterdam Assembly remained a vivid experience in Ernest Payne's mind. He met the distinguished ecumenist John R. Mott, now ageing indeed but one who was still in the ecumenical context. He was glad to be present at the session presided over by the Archbishop of Canterbury at which the World Council of Churches was formally constituted. He was deeply moved by the open Communion service held at the Nieuwe Kerk according to the Reformed tradition with ministers of different traditions including Dr Percy Evans, serving the communicants at the long tables. He was impressed by the session at which Karl Barth and C. H. Dodd introduced each in his own way, the main Assembly theme 'Man's Disorder and God's design', Barth often raising his voice and shaking a prophetic finger of warning and Dodd speaking very quietly with no gestures at all. He was fascinated by the debate about East–West relationships between Professor Hromadka of Prague and John Foster Dulles, the American politician. The British Baptists elected to the first Central Committee of the World Council of Churches were M. E. Aubrey and Ernest Brown.

To have been present in Amsterdam in August and early September 1948 was an exciting and memorable experience. Ernest Payne can scarcely have thought at the time that he would be present at the next four World Assemblies and would finally retire from the World Council of Churches at Nairobi in 1975 as one of the presidents.

In May 1949 Dr W. O. Lewis, Associate Secretary of the Baptist World Alliance who was at that time in charge of the London office asked if he might come to Oxford. There was to be a further Baptist Congress in 1950 and he was expecting to retire then. Lewis told Ernest Payne that it was his hope that he would become his successor. He wanted to prepare him for an approach and to ensure if possible his acceptance of it. All the evidence is that Lewis returned to London a disappointed man. Ernest Payne gave him little or no encouragement. His lack of interest in this possibility had nothing to do with his commitment to the Baptist World Alliance nor to the wider church. It was based rather on his conviction that now, after some nine years, he was finding himself more and more at home in Oxford. He was growingly respected and his work and opportunities were increasing in usefulness. He was being used frequently as a supervisor for theses and as an examiner by the Board of Theology. Regent's Park College was still full of students, most of whom were older and were ready to benefit from all the help which Ernest Payne gave to them through his tutorial work. In addition to that, a tutor in a Baptist college is in a remarkably independent position which enables him to play a part in the life of the denomination as well as in the college. He is not thought of so much as a representative of the college as is the principal and in many ways is a freer agent to speak frankly and to risk the arguments that inevitably follow from such speaking. Freda Payne and Ann were happy in Oxford. And these reasons added up to a strong conviction that it was right to stay in Oxford.

But there were other reasons, more personal to Ernest Payne, that caused the firm rejection of the approach from W.O. Lewis. Although he was subsequently to become an ecumenical traveller and enjoy seeing other countries, he disliked travelling, and particularly staying in hotels. More importantly, he doubted whether he would ever be able happily and indeed successfully to cope with the somewhat isolationist attitude of the Southern Baptist Convention to wider ecumenical relationships. He believed he had an opportunity better to serve the Baptist cause and his own deeply held Baptist convictions in and through ecumenical contacts that were already beginning to open up. But there is a deeper reason too. Whatever else may be said of Ernest Payne, he was never an ambitious man, nor one who ever sought position, power, or the limelight. These things as they came were thrust upon him. His friend, J.O. Barrett in letters and conversations, reproached him more than once for this apparent lack of ambition. Barrett's fear was that Ernest Payne's own hesitations would prevent him from using to the full the gifts, the great gifts, that God had undoubtedly given to him.

The Focus Group that had begun to meet in connection with the Baptist Union Council before the war, still met occasionally and sometimes there was an attempt particularly by J. B. Middlebrook to initiate talk about what each would do in the future. Ernest Payne always resisted such talk. One cause of the uneasy relationship which existed between the two men was their differing attitudes concerning personal ambition. J. B. Middlebrook was properly ambitious, well aware of the responsibility that he had to develop his undoubted gifts in places of authority within the church. Ernest Payne neither sought nor particularly enjoyed positions of authority. When authority did come to him, however, he received it with determination and guarded it - sometimes almost too jealously - finding it difficult often to delegate. But it must have been somewhat frustrating to J. B. Middlebrook that Ernest Payne, who did not seek positions of authority, constantly had them given to him in so many different contexts.

The suggestion that W. O. Lewis had made was repeated even more pressingly by Dr Theodore Adams, one of the most influential of the Americans in the Baptist World Alliance. Adams urged that he should consider the post of Associate Secretary of the alliance saying that it was his view that the acceptance of such a post would almost certainly lead to him being appointed General Secretary of the Baptist World Alliance on the retirement of Dr Arnold Ohrn. But Ernest Payne was firm in his refusal. In his reply to Adams he made it clear that although he was appreciative of the confidence put in him he did not feel as though the proposal related to him at all.

Then yet another approach concerning his future was made. There were to be changes in the Baptist Missionary Society. Dr Williamson, the Foreign Secretary, was to retire in 1951. Ernest Payne was appointed Chairman of the Secretariat Committee which was considering the possibility of restructuring the Society in the light of the forthcoming retirement. However, he was suddenly presented by a suggestion from within the committee itself that he should accept nomination. Such a proposal was not open to all the objections that had been mentioned in connection with the Baptist World Alliance approach. He still felt a very strong attachment to the missionary society, but he did not believe that it was right, except in exceptional circumstances, to go back on one's tracks. Further he knew himself well enough to know that it would not be easy for him to be the colleague of J. B. Middlebrook. He still felt that his job was at Regent's Park College. In any case he had virtually no first hand experience of the overseas missionary field. So it was that he resisted the request, and in the end it was the Rev. V. E. W. Hayward who was appointed.

Call to London

After these approaches he hoped that he would be left undisturbed. But it was not to be. M. E. Aubrey had been General Secretary of the Baptist Union since 1925 and was now 64 years old. His had been a difficult time in office. It was a period of decline in church attendance; there had been the difficulty over the joint headquarters in 1938; he had had to face all the dangers and difficulties of the war years. As there was a general desire that he should serve as President of the Union, it seemed sensible that he should be nominated as Vice President in 1949, and that his year as President in 1950-51 should coincide with his last year as Secretary. Aubrey accepted this as a wise suggestion and felt also that the time was ripe for a forward movement, so that during his presidential year he called the denomination to a united campaign that became known as 'Baptist Advance'.

A committee, under the chairmanship of Percy Evans, was set up to recommend his successor. There was widespread expectation that it would prove difficult to agree on a nomination. If the committee was unanimous on a name, then it was going to be very difficult for whoever was approached to refuse the nomination. Somewhat remarkably, it seems that Ernest Payne had no real expectation nor thought that the committee might look in his direction. Certainly he had little desire that they should. His part in the Baptist Union Council and his intervention in the debates had often been extremely critical of the official line. He had never had contact with nor been seriously under the influence of the Spurgeonic tradition which was very strong in certain parts of the country. He was known to be involved and becoming more deeply involved in ecumenical affairs. On 16th January 1950, however, he received a letter asking him to meet a deputation from the Secretariat Committee.

The meeting took place late in January in the offices of the SCM Press. There he met Percy Evans, Hugh Martin and Arnold Clark. They presented him with a unanimous and pressing invitation to succeed M. E. Aubrey. His initial reaction was one of genuine and deep dismay. He sought out Grey Griffith as soon as he could and put to him all his doubts and hesitations. Could he do the job? Ought he to do the job? What was to happen at Regent's Park College? He had few illusions about the post and what it would entail. He knew enough already of the cross currents within the denomination and the reluctance in many quarters to accept leadership from the Church House, to recognise that the job would be no sinecure. He questioned seriously whether he was possessed of the requisite gifts for the position, particularly as a public figure and as an effective speaker to large gatherings. But even if he was adequate as a person, he wondered whether he really need take the job. It would limit his chances of serious writing, and would leave Regent's Park College in difficulties at a crucial moment in its own affairs. At the heart of it, probably, was the question in Ernest Payne's mind, whether if he left Regent's now, might he not always feel that in some way or another he had let Wheeler Robinson down?

Grey Griffith answered his questions frankly. He said that he and others had no doubt that he could do what was needed at the Church House. Without any doubt he ought to accept the nomination. If God was calling him to the task then God could be trusted to have a plan for the college in Oxford. This view was confirmed by people who were deeply concerned also for the life of the College, men like C. T. LeQuesne and Seymour Price. Both these urged him to go to Southampton Row as did Percy Evans. The words of Percy Evans carried great weight with Ernest Payne particularly when he assured him that he would help him to gain the support of men within the Spurgeon tradition. He consulted his brother Philip Payne, who told him that the invitation must be accepted.

So, reluctantly, he agreed that his name should be taken to the March meeting of the Baptist Union Council in 1950 as the sole nomination. It was F. G. Benskin, one of the senior presidents of the Baptist Union, who proposed the nomination at that council. Benskin was one of the few who could still speak with first hand knowledge of Ernest Payne's parents and grandparents. The Baptist Union Council that day was convinced of the rightness of the nomination. Many spoke in support of it. There was a spirit of unanimous conviction as the council greeted Ernest Payne cordially, and told him that his name would go with the backing of the council to the forthcoming assembly with a view to appointment to the secretaryship for a five year period starting in May 1951.

The students at Regent's Park College who knew him as well as most, had little doubt of the rightness of the nomination, though they viewed his departure from Oxford with considerable sadness. When he was asked by the students if they could congratulate him on his appointment, he made a typical reply, 'You may not congratulate me, but you may wish me well.' The secretaryship of the Baptist Union was not an office that Ernest Payne ever sought. It was an office to which the Baptist Union Council and then the Baptist Assembly called him with virtual unanimity. He accepted because of his loyalty to the denomination and because he believed that the call truly reflected the call of God. He knew that he could bring nothing other than himself and the gifts that he had. During his years of service there were times when the denomination was critical of him as were some of the people within it. He was a sensitive person, but recognised that criticism was inevitable and accepted it as part of the responsibility of office. When it was well founded because of misjudgments and unwise statements, he accepted its validity. What hurt him was when he was criticised for being what he was bound to be - and what he could only be - himself. He could not have brought anything other than himself to that office, and the denomination when it called him, must have known it.

4

The London Years

1: 1951-55

The first task that faced the Payne family was to find a home in London. The search began in the winter of 1951 and fortunately it was not too long before Freda Payne discovered a house in Prothero Gardens. It was a pleasant family house, adjacent to Hendon Central Station, which would enable Ernest Payne to reach the Baptist Church House with a relatively short Underground journey. After considerable negotiations, the house was purchased, and for some 16 years it became home for Freda and Ernest Payne, and a place of welcome and hospitality for very many visitors.

Before Ernest Payne could take up office, however, there were two events of significance in the early months of 1951. The first was sad. On 23rd March, Percy Evans died suddenly. The shock to the denomination was considerable. But to Ernest Payne the loss was tragic. As he was to write years later, 'the sky darkened for many that day'.[7] The persuasion of Percy Evans, and the assurance of his support, had been one of the chief influences in his decision to accept the invitation to become General Secretary. He had promised to advise and help in all ways and most particularly in the contacts with that part of the denomination with which Ernest Payne thus far, had had all too little contact. With the death of Percy Evans he felt that the task was going to be much more difficult. And so it turned out.

The other event was quite the reverse. He received a communication from the University of St. Andrews intimating that it had been decided to confer on him an Honorary Doctorate in Divinity. This news was not only a surprise to him, but one that gave him great satisfaction and some growing confidence in the task that lay ahead.

Arrival at Southampton Row

The last Report of the Council under the secretaryship of M. E. Aubrey which was presented to the 1951 assembly gives the impression that the sentiments uppermost in the mind of the council were a mixture of bewilderment and disillusionment. The Korean War had begun, and all that had seemed so certain in the aftermath of the victory over Germany in 1945 seemed to be slipping away. There was a sense of apprehension that possibly a third world war was imminent.

So far as the denomination was concerned, the Council Report sums up the heritage that was being handed over to Ernest Payne. The Report shows that during Aubrey's secretaryship, the Superannuation Fund had been raised, the Victory Thanksgiving Fund had been gathered, the Baptist Forward Movement had been carried through and the Baptist Home Work Fund had been established. Yet these were events rather of consolidation than of progress. This was probably inevitable, for consolidation had been necessary, partly due to the problems created by the Second World War and partly due to the difficulties that all the established churches were facing of lack of support and of changing attitudes within the post war generation. But there is one particular comment: 'Nothing has been more pleasing than to see the old rather official and stand-off relations between the churches and Associations on the one hand, and the Church House on the other change into those of confidence and friendliness and easier approach so that those of us who work at the centre feel ourselves borne along by a current of good will and common purpose'. This was a foundation upon which Ernest Payne was to build.

On the Tuesday evening of the Baptist Union Assembly, farewell was taken of M. E. Aubrey who had been secretary of the Union for 26 years. As Ernest Payne listened to the speakers he must have reflected that as a student in Regent's Park College he had sat in the gallery at Bloomsbury 26 years earlier, when Aubrey made his speech following his election as General

Secretary. On the Thursday morning session, the succession of Ernest Payne to the secretaryship was briefly recognised. One might say, all too briefly recognised. Ten minutes were allocated to the welcoming of the in-coming Secretary by the President, Dr H. R. Williamson who said that he regarded it as a high and sacred privilege to induct Mr Payne into his new office. As a reminder he read from the Council Report which had been adopted on Monday by the Assembly: 'On those who have chosen him lies the moral and inescapable obligation of supporting him with their prayers and their loyalty in his heavy task of leadership. The Council looks to the future with high hopes and assures Mr Payne of its willing co-operation and affectionate solicitude for him and Mrs Payne in their new sphere.' There then followed a brief act of induction in which prayer was offered by the Rev. Murray Page who was a good friend through all the years. When Ernest Payne replied to the welcome, he indicated his apprehension about the task, and commented that he had been tempted to run away from it, and never more so than when he heard of the death of Percy Evans. Then he went on to say, 'I accept from you this solemn trust and responsibility. Relying on the pledges of this company here, and those whom they represent and relying upon God, I will serve the denomination.'[8] The date was 26th April 1951.

On the next morning, the Friday, he met Aubrey in the Church House. It was an extraordinary handover. Aubrey introduced him to the tenants of the house. He handed over a number of keys and assured him that he thought that the general administration of affairs was working with reasonable smoothness. He further told hm that one of his first tasks would be to find a first class private secretary, preferably from outside the Church House staff. However, he assured Ernest Payne that Miss Norris, his own secretary would remain for up to one year although she was already due for retirement. Aubrey then shook him by the hand, departed, and before long began an extended visit to the United States. In the years that remained of Aubrey's life, he kept quietly in the background, never interfering with Ernest Payne, and always available for consultation, and to everybody's satisfaction, not least Ernest Payne's, was ready five years later to propose to the assembly the re-election of Ernest Payne for a further term.

There were three events of that first morning, 27th April

1951, relatively trivial, but remembered nevertheless. *The Times* newspaper carried an advertisement which contained lines by Henry van Dyke. 'This is your work, your blessing, not your doom.' Secondly, after Aubrey left, Ernest Payne was sitting at the empty desk and Seymour Price came into the Secretary's room. He wished Ernest Payne well, and advised him not to look back longingly to Oxford, however great the temptation might be. Rather he should look forward to the great opportunities that lay ahead in the wider service to the denomination. Thirdly, a little later that morning, the Baptist Union accountant, Leonard Strugnell appeared. He had been in the Baptist Church House since the days of J.H. Shakespeare. Strugnell shook Ernest Payne warmly by the hand, promised his loyal support, and said, 'I always say, if one person can do a job, another can.'

At the Church House, Ernest Payne found a staff experienced and loyal. O.D. Wiles had been Deputy General Secretary of the Baptist Union since 1948 and stayed with Ernest Payne until 1960. Wiles had served in the pastoral ministry but most particularly had been a distinguished chaplain in both world wars and had been decorated for his service during both those wars. The problem, however, really lay with the definition of the post of 'Deputy'. The questions were never really resolved as to whether the authority of the deputy was limited to the times and seasons when the General Secretary was away and whether it covered all matters or only those specifically deputed to the individual concerned. Wiles proved to be exemplary and loyal and Ernest Payne supported his subsequent re-appointment.

There were others who helped Ernest Payne, particularly in those early years. Grey Griffith, having retired from the Baptist Missionary Society, was now extremely active in the Baptist Union. He was chairman of the Grants Executive, and had assisted with the organisation and supervision of the new Home Work Fund and the Scheme connected with it. He possessed an unrivalled knowledge of churches and ministers, and in spite of advancing years, he maintained an astonishing zest for life and strong radical sympathies. Ernest Payne found him a guide and friend, always unfailing with advice when requested. Grey Griffith had, of course, been a mentor of Ernest Payne in the Baptist Missionary Society days and to find him now accepting such responsibility in the Union was of tremendous encouragement to the new secretary. Another supporter was Seymour Price, who had given up business as an insurance broker to become General Manager and Secretary of the Baptist Insurance Company. He was chairman of the Ministerial Recognition Committee, and had a deep interest in Baptist history. Together with these two were Arnold Clark as treasurer and Gordon Fairbairn, as solicitor, both of whom were extremely helpful to Ernest Payne and agreed to have regular monthly meetings of the officers of the Baptist Union.

He was fortunate, too, with the presidents of the Union during his early years. The president who inducted him was Dr H. R. Williamson, a distinguished missionary and officer of the Baptist Missionary Society. He was followed by Arnold Clark, the treasurer of the Baptist Union, and then by the Rev. Henry Bonser, the remarkable and faithful area superintendent. After Henry Bonser came Robert Child, a great personal friend, of course, who had the somewhat unusual and well earned experience of being elected unopposed to the vice-presidency of the Baptist Union.

He found also at hand the ten general superintendants with whom he always tried to meet for some part of their monthly meeting. He believed that the superintendents were key figures in the denomination. He viewed them from time to time almost as a sort of diaconate. The chairman was the delightful, friendly and ever cheerful veteran, the Rev. Sidney Morris, who moulded the superintendents into an impressive, devoted and united team.

One of Ernest Payne's immediate tasks was to find himself a new secretary. Miss Norris was anxious to retire. The manager of the Baptist Holiday Fellowship was also seeking a secretary and advertised the post. Amongst those who applied was Enid Hobbs. She had had considerable experience with a firm in the City. She came from a Congregational background, but in 1951 was a member with her parents, of the Loughton Union Church. Mr Gardiner decided that she was far too good for the post that he was wanting to fill! Quite by chance he mentioned this to Ernest Payne who immediately interviewed her, recognised in her someone with whom he could work, and someone who was clearly efficient in the administrative work.

The outcome was that Enid Hobbs joined the staff of the Baptist Union in 1952 and quickly proved her worth. She and Ernest Payne shared a common outlook in many matters, and over the years he came to value her judgment as she grew familiar with a wide range of matters. The position of private secretary is never an easy one, and certainly not the secretary to the General Secretary of the Baptist Union! On the one hand, she had to be a repository of confidences and yet on the other hand must be able to deal with matters from day to day in order to protect the general secretary. This often meant a difficult and complex situation, but through the 15 years of collaboration, Enid Hobbs proved to be of inestimable assistance in the work that Ernest Payne was seeking to do.

He believed that it was wise to define objectives. This was true in his work as general secretary. Building on what Aubrey had achieved, he determined to make the Union into a visible fellowship of Baptist Churches relating to each other in and through the life of the Union, linked together in the smaller fellowships of associations, and yet well aware of the wider fellowship within the ecumenical movement. His theology of the church is reflected in his book *The Fellowship of Believers*. The local church was that place where the universal church was made manifest. Yet between the local church and that great concept of the universal church, there had to be some form of manifestation of fellowship in order that the church might not only live together in harmony but function efficiently. He believed firmly that one of those manifestations was the Baptist Union. Because of this conviction there were always those who were somewhat suspicious that he was trying to create a hierarchy within the Union to dominate the local churches. This was not his intention. He was seeking to create a fellowship in which the larger community of the Union existed for the sake of the churches themselves. His historical awareness and his knowledge of the reasons for the founding of the Baptist Union made it very clear to him where his tasks and emphases must lie. Theologically, the denomination needed to develop a functional ecclesiology of the Union. He aspired over his years in office to expedite such a development.

Specifically in the first five years, he set himself the task of ensuring that the planned Baptist World Alliance Jubilee Congress of 1955, to be held in London, should be worthily celebrated with British Baptists as effective and welcoming hosts. He believed also that the time was ripe to initiate another attempt to bring together the Baptist Union and the Baptist Missionary Society as an indication of the reality of the wider fellowship of believers. In the event, the Baptist World Alliance Congress in 1955 with which he was so greatly occupied during the first five years was a highly successful occasion. On the matter of the relationship of the Baptist Union and the Baptist Missionary Society this failed to make much progress. This was partly because of personality differences as well as immense practical difficulties, but in addition he underestimated the strength of vested interests within the structures of denominational life.

Faith and Order

It was evident that the demands made on him by the ecumenical movement were going to increase. In August 1951, there was a Faith and Order Commission meeting at Clarens in Switzerland. The main purpose of the meeting was to prepare the material for the Lund Conference of Faith and Order to be held the following year. He had already become involved in the preparation of material for this conference and in the preparatory Lund volume entitled *The Nature of the Church* there is included a statement reflecting the Baptist doctrine on this matter. Although this statement, approved by the Baptist Union Council in 1948, is based to a certain extent upon previous Baptist documents, notably the reply to the 1926 Anglican approach, it is on the whole a new document and had been prepared by a group convened by Percy Evans, in which Ernest Payne also played a significant role. At Clarens, however, it became evident that Ernest Payne would be given responsibility for one of the sections at the Lund Conference.

In connection with Clarens there occurred one of those events which at the time take on something of a nightmarish character, but in retrospect make a story well worth telling. This saga involves Ernest Payne and the then Bishop of Derby, A. E. J. Rawlinson. Unfortunately, when the bishop arrived at Clarens, he was clearly unwell. Somewhere on the journey, he had had a stroke which was rendering him increasingly helpless. He took no part in the meetings of the commission and was cared for in his room. He refused to go to hospital, and refused to allow his wife to be informed. A day or so before the meeting ended, Canon Archdall, who was a friend of the bishop, and had been looking after him, came to Ernest Payne and said that the bishop insisted on being taken back to England. Ernest Payne was surprised at this, in view of the apparent nature of the illness, but the canon stressed that this was to happen, that Mrs Rawlinson had now been told of the illness and would meet the train at Victoria. Ernest Payne expressed sympathy with the bishop, but was unclear as to what precisely it had to do with him. The canon then informed him that the bishop had made clear his firm desire that Ernest Payne should take charge of him on the return journey!

So there began at Montreux Station a quite extraordinary, and for Ernest Payne a quite frightening journey. Dr Rawlinson was almost completely helpless. With the aid of friends, Ernest Payne managed to get the bishop into and out of a taxi, and into a sleeping compartment on the continental express. It was a considerable effort because he was not an easy person to move particularly in that condition. Throughout the whole night, Ernest Payne sat beside him, attending to his needs, and apprehensive that at any moment the bishop might become worse and might even die. As the train moved on through the night, the difficulty that lay ahead of getting the bishop on and off a Channel steamer loomed larger and larger. In the early hours of the morning, Ernest Payne met a Cook's courier in the corridor of the train, and explained to him his serious predicament. The man rose to the occasion. He secured a stretcher at Calais, and persuaded the captain of the boat to allow them a cabin. At Dover, Ernest Payne and the bishop were put into a first class compartment on the train, and at Victoria, to Ernest Payne's enormous relief, he handed the bishop over to Mrs Rawlinson, and his chauffeur.

For many weeks Ernest Payne heard nothing whatsoever from or of the bishop. There then came a very brief note of thanks from the bishop informing him that he had recovered; that the doctor had told him that he had been very fortunate, particularly having risked the journey home from Montreux! In retrospect it was a strange and foolhardy journey that the bishop undertook, and that Ernest Payne had to share with him. Fortunately it all ended well, and it says something of Ernest Payne's personality that he should have been asked to accompany the bishop, and that he was ready to undertake what was asked of him.

The travelling that Ernest Payne undertook during his life was quite remarkable. He preserved a record of all his overseas journeys, which numbered over 120 and took him to every continent. These trips had to be fitted in to a very heavy programme of administrative and committee work at the Church House together with all the meetings of the British Council of Churches, the Free Church Federal Council and many other groups in England. His life involved him also in preaching and speaking in Baptist churches, for he always remembered and sought to put into action John R. Mott's dictum that a movement cannot be led from an office chair.

The work load expected of the general secretary was thus immense. Looking through his diaries, his journals and his travel records raises the question as to whether the job with which the General Secretary of the Baptist Union is presented is really one that is within the bounds of human possibility. Certainly it may be argued that each secretary will bring to it his own particular gifts and will follow his own particular interests. Yet when one has said that, there are so many *musts* within the secretary's job. Clearly he has full responsibility towards the whole denomination and an obligation to seek to move amongst the churches. Certainly he is one who has the basic administrative responsibility within the Church House. These two activities combined will help to produce the policy that will be carried through in the departments, the Baptist Union Council, and its committees. On top of all this are the responsibilities beyond the denomination. Obviously the Baptist presence in the wider circle of church life is essential. Whilst Ernest Payne was greatly helped by the loyalty of those around him, particularly Enid Hobbs, there were times when he wished that he, like an archbishop, had a chaplain who could remove from him some of the exhausting and trivial tasks of what Ernest Payne used to call in Kipling's words 'the minor damnabilities of life'.

During his general secretaryship he found holidays very difficult to arrange. When he entered into the responsibility, life had changed so much from the time when, in the earlier

(above) Mansfield College, July 1926

(below) Stone laying ceremony, Regent's Park College, Oxford, July 1938

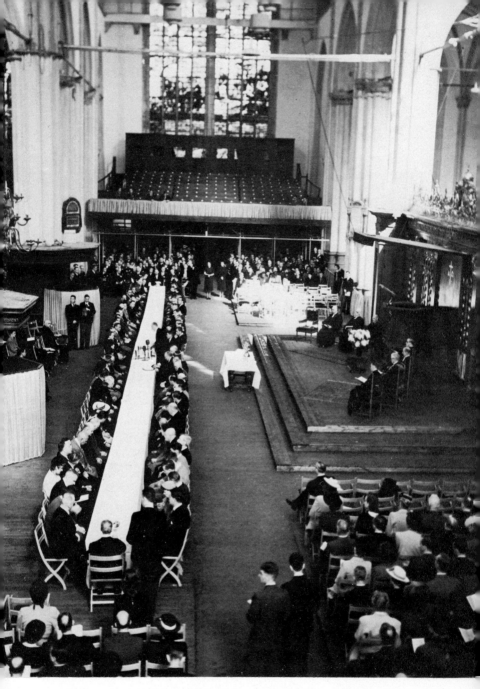

A Communion Service at the Nieuwe Kerk during the World Council of Churches First Assembly, Amsterdam, August 1948

(left) Ernest Payne
greets Franklin C. Fry

(below) Archbishop
Nikodim of Yaroslav
and Rostov receives his
delegate's badge from
Dr Payne and Dr
Visser't Hooft at the
World Council of
Churches Third
Assembly, New Delhi,
November 1961

(right) Relaxing with his grandchildren

(below) Picnicking in Canada

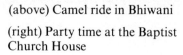

(above) Camel ride in Bhiwani

(right) Party time at the Baptist Church House

(above) Dr Payne speaking on his retirement as Secretary of the Baptist Union

(below) Dr Payne's farewell dinner at the Connaught Rooms, London, July 1967

(above) Ernest Payne and Archbishop Fisher share a joke, January 1961

(below) A meeting between Ernest Payne and J. I. Zhidkov in Paris, 1962

(above) At the World Council of Churches Fifth Assembly, Nairobi, December 1975, Vice Presidents Ernest Payne and Dr Kiyoko Takeda Cho talk to members of the African Israel Church

(below) Queen Elizabeth, the Queen Mother, in conversation with Ernest Payne and John Marsh, Mansfield College, Summer 1962

(above) Ernest and Freda Payne talking to Sir Cyril Black and the Bishop of London and Mrs Stopford at the House of Commons, September 1967

(below) Ernest Payne preaching at the Baptist Church at Yerwan in Armenia

years of Aubrey's secretaryship, the then treasurer of the Baptist Union, Herbert Marnham, used to come into the Church House after the assembly and tell Aubrey that he was sure he must be feeling exhausted, and send him for a short holiday to the South of France! August in England is generally viewed as something of a dead month and earlier secretaries had the opportunity of going away during that month, but that was in the days before the ecumenical movement and all its responsibilities. Ernest Payne found himself involved in the World Council of Churches virtually every summer. Whilst he always tried to keep Easter and Whitsun free of engagements, life became an increasing scramble, and it was only by careful husbanding of the time, that it was possible to discover opportunities for holidays. Even at Christmas he used to occupy himself during the break by drafting the annual report. Looking back now, it is remarkable that Ernest Payne survived as he did. What the cost must have been for his family life only those closest to him can really say.

Within his family he was no longer directly responsible for Gordon Holmes. Gordon's father had married again and had entered general practice at Chesham. Gordon was missed within the Payne family but close mutual affection remained. By this time too Ann had left school and had started on a course at the Domestic Science College in Bath. Philip Payne was still going to the office in Bedford Row each day, taken in a car by his faithful friend, Mr Rae, but he was becoming increasingly helpless. As often as possible on a Saturday or a Sunday afternoon, Ernest Payne went to Potters Bar to talk over with Philip matters denominational, personal and political. These meetings meant a great deal to both of them.

The annual report for 1951 showed that the hopes of Aubrey's last year in which there had been a slight increase in membership figures were not fulfilled. Throughout Ernest Payne's secretaryship with one or two exceptions, notably the year or so following Dr Billy Graham's visit to the country, the membership of the Union decreased. The stipend of the ministers on the Home Work Fund was lamentably low – still below £350 per annum. During his first year in office, Ernest Payne recognised the magnitude of the tasks to which he was called and the complexity of the issues. He laid the foundation of the organisation of the Baptist World Alliance Congress in

1955, and he determined that whatever else happened in his secretaryship, he would seek to develop within the denomination a proper organisation and administration which would not only make more efficient the running of the denomination but would have a proper caring content for the ministers and their stipends.

By the end of his first year there had already emerged a remarkable gift which he had brought to the secretaryship and which was to characterise his term of office. This was his capacity for making himself available to a continuous stream of ministers, church officers and many another who sought his advice. Sometimes he managed to meet people during the busy office schedule. At other times these contacts would take place during his lunch hour, when he would take his visitor to a nearby restaurant, give him lunch and listen to his problems, and offer advice. More often than not the person would go on his way not only refreshed in body but also uplifted in heart.

Ernest Payne's stature in the ecumenical movement continued to grow largely because of his participation in the Third World Conference on Faith and Order held at Lund in 1952. He had been asked to be chairman of the section considering the question of inter-communion. This was a very difficult assignment in 1952. A report had been prepared by a commission which reflected both the deep disagreements and also the necessity for progress. As the section discussed the report it became all too evident that there were differences not only *between* the churches but also *within* the churches. Much of the time in the section at Lund was taken up with listening to disagreements. Eventually, however, the section did produce a statement on inter-communion which remarkably was accepted by the conference in plenary session without the need for overmuch revision. This was a considerable achievement, particularly as it laid down guide lines for Eucharistic celebration at ecumenical gatherings. These guide lines were sustained and developed within the World Council of Churches from Lund onwards.

Ernest Payne was elected to the new working committee of the Faith and Order Commission. This was a responsibility which gave him many interesting, enjoyable and stimulating experiences until 1964 when he withdrew from the commission with genuine reluctance because of pressure of work. His contribution to Faith and Order showed his ability as a theologian. At heart, he was more than anything else an historian. But when it came to the discussion of theology, his mind was no less incisive and able. He cut always to the heart of a theological issue and his historical competence ensured that all was seen in a proper perspective. It was partly through Ernest Payne's advocacy that baptism grew in importance in ecumenical perspectives at a number of points, not least in Faith and Order.

India

December 1952 proved to be another significant mark in his developing ecumenical involvement. M. E. Aubrey indicated that he did not feel able to make the journey to India for the meeting of the Central Committee of the World Council of Churches. He suggested that Ernest Payne should go as his proxy. So at the end of the year he took the opportunity to be away for nearly a month and saw something of the Baptist Missionary Society work in Bengal, and in Orissa in North India as well as attending the meetings at Lucknow.

His visit to India was memorable, first because of a visit that he made to Serampore – always a place of pilgrimage to Baptists, with its links with William Carey. There he found a sense of quietness and peace in the garden planted by William Carey beside the great college. But the state of the cemetery with the graves of Carey, Marshman, Ward, and their wives and so many others whose names were familiar to him in BMS history came as a shock to him for so much of it was in decay. He felt that the present had stopped caring for the past.

The second event of importance was the Central Committee of the World Council of Churches which was meeting in Isabella Thorburn College, affiliated to Lucknow University. The chairman of the Central Committee then was Bishop George Bell of Chichester. Early in the meeting Bishop Bell read out the names of the various sub-committees which would be at work during the meetings. To his astonishment, Ernest Payne heard his name read out as chairman of the sub-committee on arrangements for the Second Assembly of the World Council of Churches to be held at Evanston in the United States of America. On hearing his name Ernest Payne stood up and said he presumed that there must have been some mistake, as he was only present as a proxy. Bishop Bell looked at him and said, 'No, there is no mistake. Mr Payne will discover that in this fellowship we try to do what we are asked.' So he accepted the responsibility which led to quite extraordinary and speedy developments of responsibility for him within the ecumenical movement. What is more, he never forgot Bell's words, and from that day on, he tried to do all that was asked of him, though many of the assignments were unexpected, and very difficult.

It was at Lucknow that he first met Dr Franklin Clark Fry, the American Lutheran, who was at that time Vice-Chairman of the Central Committee. Ernest Payne was deeply impressed with him at Lucknow, particularly on an occasion when Fry had to preside over a meeting at which the Governor of the United Provinces in welcoming the company, paid tribute to the example of Christ, but alleged that Christianity had come to India linked with imperialism, and that the day for prose- lytising – as he called it – was now over. Such sentiments would today cause far less surprise and concern than they did in 1953. Franklin Fry's reply, spontaneous and in a rather tense atmo- sphere, was memorable to Ernest Payne because in admirable, courteous and firm tones, he asserted the basic motives under- lying Christian evangelism. Soon afterwards Ernest Payne and Franklin Fry were to become closely linked in the service of the Central Committee becoming close friends and remarkable servants together in the World Council of Churches.

In India he met Martin Niemöller. He had met him once before in Mansfield College Senior Common Room in 1946 but sitting in the somewhat unlikely context of a garden in Lucknow, Martin Niemöller told him of his experiences on his first visit to Moscow at Christmas 1951. He spoke of the service at the Baptist church which he had attended and was warm in his praise of the Russian Baptists, of the quality of spiritual life he found in the church, and for the way in which they were truly a preaching church. This conversation made Ernest Payne all the more determined to make early contact with the Russian Baptists.

1952 had been for the Baptist Union a year of mixed for- tunes. Although the membership had declined by more than 3,000, Sunday School scholars had increased in number by an extra 5,500. Most remarkably there had been a spectacular improvement in the Baptist Union's financial situation. At the beginning of 1952 Ernest Payne had warned that unless there was a considerable increase in giving, there would be a deficit. Contributions to the Home Work Fund increased by the then remarkable total of £14,444, to give a total of £47,064. This was against the 1951 figure of £32,620. This year marked the beginning of a steady climb in giving to the Home Work Fund. The result was that the standard stipend could go up at last to £350, a sum which Ernest Payne felt acutely was far too small.

During 1952 he began to stress the importance of the work amongst Baptist students. He sought to concentrate resources within the Baptist Students' Federation believing that here was one of the growing points of the denomination. He encouraged constantly the student societies in the universities and the chaplains who served them, and one of his deepest regrets in the latter years of his life, was the demise of the Student Federation and of the effectiveness of many of the student societies in the universities. Most particularly during his first full year in office he had become more and more aware of the necessity to try to communicate to the denomination that the machinery of administration, intricate and often cumbersome as it seemed sometimes to be, existed solely to serve the churches. The necessity of administration was part of the necessity of mission. The purpose of the Baptist Church House was to serve the churches in their individual and corporate witness as well as to foster the Baptist advance in the broadest sense of that phrase. It was his concern throughout the whole of his secretaryship that the Baptist Union should be seen, not as an organisation which administered, but as a manifestation of the fellowship of the churches and the Associations acting together to foster the mission of the Kingdom. Already he was coming to recognise the vital importance of the work of the Associations and worked to give them more and more delegated responsibility.

A very important family event claimed his attention during the early months of 1953. Through a friend at the Bath Domestic Science College, Ann had made the acquaintance of a young officer in the Royal Engineers stationed at Shrivenham in Wiltshire. Before long Ann and the young officer, Anthony Prain were urgent in their desire to become engaged and so in

April 1953 Ernest Payne gladly gave his approval. Tony Prain came of a Scottish family, with a number of Army connections. Part of his own National Service had been spent in Hong Kong, and he decided then to remain in the Forces with his chief aptitudes and interest being in surveying. Tony and Ann were married in Hampstead Garden Suburb Church in June 1953. Their first home was in Rochester, then for two years in Germany, and their two children were born, James in 1956 and Elizabeth in 1957. The coming of the grandchildren was a welcome and exciting enrichment to the life of Freda and Ernest Payne.

In the same month that Ann was married, Queen Elizabeth II was crowned. The Baptist Union had received two invitations to the ceremony. The President, the Rev. Henry Bonser, had a place in the clerical procession, and since the letter 'B' for Baptist, came early in the alphabet, Henry Bonser led the group into Westminster Abbey. The other Baptist ticket was assigned to Ernest Payne. He has left a vivid description of the Coronation:

Our seats were on the right hand side of the main aisle just behind the Screen. Although this gave us no sight of the actual crowning, we had a fine view of the entries and exits. We had to be in the Abbey between 6 and 7 o'clock in the morning. We were there to see the gradual arrival of the great and the famous. Clement Attlee, slipping in as if, it seemed, he wished not to be noticed; the majestic Queen Salote of Tonga, striking because of her stature and her obvious excitement; Winston Churchill, magnificent in his Garter robes, giving the impression that he regarded himself as the true Master of Ceremonies; finally, the Queen herself, a vision of breathtaking splendour and loveliness. Probably never before, certainly of recent centuries, had the Coronation Service seemed to have so deep a religious meaning.

Off to the States

The summer of 1953 saw him going to the United States for the first time by air. His purpose was twofold, first to help to prepare through the Executive of the Baptist World Alliance for the Golden Jubilee Congress of the Baptist World Alliance and then secondly to go on to Evanston in Chicago, to see some of the buildings and to make certain initial plans for the 1954 World Council Assembly. His travel diaries are full of recollections of unusual and strange incidents. One of these was on this occasion at Chicago Airport. He went to Chicago to meet Dr Bilheimer, who was involved also in the Evanston preparations. They visited Soldiers Field, where there was to be a vast religious pageant connected with the assembly, in the company of a young lady called Holly Cramer, who had been asked to draft a script for the pageant. After the visit they made their way back to the airport from which they were to fly to New York. It was a sultry summer evening, and was thundering. The New York plane was held up, and a second plane was grounded by an electrical fault. Chicago in the summer, particularly when it is thundery, is very hot indeed. For some hours, Ernest Payne, Robert Bilheimer and Holly Cramer, sat waiting in the heat. Whilst they were waiting they were talking about the planned pageant. Robert Bilheimer and Ernest Payne had a Bible and passed it between them trying to convey at the same time to Holly Cramer, some of the great themes that each saw within the biblical revelation, particularly those which might be presented in dramatic form, in an arena as vast as Soldiers Field. Eventually, well after midnight, their plane left. But a year later, when the pageant was held, both Bilheimer and Ernest Payne felt highly rewarded for what at that time was a strange and uncomfortable night, for the pageant proved a most successful and impressive spectacle, and set forth clearly aspects of the biblical revelation of the Gospel.

Among further duties that came to Ernest Payne in 1953 was the invitation to serve until 1956 on the Central Religious Advisory Committee of the BBC. This body, though advisory only, wielded considerable influence on the religious policy of the BBC. During Ernest Payne's term of office, there were a number of interesting but somewhat inconclusive discussions notably on the question of Billy Graham and what should be broadcast of his mission. But most particularly it was during this time that the committee had to consider the arrangements for the new Independent Television Authority and the relationship that would have to exist between CRAC and religious broadcasting of the ITA. A strong sub-committee was set up of which Sir Kenneth Clark was the chairman, and on which Ernest Payne served. The outcome of its deliberations was that CRAC took over the responsibility not only for the religious broadcasting of the BBC, but also for that of the ITA.

Dr Billy Graham came to London in the spring of 1954. Ernest Payne and Billy Graham were dissimilar in so many ways, but both of them were convinced Baptists, and represented perhaps the remarkable and healthy diversity of approach within the denomination. From time to time Ernest Payne used the past to express the attitudes of the present – particularly his own views. In the council's report for 1954, which records Billy Graham's visit, there is a quotation from James Mursell speaking at the Baptist Union Assembly in 1874 about D. L. Moody and his meetings:

I went to the first of their meetings which I had the opportunity of attending, not without a disposition to criticise, not without much misgiving as to the soundness of the work and its probable results. But a few days' experience sufficed to cure me of my doubts and cavils ... I soon found that I had to do with a genuine, unaffected, genial-hearted man – a man utterly free from the cant and religious affectation which too often disfigure those engaged in such movements; a man, moreover evidently possessing singular qualifications, both natural and spiritual, for the work to which he had given himself ... The spell of his wizardry is the Cross – the Cross let it be understood, as meaning the bearing by the surety and substitute of guilty man, of that penalty and curse of the broken law which else the sinner must himself have borne to his eternal ruin.

This is Ernest Payne using the voice of the nineteenth century to express exactly his own reaction. He did not hesitate to acknowledge the effectiveness of Billy Graham's visit. He was impressed by the way in which night after night ten to twelve thousand people gathered in Harringay Arena, and that the closing rally at Wembley Stadium brought together one of the largest companies ever to gather at a religious meeting in England. He commented: 'Dr Graham has shown that the spiritual mood of our land is one of readiness for decision.'[9] Not surprisingly Billy Graham was invited to return for the Jubilee Congress for the Baptist World Alliance in 1955.

Enter the Russians

In 1951 contact had been made with the Russian Baptists through a group of English Quakers and there was a subsequent inter-change of letters between the Russians and the Baptist Union Council later that same year. Five months after Stalin's death in March 1953, four Russian Baptists visited Stockholm and Dr H. R. Williamson and the Rev. R. L. Child went over to meet them. At that point the chief desire in the contact from the side of the Russian Baptists seemed to be secure support for the so-called World Peace Council. Then suddenly in May 1954, Dr Townley Lord, the President of the Baptist World Alliance, received an invitation to visit the Soviet Union and to take two companions with him. He invited W. O. Lewis of the Baptist World Alliance and Ernest Payne to go with him. Both accepted with alacrity. Such a trip in 1954 was an adventure into the unknown. The three travellers left London on 16th June, spent a night in Stockholm and the next day flew to Helsinki. From there a Russian plane took them on to Moscow.

On arrival, representatives of the Baptist Council of the Soviet Union were on the tarmac to greet them. J. I. Zhidkov and Alexander Karev were there, together with an interpreter, Claudia Tortova (now Mrs Pillabeck) who spoke English well. In addition there was also an official woman interpreter. In the lapel of Zhidkov's jacket was a Baptist World Congress badge. For Ernest Payne the presence of that simple badge dispelled many of his fears and apprehensions. He knew that Zhidkov had never been to a BWA Congress and asked him how he came by the badge. The reply was that it had been given to him by one of the brethren who had been to the Toronto Congress of 1928. He had retained the badge ever since in the hope that one day Russian Baptists would renew contact with that worldwide fellowship of Baptists to which they felt they belonged. This happened at last on 17th June 1954.

All was strange to the travellers. They stayed in the Hotel Metropol in Moscow, each of them on a different floor, and they had little opportunities of being on their own or of comparing notes. They were accompanied everywhere, not only by a group of Baptists but also by an official interpreter, and usually by a photographer. The weekend saw them experiencing worship in the Baptist Church in Moscow for the first time. They were present on the Saturday evening, twice on the Sunday, and again on the Monday. All the services were crowded, and were held every night of the week except Friday. The Monday evening service was a baptismal service at which 30 candidates of varying ages, twelve men and eighteen women, were baptised.

It takes little imagination to recognise how moving an experience it must have been for the three of them to be in the Soviet Union for the first time to share in the services not only in Moscow but also in the city then known as Stalingrad, Rostoff on Don, the Crimaea, the Ukraine and finally Leningrad. The buildings were all crowded far beyond their capacity, and there was a warm welcome. At that time, partly because of the fearful Russian casualties in the Second World War – estimated at some 20 million – women predominated in the congregations, but there were a surprising number of young people. It was crystal clear to the visitors that whatever the authorities may have tried to achieve by persecution the Christian faith had survived through all the years. Whatever clever people might say about religion, these faithful folk knew better. They visited the Zhidkov family home. Jacob Zhidkov's wife was the daughter of one of the Baptist pioneers who had been exiled to Siberia in the Tzarist days. The home was not far from Moscow and like most Russian families, the Zhidkovs had suffered in the war; three of their sons had been killed.

This visit had a considerable influence on Ernest Payne and his attitude to his many contacts with the Baptists in the Soviet Union and in the Eastern Bloc countries. He always took great pains to try to understand the background of the people, and the situation in which they were living. Just occasionally little notes were furtively thrust into the hands of the visitors. When they had them translated on their return to England, it was discovered that they contained criticisms of the leaders of the All Soviet Council of Evangelical Christian Baptists for their compromise with the Communist authorities. The notes gave details of some of those who had suffered imprisonment for their protests against the Communist régime and its restrictions on religion. Thus, as early as 1954, the visitors were made aware of the existence of the group of dissident Baptists. Some measure of co-operation with the political authorities was clearly essential if any effective denominational organisation was to function. On balance, however, that first visit convinced Ernest Payne of the deep Christian sincerity of most of the leaders of the Russian Baptists, of their wisdom and of the faithfulness with which, in the most difficult of circumstances, they were seeking to maintain and extend the Baptist witness and to shepherd the widely scattered congregations. The closer contacts that he had in subsequent years did not give him serious cause to alter these opinions. He discerned too that there was growing up a second generation of potential Baptist leaders amongst whom was Zhidkov's youngest son, Michael.

Three weeks after his return from the Soviet Union, Ernest Payne was on board the Queen Mary en route for New York and the Evanston Assembly of the World Council of Churches. In 1954, Senator McCarthy's campaign against what he called 'un-American activities' was still in progress, with its violent anti-communism. At one point this campaign had even led the World Council of Churches to consider the possibility of moving the second assembly to Canada for it was vital to secure the presence of delegates from member churches in Czechoslovakia and Hungary. Ernest Payne himself was told that it might be better if he asked for a new passport and surrendered the one in which he had evidence of a visit to the USSR. He refused to follow this advice. He felt that had he been held on Ellis Island it would be somewhat inconvenient for him, but might in the long run have proved useful in combating the excesses of the McCarthy Campaign! When he reached New York, the immigration officials came on board the Queen Mary and interviewed the passengers in one of the lounges. Passports were inspected. We need to recall what the situation was in 1954. Before an American visa could be obtained, finger-prints had to be taken. Ernest Payne's hesitancy and concern about the passport inspection was shared also by Dr Visser't Hooft. He records in his *Memoirs*[10] how nervous he and his wife felt on arriving in the United States in 1954, and the relief that it was the Indian and not the East German visa which caught the attention of the official. It was with some hesitation, therefore, that Ernest Payne presented his passport and papers. The official looked it over, looked at him, and said, 'So you want to go to this economical conference?' Ernest Payne replied, 'Well, it's not very economical:' The official waved him by.

Ernest Payne's own part in the assembly was significant. The inability of the delegates to meet and partake together in a Communion service was a cause of deep perplexity and distress to many. He had been given the very difficult task of preaching at a service of preparation on the Saturday evening, at the end of the first week of the assembly. The following morning was to see a largely attended open Communion service in the First Methodist Church, followed on the Monday morning by an Anglican service, on the Tuesday by a service in Chicago, sponsored by the Augustana Evangelical Lutheran Church and on Wednesday by the Divine Liturgy of St John Chrysostom, also in Chicago. The knowledge that unreconciled church relations still necessitated such a series of services deeply affected many of the delegates, and they gathered on the Saturday evening with a sense of considerably greater emotional strain. It was the first time in the experience of many delegates of the seriousness of the divisions at the very point where unity should have been manifest, namely at the Eucharist. The sermon that Ernest Payne preached on that occasion is amongst the most effective of all his ecumenical addresses. He spoke honestly, with the utmost clarity and proper simplicity. That it had an effect over the years is evidenced from the number of people who subsequently referred to it. As late as 1977, a German Baptist who had been a student in Chicago in 1954, and who was acting as an interpreter at Evanston, reminded Ernest Payne of the sermon which, she said, she was still quoting to illustrate how it was possible, not only to live in today's divisions, but also to live in a truly Christian fashion towards others as the church struggled out of division towards unity.

In the sermon he set out the tensions that clearly existed:

We come perplexed, frustrated, in danger of being impatient with one another, of accusing those with whom we differ with obstinacy or blindness or carelessness. Some are tempted to press for majority decisions and to try to force issues. But who shall decide how heads are to be counted? And who, with the New Testament open before him, or the long and devious story of the Christian church in mind, would dare to assert that the mind of Christ is necessarily or fully expressed by either the majority or the minority in any particular Christian assembly, or even by the whole church at any one moment in its pilgrimage? The truth is that on the question of the ordering of the Lord's Table, on the question 'who should celebrate the Holy Supper and who should partake', Christians, even the Christians associated in the World Council of Churches, remain divided. Each must obey his own conscience, standing himself answerable to his Lord. To try to force the conscience of another is as wrong as it is fruitless. Even to hint at such a thing as we approach this sacred service, would be an act of sacrilege.

His conviction that freedom of conscience under God must be allowed to every individual was the touchstone of all his ecumenical attitudes.

Not surprisingly he quotes from a 17th century Puritan, William Ames, who repeated a definition of the Eucharist going back to Thomas Aquinas. 'The sacrament is a sign commemorative of the passion of Christ, demonstrative of divine grace and prophetic of future glory'. The sermon then goes on to expand those three points of commemoration, demonstration and the eschatological aspect of the Supper. He concluded by reminding the congregation that when the disciples had sung a hymn with Jesus, they went out (Matthew 26.30, Mark 14.26) and that the Lord's Supper was an occasion for refreshment and commissioning for the tasks awaiting them in the world outside.

At the close of the Communion service in this church tomorrow, at the close of the other services in the coming week, we shall go out with Christ, recommitted to a great adventure, the great task; to the making of disciples; to 'the building up of the body of Christ, until we all attain to the unity of the faith and of the knowledge of the Son of God, to mature manhood, to the measure of the stature of the fulness of Christ (Ephesians 4.12, 13).[11]

The sermon through its simplicity, frankness, incisiveness and sincerity, caused Ernest Payne to be marked out by the delegates present as a potential leader in the ecumenical movement.

It was not surprising that he was elected to the new Central Committee in place of M. E. Aubrey but rather more unexpectedly he was elected as vice-chairman to Franklin Clark Fry who succeeded Bishop George Bell. This election as vice-chairman came to him as a considerable surprise. The vice-chairmanship carried with it, not only the responsibility of presiding at some of the sessions of the Central Committee itself, and of the subsequent Assembly, but also in the chairing of certain sub-committees. He was elected immediately to the chair of the staffing sub-committee of the World Council of Churches, a position which he held until 1968. The weeks in Evanston had transformed him from being one of the ordinary delegates and functionaries to being a leader amongst them.

The Baptist World Alliance Congress

His basic responsibility, however, was still the secretaryship of the Baptist Union. When he returned from Evanston he became immersed in the preparation for the Baptist World Alliance Congress. A strong committee had been set up with Ronald Bell as chairman. Bell proved to be a tower of strength in every aspect, not least in the financial negotiations that were necessary. The policy of the alliance was to expect the inviting country to accept full responsibility once the booking fees for delegates had been agreed upon. More than once there had been difficulties over a substantial deficit, most particularly that which the Danish Baptists had had to face after the Copenhagen congress. This meant that the British Baptists had to depend largely on the number of Americans coming to the congress. The international situation in 1954 and indeed in 1955 made this somewhat uncertain. There was not immediately tremendous eagerness on the part of British Baptists from outside London to be present. But the hard work of Ronald Bell and O. D. Wiles, at the Church House with A. A. Wilson at the Mission House, helped to carry the congress through.

This congress about which so many people had considerable apprehension turned out to be a very successful event. The theme was 'Jesus Christ, the same yesterday and today'. It opened on Saturday 16th July. On the evening before, through the kindness of Sir Cyril Black, then MP for Wimbledon, the British Baptists were able to entertain the Baptist World Alliance Executive and a number of friends to dinner in the House of Commons. It was a superb warm summer evening, and after the meal the visitors went out on to the terrace of the House by the river. Many of the overseas visitors subsequently regarded that occasion as the highlight of the whole congress!

A total of 8,524 delegates registered at the congress, and of these more than 4,000 had come from the United States. This enabled the Baptist Union to close the accounts with a substantial surplus. The congress was a success not only financially, but also because it was more representative than ever before. The numbers are significant. The Canadians sent 518, the Australians 332, the Germans 330, the Swedes 285 and the British Isles supplied, in the end, some 1,700. Baptists from the Soviet Union were present but none from other Eastern European countries. The Archbishop of Canterbury had been amongst those who had welcomed the delegates at the opening sessions, and he had made a great impression upon all the delegates. Memorable was the Wednesday evening pageant entitled 'And There's Another Country'. The script and production were the work of the Rev. Arthur Davies, but it included scenes from the pageant that Ernest Payne and Kathleen Shuttleworth had prepared for the Atlanta Congress in 1939. The Albert Hall was crowded to capacity and many had to be turned away. There is a true story of one disgruntled American delegate from the Southern States who drew a gun on the manager of the Albert Hall in his fruitless attempt to get in! The final rally was in the Arsenal Football Stadium in Highbury. The main speaker was Dr Billy Graham, who once again made a considerable impact upon all who were present.

The congress had been very demanding of Ernest Payne, and there were already signs showing of the pressure that the multiplicity of his responsibilities were putting upon him. At the end of the official report it is recorded that in expressing gratitude to God, he commented: 'He enabled us to carry through this great enterprise in our capacity as hosts. He preserved us from any serious mishaps. He granted us the benediction of sunshine. His over-ruling presence was manifest in the unbroken fellowship which characterised the proceedings.'[12] The successful outcome of this congress fulfilled at least one of Ernest Payne's aims during his first five years as secretary of the Baptist Union.

During the rest of 1955, there were signs of hope to encourage him. The amount in the Home Work Fund was rising steadily, and the target was exceeded by £3,000 when the total reached was more than £55,000. There was every possibility that by 1956 the stipend for a married minister could rise to

£400 per annum. The membership of churches had increased in 1955 by 737 and the figure for baptisms by 2,000, which was probably the result of the visit of Dr Billy Graham. Whilst Ernest Payne was glad of these figures he was concerned about the difference between them. It appeared that baptism was not being linked clearly enough with church membership. Nevertheless there were signs of growing interest amongst Baptists in theological ministry which he helped to stimulate. There had been a report on ordination which had been presented to the Baptist Union Council and it was known that some younger ministers were at work in the preparation of a book on baptism. The production of this latter book *Christian Baptism* was made possible by the generosity of some laymen on the initiative of Ernest Payne who encouraged the authors throughout the enterprise.

The assembly of 1956 completed Ernest Payne's first five years in office. He ended the Report that he presented on 30th April 1956 with these words: 'Our new age hurls many problems at us. Even if sometimes bewildered, ought we not also to be reinspired by what God is doing?' This comment perhaps reflects more of Ernest Payne than he realised at the time. Whilst he had successfully completed his intentions for the World Alliance Congress and had in mind initial plans for the Ter-Jubilee of the Baptist Union there was growing in his mind a bewilderment about certain attitudes that he found. There was, on the one hand, conservatism not so much of theology, which he understood and respected, but entrenched positions, traditional attitudes, even a certain amount of ambition for position and protection of little kingdoms. Yet on the other hand, his experience over the first five years had encouraged him to the view that within the Baptist denomination there was still a clear ground swell of conviction about the gospel truths as interpreted over the centuries by people called Baptists.

The Baptist Union put on record its appreciation of Ernest Payne's achievements during the first five years:

His work has always been distinguished by meticulous attention to detail, but behind it all is a deep devotion to our Baptist cause, combined with a statesman-like vision of the larger issues of the kingdom. Today his value is recognised by ourselves and by all the

Christian communions that go to make the World Council of Churches.

It was M.E. Aubrey who proposed his re-election for a further period of five years.

In his response to his re-appointment, Ernest Payne revealed a little of his own reactions to the first five years:

I told the Council last November – though not without hesitation – that I was willing for my name to be submitted here again for re-election. That being your desire I am ready to undertake a further period of service and to do my best for you and for the Union. ... The work of the General Secretary of the Union has become, of course, very varied, at times exciting, always exacting, often more than not a little frightening. The apostle Paul spoke of the daily pressure upon him of the care of all the churches, but he was at least spared importunate questionings over the telephone by journalists wanting to know what the Baptist Union thinks of the lastest activities of the government! A more exalted ecclesiastical office than mine was once described as 'incredible, indefensible, and inevitable'. I have sometimes been tempted to echo these adjectives ... My job appears more like that of a juggler, trying to catch plates thrown at him from various parts of the stage – and occasionally by the audience – and intended not only to hold them but to put them in some kind of order!

Now about the future. When I undertook this service I said that the first five years, in addition to the regular work of the Union, would move towards the Jubilee Congress as a kind of climax. Should I be elected for a second term of office, I suggested that one of its major concerns should be the finding of new and closer relationships between the Baptist Union and the Baptist Missionary Society. I still believe that. Five years ago I should have said this was mainly necessary because of the denominational situation in this country. That is still important, but I am now convinced that it is a situation of our missionary churches overseas and the prospects facing them that make it urgent and imperative. I do not see clearly what we ought to do. But both bodies have pledged themselves to give their minds to this question – I hope it can be done with restraint, sympathy and mutual confidence. Should I be spared and we agree upon yet another term, we shall have together worthily to celebrate the Ter-Jubilee of the Baptist Union, and I would suggest, to engage in serious reflection on the theological as well as practical implications

101

of our association together as churches. Our plans for 1962-3 will have to be worked out fairly clearly during the next five years along with all the other things that have to be done. We are custodians of a great heritage, both spiritual and material in this Union. It is a great but humbling honour to have your confidence. I thank you.

II: 1956–61

So it was with the Baptist World Alliance Congress completed he turned to the initial planning of the Baptist Union Ter-Jubilee celebrations and he renewed his efforts to bring together the Baptist Union and the Baptist Missionary Society. But it was not to prove as easy as that.

After the 1955 Congress, the Baptist Union Council and the General Committee of the Baptist Missionary Society had agreed a joint declaration of intent to deal seriously with their relationships. In the light of this joint declaration, Ernest Payne drafted a memorandum dealing with various alternative procedures for opening up the matter again. He sent a copy to J. B. Middlebrook hoping that they might come to a common mind as to how best to proceed and assumed that it would be discussed with the officers of the Baptist Missionary Society. Several months went by and no response had come. His enquiries at the Baptist Missionary Society indicated that the matter had not yet reached the BMS officers. When late in 1956 Ernest Payne asked J. B. Middlebrook about this memorandum and what he thought ought to be done, Middlebrook indicated that interesting though he found the memorandum, he did not propose to act upon it as it was not in any sense an official approach by the Baptist Union to the Baptist Missionary Society. This attitude Ernest Payne felt to be somewhat evasive and caused him deep concern and considerable perplexity. He realised that he must bide his time.

Peace and war

Amongst his many duties was secretaryship of the United Board which was responsible for Free Church chaplains in the Services. In 1955 it had been suggested that the establishment

102

in the Far East would appreciate a visit by a representative of the United Board, possibly Ernest Payne himself. It so happened that in February 1956 the World Council of Churches had arranged for its Executive to meet in Australia. Ernest Payne recognised that this would be an expensive trip. However, it seemed that if he could combine a visit to the chaplains in the Far East with the visit to Australia, then the financial burden, particularly on the Baptist Union, would be eased. He was assured that the Royal Air Force would fly him to and from Singapore, and arrange a worthwhile tour. So he accepted this double responsibility for an extended trip to the Far East and Australia.

The RAF accorded him for the purpose of the journey and the tour the rank of Honorary Air Vice Marshal – a distinction for which he felt unfitted, both by experience and temperament, but one for which he was very grateful in view of the advantages it gained him in the difficult travel arrangements! For the journey out he travelled with RAF personnel in a transport plane going to India, spending a night en route in Karachi. He visited Calcutta, Singapore and Hong Kong. Everywhere he went he visited not only chaplains but also the missionaries of the Baptist Missionary Society and indeed other Free Church missionaries. When taking leave of the Air Commodore, Commander of the United Kingdom Air Force in the Far East, Ernest Payne thanked him for all the arrangements which had been made and was rather taken aback and not a little shaken by the Air Commodore's reply: 'We thank you, sir, for making the trip at your age – if I may say so.' Ernest Payne was then 54 years old!

All these visits left him deeply impressed with the work of the chaplains and by what the Service authorities were seeking to do in the way of training for the future the many young men who were doing their National Service so far from home. The visit was also beneficial to him in that he received vivid and lasting impressions of the complex social and political problems in the multi-racial communities which were so evident in the places which he visited, and which before long were to become only too common in England itself. It also enabled him to go on to Australia for the World Council Executive and gave him the chance of meeting Aunt Flossie, his father's sister who had emigrated in 1897. She had gone to Australia to join her fiancé, Edward Wallis. Aunt Flossie had been baptised in the Downs Chapel, Clapton, by Dr Tymms and claimed membership there until her death at the age of 103. Aunt and nephew kept in touch after that first meeting, writing weekly letters right up until December 1970, when Aunt Flossie died.

The Central Committee of the World Council of Churches met later in August 1956 just outside Budapest. Throughout the visit of the committee to Hungary, there was a consciousness of tension and unrest beneath the surface, but few, if any, of the members of the Central Committee at that meeting in the summer of 1956 had any idea that within two months there would be an uprising. The Christians in Hungary were clearly under considerable pressure and had a sense of foreboding. In the Sunday services which the committee shared with the Congregation of the Reformed Church in Budapest, as the psalms were being sung many of the congregation, both men and women, were in tears. Ernest Payne reflected that the addresses given by the members of the Central Committee did not and could not meet the needs of the people, and that perhaps it would have been much better for all if the Hungarians had, in fact, preached to the Central Committee.

The Autumn of 1956 fulfilled only too dramatically and in a disturbing fashion, the fears that had been felt in the earlier months in Budapest and elsewhere. In September, President Nasser seized and nationalised the Suez Canal. Weeks of fruitless negotiation followed and suddenly in late October, France and Britain, after secret discussions, committed themselves to the ill-fated and short-lived military attack on Egypt. During the same week there was a sudden revolt in Hungary. It appeared to be a spontaneous and natural uprising, and it was said that within 24 hours the fabric of communism had disappeared and a new régime was under construction, pledged to neutralism, free elections, and the multi-party system. The church in Hungary was affected by this uprising and there was a change within the hierarchy. On 3rd November the World Council of Churches sent from Geneva a message of goodwill and approval. But the USSR was already sending troops in to crush the Hungarian Revolt. The western nations were impotent. France and Britain had already lost the support of the United States of America as a result of the attack on Egypt. Within a few days of the Russian invasion thousands of Hungarians were fleeing across the frontier into Austria, and to assist them the World Council of Churches mounted one of its biggest and most demanding operations to aid the refugees. On Sunday 4th November 1956, Ernest Payne was due to preach in Leicester. Early on 3rd November however, he was called to the telephone and asked to go with the Archbishop of Canterbury, Dr Geoffrey Fisher, and the secretary of the British Council of Churches, Rev. Kenneth Slack, to represent to the Prime Minister, Anthony Eden, the concern of the churches at the Suez operation which seemed so clearly to conflict with the letter and spirit of the membership of the United Nations. There was a widespread feeling amongst the Christians that the government was flouting the United Nations and that this was morally wrong. He arranged for a substitute in Leicester and prepared to go to meet the Prime Minister. He met his colleagues at the entrance to the House of Lords, and the Archbishop then said that they were to be received not by the Prime Minister but by the Lord Chancellor, Lord Kilmuir. The delegation was courteously received by Lord Kilmuir but appeared to Ernest Payne to make little impression upon him. The Archbishop expressed the strongly felt views of the churches and the Lord Chancellor promised to convey these to the Prime Minister. At the end of the interview Lord Kilmuir came to the door of his room and said goodbye to each personally. He said to Ernest Payne that he understood that he was a Baptist, and added, 'My wife is very proud of her connection with William Carey.' It turned out that Lady Kilmuir, who was a sister of Rex Harrison, the actor, claimed an actual lineal descent from William Carey, although this was never finally proved to Ernest Payne's satisfaction! However, Lord Kilmuir did subsequently read the lesson at the Carey Service in Westminster Abbey in 1961, and very impressively he did it.

The events of the Autumn had a considerable effect on denominational affairs. The November meeting of the Baptist Union Council was to be held in Bristol. The Citizenship Committee hoped that a resolution criticising the government for the attack on Suez would be accepted and passed by the council. Sir Herbert Janes, a well-known Luton builder, was the President of the Union for 1956–57 and in the chair of the council. Before the council began he told Ernest Payne that if too critical a motion was passed on Suez he would find himself bound to resign the presidency. Sir Herbert gave Ernest Payne a letter which was to be read if and when he withdrew from the council. In the debate in the Baptist Union Council, however, it became quickly evident that the council itself was sharply divided on the Suez issue. Perhaps this debate illustrated most clearly the sharp political polarisation which entered into the churches and notably the Free Churches certainly from 1930 onwards – perhaps even earlier – and stemmed from the break up of the Liberal Party after the First World War. One section of the denomination clearly had moved to the right in politics. There were already signs that another section had moved further to the left. This polarisation politically has remained with the denomination. Possibly it says something of the compromise nature of the debate that Sir Herbert Janes felt able to accept the resolution in its final form and remained president!

In spite of international tensions, it was during 1956 that the renewed contacts with the Soviet Union bore fruit with the arrival of students from the Soviet Union to share in the ministerial preparation in the Baptist colleges in England. Two students, including Michael Zhidkov, went to Spurgeon's College, and two went to Bristol. Although the Russians asked what the full cost of training would be the British Baptists made it clear that this aspect of the matter did not greatly concern them. They were only too delighted to have the Russian young men amongst them. Their presence in England, however, brought some anxieties. It was soon learned that the authorities felt it necessary to keep a close watch on them. However, the links have proved of enduring value, particularly those with Michael Zhidkov who is now in Moscow, and Matthew Melnik, who went to Bristol. The presence of these students helped a number of people, not least Ernest Payne, of course, to have a clearer understanding of the difficulties and yet the importance of close personal contacts between East and West.

By the end of 1956 there was still much to be thankful for within the Baptist Union itself. During that year it received 24 new churches into membership which was the largest single number for many years. Baptisms were more than 10,000 for the first time since 1944, and the churches reported an increase in membership of something like 1,100. The Home Work Fund had produced a record sum of more than £63,000, and the standard stipend had been increased to £400. Whilst Ernest Payne was pleased about this, he felt it was still not good enough and the appeal for 1957 was for £72,000 to increase the stipend to £450 per annum.

Denominational tensions

But there were difficulties on the horizon which concerned him deeply. There was a shortage of ministers and a decline in men offering for pastoral service. There were signs that a number of ministerial students were going to inter-denominational Bible colleges, a fact which was going to cause increasing difficulties of accreditation for the denomination in the years that lay ahead. The disagreement that had been evidenced at the Baptist Union Council in Bristol over the Suez issue was further reflected in disagreement on the policy about Cyprus and the question of the abolition of the death penalty. Differences in theology were also surfacing, which were related to a difference of emphasis upon the doctrine of the church with, on the one hand a growing re-emphasis on the 19th century independency and on the other hand a desire for closer relationships ecclesiologically within the Baptist Union. The Baptist Missionary Society also was facing difficulties on the questions relating to the Union plans being put forward both in North India and in Ceylon. Ernest Payne sounded a warning note when he drafted the council report:

Our prejudices, whether political or ecclesiastical, are poor guides, as we seek to discern the unfolding purpose of God. Our greatest safeguards are a constant waiting upon God, close fellowship with his people: those of our own tradition, and those of other traditions, those of our own nation, and those of other nations.

The early months of 1957 saw further pressures building up. The Executive Committee of the World Council of Churches met in Geneva. The meeting was not an easy one. The events in Egypt and Hungary had placed a considerable strain on the secretary of the World Council and those who shared responsibility with him. The message which Visser't Hooft had sent on 3rd November to Budapest on behalf of the World Council, was now being severely criticised by the churches of Eastern Europe. The restored Hungarian authorities had even suggested that the World Council of Churches had been plotting against them during the meetings in Hungary during the previous summer. The council was faced with vast relief operations for the tens of thousands of refugees leaving Hungary, and already was responsible for some 150 workers in Austria alone caring for these refugees. The hoped-for discussions with the Moscow Patriarch about relationships of the Russian Church to the World Council of Churches had been postponed. It was further clear that the Suez affair had been a great shock to the Afro-Asian churchmen. The situation in Cyprus was threatening, and making it very difficult for the Ecumenical Patriarch in Constantinople. There was a sobering and difficult report on the discussions concerning the integration of the International Missionary Council with the World Council of Churches. Thanks to the propaganda of the opponents of the World Council, particularly in Scandinavia, but also in America through the influence of Carl McIntire, ecumenism was being identified with liberation, with modernism and syncretism. Much of the agenda for that executive was fraught with difficulties.

Nor was it all easy within the denomination at home. A situation developed which troubled him greatly and touched him personally because of the suffering it brought to friends. In March 1957 the Baptist Men's Movement Conference met as usual at Swanwick. It was there that Victor Hayward, the Foreign Secretary of the Baptist Missionary Society, spoke to him of difficulties within the Baptist Missionary Society. During 1956 Victor Hayward had made an extended tour in Angola and Belgian Congo as BMS Overseas Secretary. Whilst he had been in Congo, at Yakusu, he had had to try to deal with long-standing problems involving personal relationships. An adverse report had been sent to the BMS protesting about his conduct of affairs whilst in Yakusu, and the officers of the Baptist Missionary Society had asked two or three people to investigate and report on the situation. This is neither the time nor the place to go into the details of this unfortunate affair which dragged on for two years. We still stand too near to the event. Amongst Ernest Payne's papers is a fully documented record of all that went on. It is not likely to be the whole story, but it was written and compiled at the time of the events which it describes. This episode which resulted in a number of resignations of both missionaries and headquarters staff and included Victor Hayward, was a source of continuing anxiety to Ernest Payne.

At the Spring Meeting of the Free Church Federal Council in 1957, he was elected Vice-Moderator with succession to the moderatorship in March of 1958. The Baptists had thought to nominate R. L. Child who was at that point coming to the end of his service with Regent's Park College, but in view of his sister's ill health, Robert Child felt he could not accept the nomination, so M. E. Aubrey joined with others in putting forward Ernest Payne's name. His nomination was warmly received, but it meant still further responsibility.

The Central Committee of the World Council of Churches met in the summer of 1957 in the United States. He was not only involved in the normal committee work but also with a group preparing a report presenting the case for the integration of the International Missionary Council with the World Council. Ernest Payne was commissioned to prepare, with Dr David Moses, of North India, a pamphlet arguing the case for integration. It was Ernest Payne who prepared the first draft of this and after he had incorporated comments from Dr Moses, it was published in December 1957 under the title *Why Integration?* By this time he was also the chairman of the sub-committee dealing with the first article of the World Council's Constitution, the vital article entitled *The Basis*. This was proving a most difficult assignment. Extensive soundings both personal and semi-official were taken to find a way which would meet the pressure to alter *The Basis* so as to respond to pressure for a reference to the scriptures and also take into account the view of the Orthodox that *The Basis* in its original form was not sufficiently and explicitly Trinitarian. A number of members of the Central Committee felt that any attempt to alter the wording would prove divisive, and that the matter had better be dropped. In the end it was Visser't Hooft himself who worked out a proposal which was warmly supported by Ernest Payne and which won general acceptance. This was formally adopted with virtually no opposition at the New Delhi Assembly in 1961. *The Basis* now reads:

The World Council of Churches is a fellowship of Churches which confess the Lord Jesus Christ as God and Saviour according to the Scriptures and therefore seek to fulfil together their common calling to the glory of the one God, Father, Son and Holy Spirit.

Ernest Payne's sense of humour has already been mentioned. He enjoyed laughter and appreciated wit not least in committees. Some time, somewhere, somebody should compile a book of limericks composed by ecumenists as light relief from the serious and sometimes frustrating committee work. One of the most distinguished of Orthodox participants in earlier ecumenical days was Professor Florovsky. His interventions were usually offered at high speed, were always erudite, but not always clearly understood by all. He was the subject of a limerick – authorship unknown, though often guessed at – which was much beloved of Ernest Payne:

> Florovsky is at it again,
> His meaning is not very plain,
> But Franklin C. Fry says 'Never say die',
> Though it clearly gives Ernest A. Payne!

M. E. Aubrey died suddenly in October 1957. The responsibility of speaking in Bloomsbury Baptist Church at the Memorial Service fell to Townley Lord and to Ernest Payne. Some of the things that Ernest Payne said no doubt reflected his own experience:

When Aubrey retired in 1951 he had been for 26 years in a position the daily demands of which are inevitably extremely heavy. Only a strong man, physically strong, and more important, spiritually strong, could have carried the burden of responsibility so long and so successfully. Our friend was a strong man, both physically and spiritually, though his all too early death at the age of 72 indicates the price that was paid.

During 1957 the decline in membership amongst the churches of the Baptist Union continued. The Home Work Fund was short of its target by some £4,000, and a small deficit had to be declared. All in all it had been a hard year and at the beginning of 1958 it was evident that Ernest Payne was physically tired. Fortunately the Executive of the World Council of Churches in February 1958 met in London. There were considerable difficulties to be faced at that executive, not least the aftermath of the Hungarian revolt, with continuing criticism from Eastern Europe of the attitude taken by the World Council in connection with support of the régime that had power temporarily after the revolt. Difficulties were still being encountered from the hostility of Carl McIntire of the so-called International Council of Christian Churches in America. Yet again the executive turned to Ernest Payne with the request that he should answer in writing some of the criticisms. This he did in an article published in the *Ecumenical Review* for April 1958 entitled 'Some Errors and Illusions'.

In masterly fashion he marshalled the facts relating to the World Council of Churches' relationship to the churches in Hungary before and after the events of October–November 1956. The article replies to the assertion made both in Hungary and in China that the World Council of Churches was an agency which was either aimed at or had been used by others, to assist in 'the overthrow of the revolutionary government and the socialist social system'. Ironically the other matter that he deals with was the attack by Carl McIntire. This attack was quite the opposite and suggests that the World Council of Churches conceives of the kingdom of God as a visible social order patterned after the communistic economic principles and as such is a foe of the capitalistic, private enterprise system. One paragraph in particular is worthy of quotation:

The World Council is an organisation to which there is no parallel. Indeed it is not really an organisation, but rather an enterprise and an adventure. Churches of various lands and persuasions have joined hands, believing that they understand one another well enough to do certain things together. The common acknowledgment of our Lord Jesus Christ as God and Saviour is the flag under which they gather; the password by which they recognise one another, a signpost which directs them forward. They have engaged to talk together about 'the building up of the Body of Christ ... that we ... may grow up in all things into him, which is the Head, even Christ'. (Ephesians 4.12–15) When one member church suffers, 'all the members suffer with it'. So effective was the article that it circulated widely as an off-print.

The summer of 1958 was again a busy one. Ernest Payne was involved in the Lambeth Conference in his capacity as Moderator of the Free Church Federal Council, and he was appointed spokesman when representatives of the non-Anglican Churches greeted the assembled bishops in the library at Lambeth Palace. In July he was in Berlin for the European Baptist Federation, then in Zurich for the Executive of the Baptist World Alliance, and finally in Denmark for the World Council of Churches meetings. On Monday, 15th September, he was in Oxford for a committee of the International Missionary Council. He spent the night with friends at Regent's Park College, and travelled to London on the Tuesday morning. He took a taxi from Paddington to the Baptist Church House. As he stepped from the taxi on arrival at Church House he fell on to the pavement. He struggled to his feet, but was quite unable to move. The driver of the cab got out from his seat and began to help him into the Church House. At that point Ernest Payne collapsed completely. His next recollection was lying on the step in the porch of the building, with a policeman bending over him, and the caretaker of the Church House saying, 'Why, it's our Dr Payne'. Typically he thought he would be all right and simply asked to be taken inside, and allowed to rest, but an ambulance had already been sent for and as he sat in the chair which was situated in the lift, he realised that he was far more ill than he had thought, and could not cope with the situation. He was taken to the nearby Homeopathic Hospital, and after some tests and uncertainty, the heart specialist, Dr Kellner, diagnosed a coronary thrombosis.

He spent six weeks in hospital. When he was finally allowed to leave, Dr Kellner told him that he did not think that his heart had suffered any permanent damage and assured him that if he was prepared to take life more quietly, avoid emotional excitement and involvement in difficult matters, then he should be all right for at least another ten years. Ernest Payne was thus faced with a very difficult decision. There was no way in which he could go on as Secretary of the Baptist Union if he was to take life more quietly and avoid emotional excitement and involvement. He knew only too well that the stressful secretaryship of the Baptist Union could not be effectively discharged with half a person's time and energy. The question which faced him was whether he should resign or go on knowing the risk that was involved. He was fifty-six years old with still so much to do. He talked the matter over very carefully with his wife. Together they decided that he should not resign but continue in the secretaryship come what may.

At the end of the month of November he flew together with his wife to Tenerife for a fortnight's holiday. He was instructed by the officers of the Baptist Union to try resolutely to reduce the number of speaking engagements. Grey Griffith persuaded the officers that on longer train journeys he should now travel first class. Most important of all, through the generosity of friends, he and his wife were given a car. The doctors advised against Ernest Payne attempting to learn to drive and so from 1958 onwards, for the next 22 years, Freda Payne was his faithful driver. She must have driven him thousands of miles on behalf of the Baptist Union.

When he returned to the Church House there was cause enough for concern. The statistics of the denomination in 1958 reflected a severe loss of Sunday School scholars of about 21,000 together with a downward trend in membership statistics. There had been a good response to the Home Work Fund target but a growing concern about the ministerial situation. The candidate position had improved somewhat, but now the concern was about the number of men who were leaving pastoral service for other forms of vocation, notably teaching. Questions were being asked as to whether the preparation for the ministry was adequate for the challenges of the modern world, and whether the churches were facing the opportunities of the day with sufficient spiritual vigour and financial response. There was considerable apprehension within the Union and its council. Ernest Payne was determined, if he could, to change the mood of the denomination through the celebration of the Baptist Union Ter-Jubilee.

The Baptist Union Ter-Jubilee

The assembly of 1959 saw the launching of these celebrations. The President of the Baptist Union was J. B. Middlebrook who gave his support publicly to the scheme at the assembly and advocated the celebrations during his year of office. There were three emphases within the Ter-Jubilee plans. The first was commemoration and education; the second was evangelism; the third was a financial appeal for £300,000. In the proposed four part division of the appeal funds there is reflected Ernest Payne's own judgment as to denominational priorities. One quarter was to go to augment the Loan Fund so as to make money more available for development within local churches. One quarter was intended to build up the capital resources of the Home Work Fund so as to bring in more regular income to care for the union's ongoing work and make possible stipend increases. The third quarter was to be used for ministerial training, and the fourth was reserved for a series of special Ter-Jubilee projects which would be decided both during and after the Ter-Jubilee. Ernest Payne's hope had been that the Ter-Jubilee might have been an opportunity for a joint financial appeal with the Baptist Missionary Society. But this had not been agreed. It had also been his plan that the Union should offer the cost of one new church building to each of the ten areas out of Ter-Jubilee monies, but this suggestion was also rejected.

The celebration was to last for four years, from the assembly of 1959 to that of 1963. Each year was to have a particular theme; these were, in order, 'Alive to the Gospel', 'Alive to Christian Education and Training', 'Alive to Neighbourhood, Nation and World', 'Alive to our Heritage and Opportunity'. The main objects to which the Ter-Jubilee Fund was to be devoted had gained an importance in the years during Ernest Payne's secretaryship, and subsequent events have shown the rightness of the judgment for the use of the money. The Loan Fund has proved and is still proving of great importance to the development of local Baptist church life through its buildings. The Home Work Fund has always tended to be under-capitalised, and without the injection of the Ter-Jubilee capital, its financial difficulties would have been all the greater. Ministerial training was then as now in need of support from the totality of the denomination. This part of the appeal meant, incidentally, that for the first time the denomination as a whole responded unitedly to an appeal for ministerial training. The distribution of this particular quarter of the fund made it possible to grant £20,000 to the new Northern Baptist College, which was coming into being through the linking of Rawdon and Manchester Colleges. Without this help, the Northern College Appeal would have faced very serious difficulties and the effective completion of the project been jeopardised.

£15,000 was given to help with the salary of a special Church history tutor at Regent's Park College, and the appointment of Dr B. R. White as tutor on the staff at Regent's would have been most unlikely without this help. The variety of usages to which the fourth quarter has been put has revealed the wisdom of leaving flexibility for the dispensing of some of the money.

The summer of 1959 took Ernest Payne to the Central Committee of the World Council of Churches at Rhodes. On arrival in Rhodes, Franklin Fry was unwell. This meant that Ernest Payne had to preside at the session when the representatives of the Orthodox Church welcomed the World Council to its first meeting on Orthodox territory. Those who are involved in the ecumenical movement experience from time to time what appears to be 'divine irony', or perhaps a better description would be a 'divine rebuke', tempered always with divine promise. The Orthodox Churches and the Baptist Churches stood far apart both in theology and also in any real personal relationships. Yet here was the full weight of Orthodox ecclesiastical authority extending all the warmth of its hospitality to the Central Committee of the World Council with a Baptist presiding and responding. Not only must it have been a salutary experience for all concerned but it was a moment also – however fleeting – of prophetic ecumenism, a momentary glimpse into that desired day when divisive denominationalism is dead.

In the midst of all the denominational and ecumenical activities, Ernest Payne completed his year as Moderator of the Free Church Federal Council. He had found himself drawn very much into discussions concerning building grants for denominational schools. The Roman Catholics were finding it increasingly difficult to provide sufficient schools for the growing Catholic population and, supported by the Church of England, which was becoming unhappy about the reduction in the number of their schools since 1954, were seeking a substantial increase in the 50% capital cost of new schools that could be obtained from public funds. Most nonconformists were still, in theory, opposed to grants of this kind. In practice it seemed, however, most had lost their desire to fight with any real conviction on the matter. But there was still a case to be argued. Ernest Payne wrote an article for the *Free Church Chronicle* under the title 'Denomination Schools – Are the Free Churches Being Unreasonable?' which gained considerable circulation as an off-print, and he soon found himself involved in a deputation to meet government ministers, notably Mr Edward Boyle, the Minister of Education, and Mr R. A. Butler, the Home Secretary, who as Secretary of State for Education, had piloted the original 1944 Education Act through the House of Commons.

The outcome of the negotiations of 1958–59 was that the grants were raised to 75%, and certain assurances were received as a result of the representations. One of these assurances was the setting up, with the encouragement of the Ministry of Education, of a central Joint Anglican – Free Church Education Policy Committee which was able to discuss particular situations where friction arose, and tried also to look ahead at likely changes in general educational policy. The chairman of this group was to be the Bishop of London, and after a few years the bishop raised the question about an unofficial sounding of the Roman Catholics as to whether they would welcome private talks. This led in May 1963 to the first meeting of a group of nine; three Anglicans, led by Dr Stopford, Bishop of London, three Free Churchmen, led by Dr Aubrey Vine, then Secretary of the Free Church Federal Council and including Ernest Payne, and three Roman Catholics, led by Bishop Beck, later Archbishop of Liverpool. This group met about twice a year. The members reached such a measure of mutual confidence that, as we shall see, in 1965 the representatives of the three main Christian groups were able to go together to the Minister of Education for discussions about a further increase in building grants for denominational schools. Not surprisingly, the meetings of the nine were regarded with some suspicion by certain Free Churchmen, but on the whole Ernest Payne always considered that the meetings were fully justified and valuable.

What became clear to him in the late 1950s and early 1960s was that the Free Churches were viewed by successive governments as being no longer politically important. This had been only too clear when Free Church protests relating to the introduction in 1956 of Premium Bonds were ignored. One of the problems was that there was no longer a network of effective local Free Church Councils covering the country to voice the Free Churches' views or to monitor the educational situation. Yet he was convinced that it was important to recognise that in a number of places where there were only church schools,

116

the Free Church children and their parents could still be placed at some disadvantage if the attitude of the local clergymen was not as enlightened and as friendly as that of his diocesan bishop. He believed that the Free Church view of education needed clear restatement and this he always tried to do in writing and speaking. The Free Churches believed and still believe that in a mixed society it is right that the children of the nation should be educated together and that they are not subject while in school to denominational pressures. Whilst there must always be the right of parents to withdraw their children from the national system in general or from religious instruction in particular, any schools which are built for such children to be educated separately should not be erected at public expense. Great as has been the service rendered to education by the Christian church, history has many warnings against ecclesiastical control both of schools and of universities. Since this particular controversy, however, the educational system has become more complex with the growth of the multi-racial society and the problem now is not only of different denominations of Christianity but of the educating together of children of different faiths. This problem has moved on since Ernest Payne was wrestling with it, together with his Free Church colleagues in the 1960s.

Baptist Union–Baptist Missionary Society

During 1959, the difficulties in the Baptist Missionary Society finally came to a head. The Baptist Union Report for that year expressed concern at the conflict of policies and personalities which had clouded the affairs of the Society. A number of resignations resulted from the difficulties including those of the then Foreign Secretary, the Rev. V. E. W. Hayward, Dr Ellen Clow, the Rev. Leslie Taylor, and Dr Stanley Browne. Although each of these went on to valuable service in the life of the Christian church in different spheres, their loss to the society was considerable.

The Council Report of 1959 expressed concern at the slowness of progress in BMS and BU relationships. Ernest Payne felt the failure to relate very deeply. He had a deep love for the Baptist Missionary Society as well as the Baptist Union which

117

he served. In 1953 it had been agreed that the formal consultations needed to be delayed until the celebration of the 1955 Golden Jubilee Congress of the Baptist World Alliance had been completed. During 1958 and 1959 the officers of the Baptist Union and of the Baptist Missionary Society met some 15 times, but made little or no progress on the main issue. An interim report on the situation was presented to the Baptist Union Council in November 1959. The Council showed itself dissatisfied with that report and referred the matter back to a joint meeting of the officers.

At the beginning of the 1960s the Joint Officers' meetings had been widened to include the officers of the separate Baptist Unions of Scotland and Wales. From many points of view this was a sensible and advantageous arrangement, but it did have the effect of slowing down and complicating discussions regarding a new headquarters. With the presidents changing annually this brought also a growing problem of continuity of discussion. It became evident that another of the difficulties arose from the different constituency in which the BMS was involved. The presence of the Baptist Union Officers from Scotland and Wales was a constant reminder that the Baptist Missionary Society had to be aware of its own commitment to the other unions and this was complicated during the next decade by the developing sense of independence – linked in some ways to nationalism – being asserted by the other two unions, notably that of Scotland.

During the final years of his secretaryship, Ernest Payne found the Joint Officers' meetings with their constantly changing personnel more and more frustrating. In his journal he comments somewhat ruefully that he read a life of Dr John White (1867–1951) written by Augustus Muir in which the author recounts some of the difficulties that John White had experienced in seeking to bring closer together the Scottish Presbyterian Churches. White's comment seemed to fit so many Baptist situations:

Not only were we cautious, but we paced round and round in a circle, coming back again to the point from which we had started, not making any headway. The greatest difficulties we faced were psychological and temperamental – but these are never insuperable. They go out by Conference and by prayer'.[13]

118

Another quotation from the same book Ernest Payne discovered applied, he thought, to very many relationships, not only within churches, but also between churches:

The most powerful causes of continued separation are to be found in misunderstanding and irritated feelings. In all ages, these have done more than intellectual convictions to create and continue the divisions in the Church of Christ.[14]

It is relevant and revealing at this point to insert a note which Ernest Payne left amongst his papers:

My reiterated prayer throughout the 1930s and the 1940s and well into the 1950s was for 'a clear head and a stout heart'. In my early years at the Church House I offered it daily as I crossed the threshold. After my illness in 1958 I began to add a prayer for greater sympathy with those who tried me by their inefficiency, ignorance and unreasonableness, and for a greater charity. Gradually prayer for personal forgiveness came to have a larger place.

The Joint Officers' meeting, however, in February 1961, agreed 'on the immediate re-opening of the matter of headquarters'. There seemed at that point to be two possibilities. The first was to reconstruct, perhaps completely to rebuild, the Baptist Church House. The second was the demolition and rebuilding of the Bloomsbury Central Church. What could be done on the Southampton Row site depended upon the accommodation on which the Baptist Union and the Baptist Missionary Society both insisted. This was a delicate matter, and on both sides there was probably a considerable difference between what was actually asked for and what was really essential. Much depended, of course, on whether or not any of the separate departments of the two organisations could and would be amalgamated, but it depended also on whether some of the larger demand units such as the BMS Visual Aid Department with its exhibition equipment and van, could be housed off the site in rather less expensive premises. In addition there remained the potentially thorny question about who should hold and control the headquarters, whether at the Church House or anywhere else, if it was to become the home of both the Union and the Society with each maintaining its separate identity.

The reconstruction of Bloomsbury had become an urgent

necessity if it was to be maintained as a worthy Central London church. This was clearly something of denominational importance. In 1958 Dr Townley Lord had been succeeded by Dr Howard Williams who was faced with the difficult and daunting task that congregations had been declining. Howard Williams proved immediately an effective, though for some Baptists, a radical pulpit figure. It was suggested that possibly a new block of buildings on the Bloomsbury site which was not far distant from the Church House might provide for the needs both of the Bloomsbury Church and for some of the denominational departments. It was suggested that perhaps some of the senior secretaries of the Baptist Missionary Society could then be accommodated in the Church House, leaving, perhaps to the next generation, the decision as to whether or not it should be reconstructed or replaced. That this idea came to nothing was due in part, at least, to the strong feeling held by the Baptist Missionary Society, and understandably by J. B. Middlebrook, that there must be provision for the housing of all the departments of the Baptist Missionary Society under one roof. This deeply held point of view made it very difficult to envisage the possibility of altering the Church House satisfactorily. Investigations continued, however, and it became clear that the discussions about joint headquarters were still going to be extremely difficult and tedious.

That it was still the intention of both the Society and the Union to come together was emphasised by a resolution prepared by Ernest Payne, seconded by J. B. Middlebrook and enthusiastically passed by the assembly in 1961 in the following terms:

This Assembly gives Council full authority, jointly with the Baptist Missionary Society, to build or acquire premises which, in the opinion of the Council, will be suitable as denominational headquarters. The general aim should be to make provision for the present and estimated future requirements of the Union and the Baptist Missionary Society and such other organisations and activities as may be conveniently housed or conducted in the same building or buildings.

A similar resolution was passed by the BMS members' meeting, being moved by J. B. Middlebrook and seconded by Ernest Payne. This resolution still remains operative today.

Changes, however, were coming in the Baptist Missionary

Society personnel. In 1962 Bruce Glenny was appointed as Baptist Missionary Society accountant, a younger man whose appointment seemed to give hope that there could be a wind of change blowing in the whole denominational situation. Bruce Glenny was a man of wide sympathies, sound judgment and great integrity. Ernest Payne and many others placed high hopes in the possibilities which were opening up with his appointment. Tragically for the whole denomination Bruce Glenny was suddenly taken ill and within two years had died. J. B. Middlebrook was to retire in 1962 and his successor was to be the Rev. A. S. Clement, the editor of the Carey Kingsgate Press. A. S. Clement was one who showed himself ready to join in trying to work out the possibilities of joint headquarters, but the difficulties facing both houses grew rather than diminished as the years went by, and the headquarters situation remained unsolved throughout the rest of Ernest Payne's secretaryship.

The year 1960 saw changes within the Baptist Union headquarters staff. The Rev. O. D. Wiles retired from his post as Deputy General Secretary of the Union, and the Rev. R. W. Thomson was appointed Assistant General Secretary, thus abolishing what Ernest Payne always felt to be the somewhat ambiguous post of Deputy General Secretary. R. W. Thomson had come into the Church House in 1958 from a pastorate in Loughborough, and had taken on immediately the responsibility for the minutes of a number of sub-committees and had also become Secretary of the Psalms and Hymns Trust. It was a good appointment, for he proved meticulous in his work and a loyal assistant to the General Secretary. Unfortunately at the same time, Mr Strugnell was falling a victim to severe arthritis. Indeed, from 1958 to 1960 he was away from the Church House for a considerable period and Ernest Payne found that he was having to deal with salary cheques of heads of departments and certain other of the Union employees and pensioners. The situation was satisfactorily resolved when in 1961 the Rev. A. E. Bastable, who had had training as an accountant before service with the Baptist Missionary Society in China and India, was appointed to the accounts department, and proved a most reliable colleague to Ernest Payne for the rest of his time in the Baptist Church House.

III: 1961–67

Ernest Payne was reappointed for a further five years at the assembly of 1961. The resolution was moved by Grey Griffith with his usual vigour and discernment. He knew Ernest Payne as well as anyone outside the family. What he said took on particular significance as he died later that year – to the denomination's and particularly to Ernest Payne's great loss. He described Ernest Payne as a man with a sense of what was vital, possessed of the courage to proceed when others doubted, and he cited the Ter-Jubilee celebrations as an example. He suggested that Ernest Payne could see the problems that required solving, and although to see a problem is not to solve it, never to see it is never to solve it. He recalled that Ernest Payne never spoke without having something worthwhile to say; that he never spoke except relevantly to the occasion of speaking; that he was possessed of hindsight, insight and foresight, knew which was which and which to use at any given moment. He reminded the assembly that the then Archbishop of Canterbury was reported as having said, 'The one man I would like to be would be Dr Payne'. The resolution was seconded by David Coates and accepted with acclamation by a standing vote.

The first Swanwick

The month after that assembly the first Denominational Conference was held at Swanwick. It was Ernest Payne's idea and was to be seen as part of the Ter-Jubilee Campaign. The intention was to stimulate further the thought of the denomination about its mission, its heritage and its life. Places were allotted to each of the ten areas, to Scotland, Wales and to the Baptist Missionary Society. 271 Baptists came together at The Hayes, Swanwick, from 23rd to 26th May.

In a brief introductory address, Ernest Payne quoted a recent sermon in which the Archbishop of Canterbury had claimed for the Anglican Church 'the quality of a robust holiness'. He doubted whether any would dare, at the present time, to put forward such a claim for the Baptist denomination, but it was his hope that the Swanwick Conference might point forward along a path leading to that claim being made for us at some future time. He made it clear that the absence of any directive to the conference from the Baptist Union headquarters was deliberate. The end was to be left open to the movement of the Spirit. For him, there was an element of a dream come true in the unparalleled constituency of the conference. Upon this he looked with gratitude and expectancy, and with the hope that, under God's blessing, the gathering might prove historic. He recalled that 300 men had been enough for God and Gideon. There were 271 people at Swanwick; they too could be enough!

The conference heard a notable address from Dr Champion, pin-pointing the state of the denomination and calling for more and deeper theological thought and study. There were Bible studies and much discussion. The findings of the conference were summed up in a statement which reflected the cross-section of the denomination represented. It has considerable interest in that it stimulated a great amount of thinking, talking and writing, and undoubtedly played a significant part in shaping the future life of the denomination. Seven main topics emerged in all.

● First and foremost it was accepted that independency needed now to be supplemented by a much clearer realisation of the necessity of interdependency of the churches, based upon the teaching of the New Testament and indeed teaching which is implicit in Baptist principles and clearly expressed in the 17th century confessions.

● There was agreement on the importance of the associations for the healthy development of denominational life, and a general feeling that there should be an examination of the functions, workings and even boundaries of the associations.

● Questions relating to the ministry of the church were fully discussed. Whilst all were agreed that it is the total membership of the church which is involved in the ministry, nevertheless, there were questions relating to the specialist ministry which needed careful consideration amongst Baptists at that time. The matters mentioned are:
   (a) the method of settlement and removal of ministers.
   (b) the status of both deaconesses and probationer ministers.

(c) the recognition and ordination of men over 40 years of age.

(d) the desirability of clearer distinction between full and part time ministries.

(e) the possibility of a system of increments to stipends based on length of service.

(f) the need for training and refresher courses for lay preachers.

● There was a recognition that pilot schemes needed to be developed to meet the peculiar situations, for example in areas where the movement of population was sudden, such as new housing estates, new towns, and village churches. The rural situation in particular was noted as being a special area for consideration.

● There was an urgent need for sustained teaching of church members involving Christian doctrine, witness, service, as well as Church history and Baptist principles.

● It was suggested that the Baptist Union needed to appoint a commission to look at a number of these issues and that the results should be sent for study not only to the churches but also to the associations.

● Finally there was a recognition of a lack of knowledge on the part of many members of the world situation. It included both lack of knowledge of world Baptists and also of the wider ecumenical movement.

On the whole, the first denominational Swanwick was judged at the time to have succeeded in its intention to stimulate thought which would lead to action. In the *Baptist Times* of 1st June 1961, the reporter concluded his account with the comment: 'One observer, at least, feels Swanwick 1961 has brought the denomination to a point in its developing life from which it will not look back.'

Looking back now over the twenty years since Swanwick 1961, it is evident how much of the discussion has been taken up into denominational thought and practice. Whilst it would be too much to claim that all of this has stemmed from the impetus of Swanwick, the fact remains that all of the seven points in the statement have been further developed. There has been much deeper thinking theologically on the relationship of local churches to each other, to the associations and to wider fellowship in the Baptist Union. There has been considerable concentration upon the role and functioning of associations. There has been considerable reflection upon and action on the nature of Baptist ministry, its financial support and its continuing training. Denominational education of church membership received a great boost even during the celebrations – some 30 booklets of various kinds were published. This development led ultimately to the Christian Training Programme.

One of the results of this theological reflection, however, was growing evidence of the tensions which exist within the denomination. The years that followed Swanwick marked a time in which theological polarisation began to become apparent. Within so diverse a denomination this was inevitable, but on the whole the various strands of theological thought were held together in creative tension. During his final period as secretary, Ernest Payne, a great advocate of religious freedom, tried to create a climate of proper tolerance to allow the free expression of differing points of view. At the same time, he believed that the diversity must have its proper limits controlled both by doctrinal orthodoxy and by the necessity to maintain denominational unity.

Friendships new and old

In December 1961 Ernest Payne was in New Delhi for the Third Assembly of the World Council of Churches. This assembly was fascinating not only because of the Indian setting but because of what was achieved in the business sessions. The change in the basis of the World Council, which had caused the sub-committee (of which Ernest Payne was the chairman) several years of anxious consultation and debate, was accepted almost unanimously and brought into the basis a more definite doctrinal emphasis. The integration of the International Missionary Council and the World Council of Churches, which Ernest Payne had helped facilitate, was carried through without any serious opposition. But the greatest public interest centred on the application from the Moscow Patriarchate and the Orthodox Churches of Bulgaria, Romania and Poland to join the council. There were 23 new churches received into membership at New Delhi and these four Orthodox Churches

125

were amongst those so received. It was significant that of the others no fewer than eleven were from Africa, two from the Pacific Islands, and two Pentecostal churches from South Africa. The constituency of the World Council was becoming more truly ecumenical.

One of the most pleasurable of Ernest Payne's experiences at New Delhi was when, as Vice-Chairman of the Central Committee, he found himself in the chair of the business session of the assembly when Archbishop Nikodim of the Russian Orthodox Church and representatives of the other new members were welcomed and seated in the assembly. His contact with the Russian Baptists had already begun, but they were soon to develop also with the other churches. Archbishop Nikodim then of Yaroslav and Rostov, but soon to be translated to Leningrad, was to prove an important figure in World Council affairs during the next two decades. He was always something of a controversial figure, but no-one could ever doubt his remarkable ability. He and Ernest Payne became cordially related not only within the affairs of the council but also as personal friends.

Franklin Fry and Ernest Payne were again appointed to the Central Committee. There had been considerable discussion in the Nominations Committee concerning their re-appointment. The consensus of opinion was seemingly in favour of the re-election of the two of them, though this would in the end have to be done by that committee itself. There were some who were a little hesitant about re-electing Franklin Fry, for he had had a long tenure in the chair. There were even a few who indicated to Ernest Payne that they hoped that he would replace Fry. Ernest Payne had no wish to become Chairman of the Central Committee and indeed did not really think himself fitted for the public demands involved in it. His own view was that it would probably be wiser for others to be appointed since Fry and he had had seven years in office. On the other hand the retirement of the Secretary of the World Council, Dr Visser't Hooft, was anticipated within the life of the newly elected Central Committee. A strong and experienced chairman was therefore thought to be desirable. An informal approach was made to Fry from the Nominations Committee about the future, and he indicated that he would be willing to continue in the chair, but only if Ernest Payne continued as vice-chairman. This

126

clearly forced Ernest Payne's hand. He had no wish to make Fry withdraw nor to endanger his re-election. When the new Central Committee had its first meeting, immediately after the assembly, they were both re-elected to office without challenge.

It was evident that this second term was likely to be far more exacting even than the first one. At the back of Ernest Payne's mind was always the fear that something might one day happen to Franklin Fry, which would leave him with the main responsibility. Perhaps it was just as well that at New Delhi he did not know exactly how demanding, difficult and challenging the ensuing years were to be in his service of the World Council.

Franklin Fry and Ernest Payne formed a formidable and effective team in the responsibilities of the Central Committee. Fry was a natural leader, big in stature, big in heart, competent in chairing, firm, some would even say, over-firm. But he was a man of very great charm and conviction. Ernest Payne was very different physically, a smaller man, somewhat retiring, naturally shy, not one with any enthusiasm for the chief seat nor one who easily responded to the spotlight in public gatherings. He was recognised as an able chairman, scrupulously fair, with a skill and incisive ability to see through problems created by differing opinions and, more importantly, to suggest how they might be reconciled. He possessed an extraordinary ability, in the midst of a debate, to produce an amended draft of a proposition which expressed what all really wanted to say. In the most positive sense of the words, he was a Christian diplomat and a master of proper compromise. A distinguished Orthodox priest once commented that if he was on trial for his life and could choose his judge, he would choose Ernest Payne!

Changes in personal relationships were on the way for Ernest Payne. On Easter Sunday 1962 there came a considerable personal blow to him and a great loss to the denomination when John Barrett, who was then the area superintendent for the North East, suffered a severe stroke which left him for a long period completely helpless and speechless and then permanently crippled. John Barrett was 61 at the time and had been a close friend of Ernest Payne since their student days. Ernest Payne had been best man at John Barrett's wedding, had met him frequently, and most importantly they had corresponded together regularly through the years. The correspondence which Ernest Payne kept provides a valuable commentary on personal, denominational and ecumenical matters. In spite of the changed circumstances John Barrett remained a great encourager of Ernest Payne and the correspondence continued.

During 1962 there were changes in personnel in the Baptist Union. Gordon Fairbairn, the honorary solicitor, a man whose counsel Ernest Payne had greatly valued, retired. He was succeeded by his son Richard Fairbairn. At the same time Hugh Martin retired from the British Council of Churches, where his experience and judgment had been wisely used as Chairman of the Executive Committee. Ernest Payne was elected to succeed him. This was a somewhat unexpected election as both of them belonged to the same denomination. As events turned out Ernest Payne was twice re-elected, and held office as Chairman of the Executive until the Spring of 1971. It is one of the continued ironies of British church life that Baptists, who on the whole are judged by most of the media to be extremely slow and backward ecumenically, have supplied a number of the leading officers within the organised ecumenical movement, particularly in the British Council of Churches and the Free Church Federal Council.

That same summer saw Ernest Payne at meetings of the World Council of Churches in Paris. At these meetings the All Soviet Union of Evangelical Baptists was received into membership of the World Council. J. I. Zhidkov was present as its leader. For Zhidkov it marked the culmination of years of leadership, responsibility and some suffering. He had seen the church in the Soviet Union through the difficult years of oppression prior to the Second World War; he had shared personally in the tragic losses of that war – a war which at the same time had brought increasing freedom of action to the churches; he had piloted the Baptists through the post-war years of fluctuating freedom and oppression and now he rejoiced as they were welcomed as part of the World Church. At that Paris meeting too after a very careful debate, and expressions of some hesitation, the decision was taken to accept the invitation to send observers to the Second Vatican Council which was to begin a few months later. That this decision was of the highest importance may be seen more clearly now than when it was first taken. It began a relationship between the World Council and the Roman Curia, which has developed considerably over the intervening years, so that there is now an almost permanent contact between Geneva and the Vatican.

During the same summer the Executive of the Baptist World Alliance was faced with a similar question as to whether it should accept an invitation to be present at the Vatican through observers. The Secretary for Christian Unity in the Vatican, Monsignor Willebrands, had made it clear that the secretariat did not wish to embarrass the Baptist World Alliance by sending an invitation to the Vatican Council which would have to be refused. So the question with which the executive was faced, was, whether the Alliance would wish to have an invitation. If so, one would gladly be sent. A number of members of the Alliance executive shared Ernest Payne's view that Baptists should be represented with other churches, and that no real dangers nor compromise would be implied. Interestingly enough this view was supported by the leader of the Italian Baptists, Manfredi Ronchi, who said he wanted to have the right to walk into St Peter's and the Vatican along with representatives of the other churches. But there was considerable opposition from Baptists in other parts of the world, notably from South America and the Southern Baptist Convention in the United States. There seems even to have been some threat of serious division within the Alliance if a positive answer had been returned. If a straight vote had been taken it might well have been a close decision which ever way it had gone and the result would certainly have damaged the fellowship in the Alliance. It seemed best, therefore, to recognise that Baptists were not yet ready to adjust themselves to the changes which were taking place in Protestant-Roman Catholic relationships and a negative answer was returned to Willebrands.

As it turned out the Baptist World Alliance was the only world confessional body not represented at the Vatican Council. This may not have been entirely a bad thing, in retrospect, in that at that time it was probably a good thing both for Baptists, and indeed for the Vatican itself, that one large world body remained unconvinced of all the implications and possibly all the motivations of such an invitation, and stayed outside, interested and watchful. Two Baptists managed to get to Rome. Dr J. H. Jackson, a negro Baptist leader, who was an extraordinarily forceful individual, claimed that he had been encouraged to be present during interview with Pope John

XXIII, and that being so it was decided by the Roman authorities that he had better have a place as a refusal might have been interpreted at least as racial prejudice! Dr Stanley Stuber of the American Baptist Convention also got to Rome with the help of Roman Catholic friends. It would have been possible for the Alliance to have changed its attitude a year later when, following the death of Pope John, the council was reconvened in a second session. But there was no disposition to change the Alliance point of view.

For the Baptist Union, 1962 was a year that had special associations. Not only was it the 150th anniversary of its own foundation, but it was the 350th anniversary of the return from Holland to England of Thomas Helwys, to found the first Baptist church at Spitalfields in London. On 7th April Ernest Payne unveiled a plaque commemorating Helwys at the new Bilborough Baptist Church which was just a short distance away from the site of Broxstowe Hall, in Nottinghamshire, which was once the home of Helwys. 1962 was also the 300th anniversary of the Great Ejectment of 1662. It delighted Ernest Payne that this particular commemoration showed no marks of the bitter controversies of earlier generations. A special ecumenical service at the City Temple was attended by both Archbishop Michael Ramsey and his predecessor Lord Fisher. In the same year the new Baptist Hymn Book was published and again to Ernest Payne's pleasure, it was widely welcomed and warmly received.

Ter-Jubilee review

The year, then, proved a fitting climax to the Ter-Jubilee celebrations, although another year was to pass before a final assessment could be made. Already it was evident that the Ter-Jubilee was intended to be seen not as an end but as a beginning. Through it, Ernest Payne tried to engender a commitment within the denomination to an enterprise for God and the Gospel in the world. Just as M. E. Aubrey before him had initiated 'Baptist Advance' and as David Russell after him was to stimulate a 'Call to Commitment', so he saw the Ter-Jubilee as a challenge to the whole of the denomination to be true to its calling to mission at home and abroad, but for him this mission had to be within the context of the world church. The report which he presented to the 1963 assembly made this clear:

The task is one, whether overseas or in this land, and ways of making this clearer, theologically, organisationally and practically must speedily be found, if the task is to be adequately carried out anywhere. The task is one to which the whole people of God is committed; it is not one that Baptists can or should attempt alone.

It was at the assembly of 1964 that Ernest Payne presented the final report on the Ter-Jubilee Campaign. He linked this with the presentation of the 150th Annual Report of the Baptist Union itself. This he did in typical fashion, for it gave him the chance to remind the denomination of the reason for the union's existence and to quote again the purpose of its foundation:

To afford to the ministers and churches of the denomination the means of becoming better acquainted with each other, with a view to excite brotherly love, furnish a stimulus for a zealous co-operation in promoting the cause of Christ in general and particularly in our own denomination and especially to encourage our missions.

A further quotation warned that the realisation of this aim was slow in coming. As J. H. Hinton, who had served as secretary for more than 20 years commented in 1863: 'denominational union amongst Baptists has been slow in manifestation and difficult of cultivation.' Moving from the past to the present there was reference to a quotation from the book *The Pattern of the Church*, written by four younger ministers, which argued the importance for Baptists to think theologically about what the Union really is: 'Baptists inherited an ecclesiology which was based on the independence of each gathered company of believers and yet one that, from the first, recognised that there could never be forgotten the wider fellowship of Christians.'[15]

Ernest Payne quite clearly had been distinctly irritated by a quotation from the *Australian Baptist* about the conclusion of the Ter-Jubilee which read: 'The end has brought with it a sense of relief rather than a glow of triumph ... endurance rather than inspiration has marked its progress.' This quotation stimulated Ernest Payne to make what was for him an impassioned speech reflecting on the Ter-Jubilee Campaign. Speaking of the outcome of the evangelical outreach he said:

Would to God we had set the heather alight as did Whitefield and Wesley in the 18th century, but it seems that the leaves and twigs are not yet dry enough for the fire from heaven to descend, or perhaps God's new prophets have not yet had his word put into their mouths, or perhaps we are looking backwards too much and are not recognising that he is doing in our midst a new thing. What certainly has happened is that there are few churches that have not been challenged by that uncomfortable word 'evangelism', few diaconates which have not looked more seriously at their responsibilities, few groups of Sunday School teachers who have not been reminded of the importance of this task. All our churches have at least been called to a spiritual check-up. All over the country there are those who have been challenged, encouraged and helped to be more venturesome in their witness. All this has been worth doing.

Speaking of the second emphasis, that of education in Baptist history and principles, he said:

There is a quotation which says 'The history of a nation is the sap of its life and death is certain if the flow is stopped'. In the Ter-Jubilee celebrations the sap has been made to flow more freely. The materials have been provided for teaching a new generation our Baptist history and principles. We have retold the story of 1612, or 1662, of 1812 and the notable developments of the past 150 years. If we look in the Ter-Jubilee Book of Remembrance, with its hundreds upon hundreds of names of parents and grandparents, of pastors, Sunday School teachers, Bible Class leaders, friends, all gratefully remembered at this time of celebration by loved ones and by those whom they have influenced for the Christian faith because they were those who mediated the Grace of God, all this would cause one to realise the importance of remembrance.

Of the financial appeal he affirmed that

$\frac{14}{15}$ths of the £300,000 will have been raised when finally the covenants and the promises are redeemed. Naturally it is a pity that the target was not quite reached and indeed exceeded. It could have been. Perhaps if all had given as they might, it should have been. But its value has already been proved. The money has at once been ploughed back into urgent denominational tasks. There have been loans at cheap rates - only 2% to new causes - for 45 churches. The Home

Work Fund capital has been built up. Gifts together with the Ter-Jubilee Fund have enabled building of the new Northern College to begin. New possibilities of teaching, and studying Baptist history at Oxford have been opened up. The Superannuation Fund has been able to increase its benefits earlier and by a larger amount than could otherwise have been possible. Whether all this lacks inspiration is a question that others must judge. But we have to remember that whilst all this was happening, the Home Work Fund giving has gone up by 30%.

Commenting further on the word 'endurance' used by the *Australian Baptist* he drew attention to the New English Bible translation of Romans 5: 'Endurance brings proof that we have stood the test and this proof is the ground of hope. Such hope is no mockery.' He added, 'Perhaps, after all, endurance was the right word to use,' and concluded with these words:

Many years ago when I was a boy, one summer afternoon in a garden at Frinton, I watched with fascination and awe a gaily coloured butterfly struggle out of its chrysallis and spread its wings. The remembrance of that miracle came back to me last Sunday morning, as I worshipped in the renewed, transformed Bloomsbury. For so long there perhaps, and in many other places, life has been closely cocooned, shut up in the dark. May not the outward transformation that has been wrought at Bloomsbury be a piece of prophetic symbolism, an acted parable of what God would – will – do for this denomination of ours, and for the other churches of this land. Who can tell? At any rate, let that hope sustain us as we move on into another year.

New World Council of Churches Secretary

The committees of the World Council of Churches met in the summer of 1964 at Colgate Rochester in the United States of America. One of the main matters to be decided by the Central Committee was the procedure for the nomination of a new general secretary. Dr Visser't Hooft had indicated that in 1965 he would reach his 65th birthday and that seemed to him to be the time for his retirement. Franklin Fry's first suggestion had been that a nomination sub-committee should consist of the six presidents and the chairman and vice-chairman of the Central Committee. Ernest Payne did not agree. Neither did the Executive Committee which rejected this suggestion and favoured a committee elected partly by secret ballot in the Central Committee with additional names appointed by the executive to remedy any geographical or confessional imbalance. When the matter came before the Central Committee, however, this idea was also rejected, and it was speedily agreed that the executive itself be the Nomination Committee. This proposition was carried with virtually no debate. A brief meeting of the executive was held at Colgate Rochester, and Ernest Payne was asked to act as secretary for this particular enterprise. Private interviews with various heads of the divisions of the council were arranged to assist in defining the quality and characteristics of the person required. The difficult business of finding a successor to Visser't Hooft was to overshadow and indeed to complicate much of the life of the World Council of Churches during the next two and a half years. The complexity was due not only to the difficulty of discovering the right person but also because of the way in which personal relationships entered into the process. In view of the importance of the issue and the part which Ernest Payne played in it, it will be as well to tell the entire story as he recorded it at the time.

In February 1964 the Executive of the World Council of Churches met in Odessa. At this meeting there was a slow but steady movement of opinion amongst members towards one name, that of Lukas Vischer of the Faith and Order Department. There had been some suggestion that Visser't Hooft should be asked to continue until the Fourth Assembly of the Council planned for 1968, but the final decision was that on the whole it seemed wise that his original intention to retire at 65 should be encouraged. At Odessa Franklin Fry informed Visser't Hooft of the direction in which the executive was moving, and it was agreed that it would be wise for Fry to try to see Vischer in Geneva on his next visit. Ernest Payne was instructed to see the Archbishop of Canterbury and to tell him of the decisions thus far and also to inform Archbishop Frank Woods of Melbourne. In April 1964, Franklin Fry and Ernest Payne met Lukas Vischer in Geneva. Ernest Payne's own note of the interview is perhaps worth recording:

Lukas Vischer rightly said that he must think over the suggestion and that a number of contrary reasons at once occurred to him,

134

including his youth, his limited knowledge of the constituency, and of the work of general secretary and indeed his own health which had from time to time been somewhat uncertain. His immediate response and comments confirmed the impression that he is the right kind of man.

Two months later, Vischer returned a negative answer to Fry. Franklin Fry was not prepared immediately to give up and he arranged that he and Ernest Payne should meet Vischer at the Skyways Hotel near London Airport. At this interview Vischer indicated frankly the many hesitations which had caused him to refuse the nomination. Franklin Fry sought to reassure him of the growing conviction that he was the right man. He was able to assure him that the Archbishop of Canterbury was enthusiastic as indeed were representatives of the Orthodox Church. At the end of the interview, both Ernest Payne and Franklin Fry felt optimistic. However, it was not long afterwards that a letter was received from Lukas Vischer declining nomination.

In August 1964 there was a World Council consultation at Rummelsberg near Nuremberg, concerning relationships with the Roman Catholic Church. At this consultation Ernest Payne and Franklin Fry took soundings of executive members present. There was a general feeling now that certainly it would be necessary to ask Visser't Hooft to continue in office until 1966. There were again voices raised to suggest that he really ought to be asked to go on until 1968. But another possibility was by this time emerging, namely that of Patrick Rodger who was at that time working in the World Council of Churches, also in Faith and Order. When the Executive Committee met later in August 1964 there was a general consensus supporting the name of Patrick Rodger, and the final vote was unanimous to invite him. After consultation with Dr Visser't Hooft it was arranged that Franklin Fry should try to meet Patrick Rodger at Munich. Franklin Fry returned to the Executive Committee indicating that a reply from Rodger would be received by phone the following day. Whilst all this was happening, evidence was emerging of a restlessness amongst some members of the World Council staff. Apparently the name of the nominee had got to the ears of the staff members with the result that there was division of opinion about the suitability of the nomination. However, when the phone call came from Patrick Rodger to Franklin Fry, the answer was in the affirmative.

The next decision to face the executive was whether to withhold the announcement of the nomination until the Central Committee planned for the following January in Nigeria, or whether to risk announcing it immediately. It was decided that it would be virtually impossible to hold the announcement for five months and so it was decided to announce the nomination. Ernest Payne helped to draft a telegram to absent members of the executive and a letter was written to all members of the Central Committee. A communiqué was prepared for the press. But it was quite evident that this nomination was not going to have an easy passage. There was growing restiveness within the World Council staff.

Ernest Payne was at the British Faith and Order Conference at Nottingham in September 1964 and met Visser't Hooft who expressed some concern at the way in which the situation was developing. Soon after the executive meeting of the World Council, there had been a meeting of the Reformed Presbyterian Alliance and in the same month of August there had also been a meeting of the Faith and Order Commission at Aarhus. At both these meetings there had been considerable discussion of the issue, and information was being spread that the nomination had been badly received in Geneva. Certainly there was canvassing of opinion at Aarhus and indeed some attempt there to organise opposition to the nomination. Thus by the Autumn Ernest Payne was aware of an ugly situation that was developing. In November 1964 he was in Geneva for a structure committee and met Franklin Fry. There was now known to be division over the nomination and real difficulty. The danger was looming that the Central Committee might reject the executive's unanimous nomination.

It was with some very real trepidation, therefore, that Ernest Payne set off in January 1965 for the meetings of first the Executive Committee and then the Central Committee at Enugu in Nigeria. The executive first met in closed session. Although indications were given of the difficulties surrounding the nomination, the executive members nevertheless reaffirmed the recommendation of Patrick Rodger. Visser't Hooft was in an increasingly difficult position. He was willing to continue in office until 1966 but there were those who were seeking to persuade him to continue in office until 1968. Franklin Fry spoke informally to him and it was understood that he would be prepared to continue in office until 1966 but would delay his decision until he saw how things developed in the Central Committee.

The Central Committee was held on 13th January 1965. Ernest Payne was in the chair because Franklin Fry had to present the report of the Executive Committee. It was the most difficult and responsible task that he had thus far undertaken for the World Council. As soon as the meeting opened and the executive recommendation was moved, notice was given of a motion to set aside the recommendation of the executive and to ask Visser't Hooft to continue in office until 1968. A number of speeches somewhat similar in content were made supporting the counter-recommendation. Many of the Central Committee were by this time somewhat bewildered by what was going on. It was evident to Ernest Payne that if a vote were taken on the recommendation of the executive, even though it might be carried, there would not only be a considerable negative vote, but such an outcome could lead to the resignation of certain members of the World Council staff. On the other hand, if the recommendation of the executive was put and lost, he knew that Franklin Fry would undoubtedly resign as chairman and all the members of the executive as the nominating committee would be placed in a very difficult position.

Ernest Payne decided that he must try to find a way of avoiding the disastrous breach which a direct vote on the executive recommendation would cause. He talked first with Visser't Hooft and suggested that a possible way of avoiding a head-on collision might be found if he would make clear that 1966 was his deadline particularly if at the same time Patrick Rodger indicated that he did not wish any immediate vote on his name. This would enable a new nominating committee to be elected and to look afresh at the situation. To this suggestion Visser't Hooft readily agreed as did Patrick Rodger. It is evident that both acted helpfully in the situation. Franklin Fry suggested that it would be a good thing if on such an important matter a written note from both could be issued. Both Visser't Hooft and Patrick Rodger wrote their notes and handed them to Ernest Payne. Armed with these two notes he started the new session of the Central Committee on the morning of

Thursday 14th January. There was first a continuation of the somewhat general and lengthy discussion on the next step. However, finally a proposal was put that Visser't Hooft be invited to continue until 1966 and that no action should be taken on the executive's recommendation nominating Patrick Rodger. In the end this motion was carried by a small majority.

Next it was agreed that the nominations sub-committee of the Central Committee should meet with the executive to deal with the setting up of a new committee on the secretaryship. This joint committee was held two days later and both Ernest Payne and Franklin Fry made it clear independently that they did not feel that they should serve on this new committee as they would later have to handle any of the further questions and nominations which might arise. In the end it was decided that each member of the Central Committee should write down ten names and that from those well supported the nominations sub-committee should prepare a list of 18, with due regard to confessional balance. The new committee was formally appointed on 18th January with Bishop John Sadiq of Nagpur as chairman.

The Executive Committee met in July 1965 at the same time as the formal opening of the new World Council of Churches headquarters in Geneva. When Ernest Payne arrived in Geneva he found that the developing situation concerning the secretaryship was again delicate. Franklin Fry had heard that Bishop Sadiq's Committee might nominate an American, Eugene Carson Blake, as Visser't Hooft's successor. The problem this created was not that Franklin Fry was necessarily opposed to this possible nomination, but that he felt it created extreme difficulties if an American were to be appointed to the secretaryship when the Chairman of the Central Committee was also American.

When the executive met again in February 1966 prior to the meeting of the Central Committee, Ernest Payne soon learned that Fry was intending to resign from the chairmanship if the nomination went through. A suggestion was made that Ernest Payne should succeed Franklin Fry and that Hans Lilje should become vice-chairman. It became growingly evident that Bishop Sadiq's committee was indeed going to nominate Carson Blake, and Fry consulted again many of his Lutheran friends both in the United States and outside. Most shared the view that the Chairman of the Central Committee and the General Secretary ought not both to be Americans. Further, it would be undesirable for emergency statements, which were issued on behalf of the World Council to appear signed by three officers, two of whom were Americans and the other British. Ernest Payne's position was difficult. If he resigned with Fry it might all too easily appear that the cause of the resignation was personal animosity to the nominee. If Fry did resign, Ernest Payne wondered whether it would not be better for Lilje to become chairman and for him to remain vice-chairman. Then another possibility occurred to him in that if it were possible to appoint a second vice-chairman in addition to himself, preferably from the Third World, then the situation would be greatly eased.

On 11th February, Carson Blake was elected by a large majority to succeed Visser't Hooft in 1966. At the Executive Committee, Fry duly offered his resignation in the light of the rule which existed about geographical considerations governing the choice of officers. All the executive members emphatically favoured his continuing in office. At this point Ernest Payne put forward his suggestion that there should be the appointment of a second vice-chairman. After considerable discussion there was a general consensus that, at the Central Committee, Franklin Fry's statement should be read in full but that it should then be moved by Ernest Payne on behalf of the executive that Fry should continue in office and that a second vice-chairman be appointed. The executive finally decided that there should be a division of these two actions. It was further suggested that when the first resolution was moved, confirming Fry in office, intention to move the second should be indicated.

On 14th February there was a closed session of the Central Committee at which Ernest Payne had to preside. He presented the statement that Fry had previously made to the Executive Committee. He described the executive's reaction to it and explained the two actions proposed. There was general agreement that Fry should continue, and warm tributes were paid to him. After considerable discussion the executive proposals were both accepted, and statements to this effect were given to the press. A second vice-chairman was elected in the person of Russell Chandran, a distinguished Indian theologian, and a former pupil of Ernest Payne. This satisfactory outcome was, on the whole, a great relief to all.

Back home

While all this was going on there had been considerable changes both in Ernest Payne's personal life and in the denominational situation in England.

During 1964 Gordon Holmes went abroad to teach geography and economics in Uganda. Some weeks earlier he had been able, together with Ernest and Freda Payne, to visit a Northamptonshire village, to see and commend a new home which they were in process of purchasing. This was Elm Cottage, at Pitsford, which was two cottages now linked together into one and partially modernised. It had always been the hope of the Paynes and particularly of Freda to return eventually to Northamptonshire, and when they saw this property they immediately decided that this was a possibility to be looked at very seriously. Philip Payne also went down to look at it and approved. The outcome was the purchase of the cottages and a strip of land sufficient to build a garage. Subsequently on the advice of their friend, John Wilmshurst, a surveyor, they were able to acquire a further piece of ground to make a small garden. They were able to spend the Christmas of 1965 in Pitsford, and finally took up residence in Elm Cottage in August 1967 just after Ernest Payne's retirement.

Baptists had participated in the British Faith and Order Conference at Nottingham in 1964, an occasion which has affected church relations, certainly in England, ever since. A number of important resolutions were passed including one which called upon the churches to covenant together for unity by Easter 1980 or to state clearly why they felt unable to do so. Although the hopes of this conference and its resolution were not fulfilled in the way that the movers had hoped, it helped to create a new climate in ecumenical relationships. This was encouraged in a quite startling way by the changing attitudes of many within the Roman Catholic Church following the Second Vatican Council. The Nottingham report asked for responses from the churches and in November 1964 the conference's report with its resolutions was referred by the Baptist

Union to the Advisory Committee on Church Relations. In March 1965 the council charged this committee to prepare 'a comprehensive statement to help clarify and shape British Baptist opinion and policy regarding both the changing pattern of church relations in the British Isles and the more general question of Christian unity and to ensure by careful consultation that the statement takes account of the different theological and ecclesiastical opinions within the denomination.'

This was a formidable resolution with formidable terms of reference. It marked the origins of the report *Baptists and Unity* which was received and adopted by the council finally in March 1967. It was widely recognised as a good and useful report. It is significant perhaps that it was accepted at the assembly at which Ernest Payne laid down his office. Ernest Payne hoped, however, that the report would satisfy the different view points within the denomination and might relieve whoever was to succeed him of anxiety about the ecumenical issue, at any rate for a few years. In the event this proved a vain hope for within the denomination there were signs that the theological polarisation was spreading to the ecumenical issue.

In the early weeks of 1965 shadows were coming close to Ernest Payne in a very personal way. His former colleague and friend, Robert Child, was seriously ill. At the same time, in February, his brother Philip had had to be moved to hospital at Potters Bar, and it was soon clear that his long and heroic fight against the crippling weakness was nearly over. Philip Payne died on 25th February 1965. No-one – and certainly not his brother – would have wished Philip Payne's ordeal to be further prolonged, but his death left Ernest Payne with an awareness of a very great gap in his life. He had relied greatly on Philip Payne's advice on all important matters, talking over with him not only major decisions in his own life, but also difficult decisions whether related in the earlier days to Regent's Park College, or later to Baptist Union and ecumenical affairs. The result of Philip's death was that he was left in a more isolated position personally than he had ever been before.

Perhaps nothing illustrates the demands made by public office more starkly than this: on the day after Philip's death, Ernest Payne had to attend an important meeting of the joint General Purpose and Finance Committees of the Baptist Union and the Baptist Missionary Society. There was discussion about the possibility of the joint headquarters being shared at the site of the Beechen Grove Church in Watford. For a time it appeared that here might be a possibility and that an acceptable and viable scheme could be worked out. Certainly Watford was some distance from London, but in the judgment of many, the officers of the two bodies could operate from there and it would be easier for staff and staff housing. However, it became clear that a move of even so short a distance from London would not be easy for many to accept, and in any case it transpired that the site was barely large enough for effective development or dual purpose. To buy any additional property would be very costly, and there was, in the end, not sufficient enthusiasm to carry the scheme very far.

In the summer of 1965 yet another approach was made to Ernest Payne inviting him to consider a different office within the Christian Church. As Chairman of the Executive of the British Council of Churches he was presiding over the committee seeking a successor to Kenneth Slack as Secretary of the British Council of Churches. The search was not proving very easy. Unexpectedly the other members of the Committee turned to Ernest Payne indicating that, although they had set out to find a suitable Anglican and believed close collaboration with the Archbishop of Canterbury to be essential, they would all, nevertheless, support his name if he were willing to accept nomination. The committee members told him that they thought that his standing and experience would make him generally acceptable to the Anglicans.

He found this approach both gratifying and extremely embarrassing. He had resolved that he would not continue as Secretary of the Baptist Union more than a few months beyond his 65th birthday. He had said this at the time of his appointment and believed that 65 was the right age for retirement from a post of this kind. If he accepted the appointment of the British Council of Churches, he would have a responsible job which would last until 1969 or 1970 far beyond his 65th birthday. Following this approach, he had gone to Geneva in July 1965 for the opening of the new headquarters of the World Council of Churches, and friends whom he consulted were encouraging and asked him to consider the proposal seriously and sympathetically. He could not, however, feel that it would be right to leave the Baptist Union two years earlier than had been anticipated. There were a number of matters that he believed should be dealt with during his secretaryship. There was, for example, the report concerning Christian unity in response to the Nottingham resolutions. There was a report of a commission on the associations which had reported to the Baptist Union Council in 1964 and to the assembly in Leeds in 1965. There were a number of complex matters arising from this Report that he felt required his presence to evaluate. In addition he did not feel drawn any longer to an extended period of new, heavy and delicate responsibility. So he refused to be considered for nomination. As it turned out the search for a successor to Kenneth Slack was successfully concluded with the appointment of Kenneth Sansbury, Bishop of Singapore.

Retirement looms

From all this it is evident that by 1965 he had begun to reflect upon the approaching question of retirement. All that was happening to him was confirming his view that he should retire at the age of 65 or soon afterwards. It seems that later in 1965 he came across a remark in Agatha Christie's book, *Cat Amongst the Pigeons*, made by a headmistress, Miss Bulstrode: 'To know when to go – that was one of the great responsibilities. To go before one's powers began to fail, one's sure grip to loosen, before one felt a faint staleness, the unwillingness to envisage continuing effort'.[16] This was wise advice, and he took it! For whatever else the approach from the British Council of Churches did or did not do, it certainly concentrated his mind on the growing recognition that after 14 years in the Church House, the time for him to go was fast approaching.

One of the constant frustrations to him personally was the failure to develop the joint headquarters project with the Baptist Missionary Society. It is a recurring theme of the Ernest Payne story. He had worked in both headquarters and was utterly convinced that closer integration in every way would be of mutual benefit, not only to the Union and the Society, but also to the total Baptist mission at home and abroad. After the failure of the Watford possibility, there came unexpectedly in 1966 news of a site at the junction of Hampstead Road and

Euston Road. The Borough of Camden was engaged in substantial redevelopment schemes and it was suggested that the Camden Council would welcome an imaginative proposal for this particular site. There had already been an examination by the Baptist Union and the Baptist Missionary Society of a possible joint headquarters scheme to be based on the site occupied by the Drummond Street Church which was also in Camden. This had come to nothing. This new site, however, offered much greater possibilities. It was far larger than Baptists required for their own purposes. It was known, however, that before long the British Council of Churches and possibly also the Conference of British Missionary Societies would be seeking new premises. It was also thought that a number of others might be interested; for example, the Congregationalists were likely to be leaving Memorial Hall and particularly if they joined, as seemed likely, with the Presbyterian Church of England, then the question of a new headquarters would arise for the new church. It was suggested that perhaps an ecumenical centre with many shared facilities might be possible. There was some initial discussion with Camden and with the other parties who might be interested. But there was considerable caution on the part of the other possible sharers in the project. There was a feeling that a concentration of forces in the Westminster neighbourhood, where the Anglicans had their headquarters in Church House, would have a more immediate appeal. The conditions on which Camden would have insisted were making it more and more difficult to fulfil the development. The total cost of a satisfactory scheme would have been high, and a really comprehensive united scheme would be difficult to negotiate. Once again disappointment loomed, and another opportunity was missed. The discussions dragged on for many months and indeed well past the date of Ernest Payne's retirement. In the end the idea was abandoned partly because of the credit squeeze, and partly because of the complexity of relating together various potential sharers of the site.

The year 1965 had seen further evidence of growing theological diversity within the denomination. Not surprisingly Ernest Payne began the Council Report for 1965 with a reminder of the history and background of the Baptists, pointing out the considerable diversity which has always existed within the denomination, and yet which has not caused substantial permanent division. It is a diversity with which each generation of Baptists has to live. Twentieth century Baptist life has been remarkable for the richness of its diversity with such people as F. B. Meyer, T. R. Glover, Henry Wheeler Robinson, H. E. Fosdick, K. T. Latourette, Billy Graham and Martin Luther King. The council's report warns: 'These men differed widely in their theologies. Let him pause who would draw the boundaries of our fellowship so narrowly that any of these names must be repudiated and banished.'

Amongst other things, the writer had in mind the forthcoming presentation of the report on *Baptists and Unity* which was likely to come to the 1967 assembly. At the beginning of 1966 that report was in the hands of the associations and the churches for comment.

On the 11th May 1965 Ernest Payne wrote to the President of the Baptist Union, Dr Howard Williams, pointing out that at the assembly of 1966 he would complete the third period of five years as general secretary. He made it clear that when that assembly met, he would be within ten months of his 65th birthday and that he had always been convinced that it would be right to retire at the age of 65. He suggested that there should be a special committee set up to consider, not simply the question as to whether he should be appointed for a further year, but also the question of his successor. The last paragraph of the letter reads thus:

Perhaps we never achieve all that we hope. Certainly I have not done so. But I believe the general situation of the denomination is at the moment more promising than it has been for some years. The transition to a new and younger leader should be made without too long delay. I shall, of course, leave it in the hands of yourself and your fellow officers when and how you deal with this letter.

The outcome was that Ernest Payne was asked to continue for a further year until August 1967 and that the name of Dr David Russell was taken to the 1966 assembly as a nomination to succeed Ernest Payne. There is some evidence to suggest that early in 1966, when he was told of the decision to invite him to continue for just one year beyond 1966 his initial reaction was one of diasppointment. It is often suggested that three years before retirement it cannot come quickly enough,

145

but that when the moment to go actually approaches, then there is a marked reluctance to accept it. Possibly this was so with Ernest Payne. His own records and actions all suggest that he had little doubt but that he should retire in 1967. It may be that if the initial reaction was one of disappointment, then it stemmed from his not being invited to continue beyond one year – an invitation which he would have certainly declined!

Events quickly proved the rightness of the decision that he should retire for he was not at the assembly in 1966 to respond to his re-appointment. Whilst he was in Geneva in February 1966 for the crucial meetings relating to the appointment of Carson Blake, he began to feel somewhat unwell. Walking up the hill from the hotel where he was staying to the World Council headquarters had begun to tire him and worse still to bring on a pain in his chest. In those early weeks of 1966 he found himself in difficulties walking from Hendon Central Station to the house in Prothero Gardens, particularly if he was carrying a case with books and papers in it. He brushed it off with the thought and hope that it was simply old age coming on.

However, at the end of March 1966, when the Free Church Congress met in Newcastle-on-Tyne, the hotel in which he was staying did not have a lift and was some distance from the meeting place. He found that walking, even on the level, made him uncomfortable. On the second day in Newcastle he realised that something was seriously wrong. He mentioned it to Walter Bottoms and to Kenneth Slack, but said that he was sure he could probably get home all right. On the last morning of the congress, Enid Hobbs telephoned him with a request to go to London Airport and to meet a visitor from overseas. He refused the request and at the same time told her that he had not been feeling well and that she had better find out when he could see his doctor. The doctor called to see him at his home the next day. He warned him that he had extremely high blood pressure and told him to stay in bed. He did so for the weekend. When the doctor came again tests were rather more re-assuring. In the early hours of the Tuesday morning, however, he woke with an intense pain and was soon in the throes of a second coronary attack, far more severe than the one he suffered in 1958. For an hour or so he wondered whether he was going to survive, and even when the doctor arrived, he was in a serious condition. After an ambulance journey he found himself in the University College Hospital. Here he was to stay from 30th March to 8th May.

So he missed the assembly of 1966 and was not present for his re-election for his final year as General Secretary of the Baptist Union. But it was with real pleasure that he learned that David Russell had been invited by the assembly to succeed him in the summer of 1967.

He gradually recovered his strength, and fortunately suffered no relapse. When he left hospital, however, he had to face the fact that a valve in his heart had been damaged in the incident. He would need to be kept under regular observation and would have to discover the limitations with which he must live. After a few weeks at home in Prothero Gardens and a short stay at Elm Cottage in Pitsford, he returned to the Church House on 1st June 1966. His ability to carry on for this final year was made possible by his wife who drove him to Southampton Row for some months and fetched him home almost to the day of his retirement at the end of July 1967.

Baptists and unity

A most pressing and substantial task that he had during the summer of 1966 was to put in order the final version of the report *Baptists and Unity*. This had been drafted by various members of the committee and was finally edited by Ernest Payne. It was a report of considerable value both from the point of view of the historical reflections within it, and also the theological discussions which it stimulated.

The most significant chapter is the one entitled 'Biblical and Theological Principles concerning the unity of the Church'. The tenor of the report was, on the whole, positive towards church relationships, and is best summed up in the last paragraph of that penultimate chapter:

For the visible unity of Christ's church is a concept rooted in the New Testament and we cannot, as true followers of Christ, ignore what the Spirit is doing in the churches today. Do any of us really believe that it is not the Spirit of Christ who is drawing churches out of isolation into discussion and activity together? The realities of the church's unity that have engaged our attention surely demand some effort be made to embody them in the empirical – the life of the church; is it really God's will to cease such efforts and leave the appalling *status quo* to the Second Coming of Christ and the Last Judgment? And what will the Judge say to us if we do? If the unity of the church is of moment to him, ought it not be of concern to us? It is clear that opinions differ as to how the Church's unity is to be known and expressed; such difference calls for the participation in the discussions that are proceeding amongst the churches, that we may together learn the mind of the Spirit for the Church today.

This remains the formal Baptist position to-day.

The attitudes towards the various resolutions from Nottingham made it clear that Baptists were not able to agree to enter into covenant, to work and to pray for the inauguration of the union by 1980. They did, however, wish to continue in the exploration of what covenanting might mean and on the conditions it might become possible for Baptists. It is a typical Baptist response of cautious desire to participate and yet real hesitation to commit the denomination towards a path which might lead to union. The report was adopted at the council meeting on 7th March 1967. It was sent to the churches for careful study and the Advisory Committee on Church Relations was required to review the situation in a year's time in the light of expressions of opinion within the denomination. When the report came to the assembly in 1967, although there were voices raised against it, it finally carried the overwhelming support of the delegates.

Ernest Payne found the last year of office increasingly trying. It was not only that he was still in a stage of recuperating from his illness. There was the unresolved problem of the relationship with the Baptist Missionary Society and joint headquarters, and there was concern about the pressures within the Union to set up a separate Children's Department and an Education Department. The demands of travel and preaching were bearing more and more heavily upon him too. Although perhaps he may have wanted to have been asked to go on still further, he knew in his heart of hearts that the time had come for him to go. He must prepare the way, as best he could, for David Russell – the future belonged to him.

During this last year his involvement in the World Council

148

of Churches was still demanding. In February 1967 the World Council of Churches Executive met in the precincts of Windsor Castle in the new Conference Centre of St George's. For the members of the Executive Committee the meeting at Windsor was exciting because of the involvement with the Royal Family. The Dean of Windsor had been able to arrange for Her Majesty the Queen to receive the company before lunch on the first day. The Queen spent nearly an hour with the committee and spoke individually to everyone. But problems still beset the ecumenical movement. It was the time of the Vietnam War and an attempt had been made to make a joint World Council of Churches–Roman Catholic Statement on this but this had proved impossible. Even within the Executive Committee there were difficulties in getting agreement as to the sort of statement that should be made about the Vietnam situation. It was further clear that the World Council was running into financial difficulties and the preparations for the Uppsala Assembly were behind schedule.

The Report of the Council for 1966 was the last Ernest Payne drafted. Within it, only thinly disguised, are his personal reflections as he came to retirement. There is confidence in the purpose of God in history. The people of God are called to steady the nerves of mankind, to remind man that he is a creature, yet at the same time to assure him that a redemptive purpose is being worked out in history, which will one day be more fully disclosed than is at present possible. The denomination is warned against hasty judgments which have time and time again proved wrong. Baptist history illustrates this vividly. In 1769 Daniel Turner of Abingdon was convinced that all things were now going wrong with the denomination. The report continues:

Turner could not know that not many miles away from Abingdon where he was writing were growing up four boys who were destined to transform the fortunes of the Baptist denomination and through it the Church Universal. Their names were Andrew Fuller, John Rippon, William Carey and Robert Hall. Those who today are tempted to speak or think in similar terms to Turner should remember how little they really know of what God is at in 1966.

In assessing the state of the denomination the Report notes the decline of membership but points out the way in which

149

there has been considerable growth in giving to the Home Work Fund and the consequent increase in the minimum stipend. In 1951 the Home Work Fund had produced £32,620; in 1966 it produced £132,435. The minimum stipend in those 16 years had increased from £325 to £600. 'This will mean that the new General Secretary can enter upon his work with confidence so far as the finances of the Union are concerned, and that a further substantial increase in the minimum stipend should be possible in 1968.' The roaring inflation of the 1970s still belonged to the unknown future!

The Times newspaper on 19th December 1966, had commented:

In a way it is courageous for the Bishop of Chester, Chairman of the Church of England's Committee (on the Ordination of Women) to admit that the fact of people's prejudice, however right or wrong in theory, is a humanly relevant factor in the case. At least this avoids the danger of hypocrisy, which more dogmatic assertions do not. On the other hand, when pragmatism is all, there is danger of improvisation, based on instinct, propped up by rationalisation. There is also a more troubling question; how far is pragmatism an adequate expression of the revolutionary love and vision of Christ?

This quotation introduced Ernest Payne's conclusion to his final report as secretary of the council:

The council believes that these words from *The Times* are words it would be well for Baptists to ponder and apply to their own situation. They have relevance to the question of the right Baptist attitude to closer relations with other Christian traditions. They have relevance to the relation of local churches to one another and to the union. They have relevance to the Baptist Union and the Baptist Missionary Society; during the year little or no progress has been made towards a joint headquarters, or the more important matter of closer integration of the activities and structures of the two bodies. The words have relevance also to the relation of individual Baptists to one another when they differ in theological emphasis, in social behaviour and in political judgment. Our point of reference should be the revolutionary love and vision of Christ. It is in His light that we shall see light.

This concluding paragraph of the report thus provides us with Ernest Payne's final official comment in his capacity as

150

Secretary of the Baptist Union. He left it recognising its great potential as part of the people of God, calling people to redemption, but he left it recognising too that there was a growing polarisation within the denomination. He was saddened that the decline in membership of the churches had not been halted, but believed that the Union's financial situation had stabilised. He pleaded that as the denomination went on to face the crucial questions of wider church relations, of the relationship between associations and the Union, between the Union and Missionary Society, between Baptists as individuals, it should recognise that all must come closer to Christ and his light. Only then will God's way forward be revealed. Ernest Payne was calling the denomination to hold fast to Christ and for the rest be totally uncommitted. Whatever else he may or may not have done for the Baptist denomination, he made it impossible for it to escape from facing the right questions.

So the time came for the denomination to say a formal farewell to Ernest Payne. The Baptist Union Council had taken leave at its meeting in March 1967, when Sir Donald Finnemore the President of the Baptist Union presented a monetary gift on behalf of the members, and the council itself granted him honorary membership. But it was the assembly that took particular leave of Ernest Payne in a significant way.

A backward look

The Tuesday evening session of the assembly was given a special farewell character. Dr Champion spoke and presented him with a copy of the Festschrift which he had edited. It was entitled *Outlook for Christianity* and had been written by a team of people from many churches and from many lands. The main address that evening was given by Franklin Fry. At Ernest Payne's request Fry spoke about the *raison d'être* of the ecumenical movement and most particularly of the World Council of Churches. But he spoke also of Ernest Payne and said, 'In the eyes of the World Council of Churches he had been paramountly **the** Baptist. He had given the image of the Baptist communion more clearly than any other individual.' Fry turned to the assembly and said, 'And you, all of you, can

151

be very grateful for it.' In his address he went on to speak not only of Ernest Payne's contribution as vice-chairman of the Central Committee, but revealed also that at the meetings of that committee, the last session of worship had always been led by Ernest Payne. Fry went on, 'He has never slouched or sidled into the presence of God. He has been God's respectful son, and has been able to lead many of us along the paths of worship. We honour a man tonight with profound gratitude to God, a man whom I love, and whom you love.'

In his reply Ernest Payne spoke first of the Festschrift which was undreamed of and undeserved. He went on to say that his experience in the whole life of the church echoed that of Reuben Nelson, the distinguished American Baptist, who once said that his work 'brings one into fellowship with men and women so great in spiritual stature that I must almost stand on tiptoe, as it were, to reach their insights and their dreams.'

He paid tribute to Freda Payne. In doing so, typically, he quoted from the past, from Richard Baxter, who said of his own wife: 'it was one of the conditions of our marriage that she should regret none of my time which my ministerial work would require'. He pointed out that when Freda Payne married him he was in the situation of being a Baptist minister in a Northamptonshire village, and those were the prospects into which she came. There was no inkling and indeed no chance for preparation for marriage to someone whose life was to change into that of a peripatetic minister, working first in the Baptist Mission House, then in a college, and finally in denominational headquarters. Yet for 35 years of their marriage, that was the life that he led, and which she understood that he had to lead. That very fact and many other things too asked much in patience and sacrifice which she gave unstintingly. He paid tribute to the way in which over the years he had been served by others. If the secretary of a denomination was significant, so was the secretary of the secretary. He reminded the denomination that Aubrey's parting words to him had been to 'find a good secretary'. He had found one in Enid Hobbs, who had stood by him and also just simply stood him, for fifteen years.

He noted four things upon which he looked back with special satisfaction. First what had been done for ministers and for deaconesses, both active and retired, in the developing of the Home Work Fund, in the raising of the stipend, and of giving to them greater satisfaction and security in their jobs. Much still remained to be done, but he believed the foundation of proper support and security stood firm. In connection with this he expressed his satisfaction with the collection of the Ter-Jubilee Fund and the way in which this had been carried through without producing deficits on other accounts. Secondly, he spoke of the way in which he had shared in renewed links with Eastern Europeans, notably in the Soviet Union, Hungary and Poland. Thirdly, he spoke of his pleasure in having a share in providing a new hymn book for the denomination, and that together with Stephen Winward he had provided a minister's service book, and on his own had had the opportunity of writing a history of the Baptist Union. Fourthly, he rejoiced at the privilege of representing Baptists beyond denominational boundaries and hoped that he had had the opportunity of correcting some of the mistakes and misunderstandings and unfortunate impressions. His daughter Ann was once introduced to someone in the West Country who when he heard who her father was said 'Ah, that man, he's a militant nonconformist'. 'Perhaps', said Ernest Payne, 'that represents the typical Baptist.'

He went on to speak of the things that he had most regretted during his time in office. First, the failure to bring the Baptist Union and the Baptist Missionary Society together, if not under one roof, at least to a better integrated organisation, and of this he commented, 'It could have been done; it ought to have been done; it can be done; it must be done.' Speaking on this issue he quoted Emerson: 'One may strike while the iron is hot, or one may strike until the iron is hot.' He went on, 'I thought the iron was hot enough, but cold water was poured on it, so we must go on striking until it is hot enough to fuse one organisation and mould it to something more effective, for meeting the challenges of the 20th century.' Secondly, he re-gretted the tarrying of revival and renewal. He reminded the assembly of the 18th century yet again, when there was a hidden gathering of forces in preparation for a new advance. He spoke of his confidence in the future, both in his successor, and in the younger men and women in the denomination who are ready for leadership. He hoped that he would not only watch them but be allowed to help in various ways. He ap-pealed for unity within the denomination. He believed that the theological differences had to be seen within the context of the diversity within the one unity in which Baptists believed. Yet again, he used the familiar argument that if you start from John Bunyan you can, on the one hand, come down a line which will lead through Spurgeon and F. B. Meyer to Billy Graham, and you can come down on another line which will lead through John Clifford, Harry Emerson Fosdick, to Martin Luther King. He pleaded that differences should not be allowed to degenerate into bitterness or division. He reminded the assembly that the Church is **all** the people of God. All are summoned, called together, for worship, witness and service. He concluded with two quotations. The first was from Romans 15: 4–6 in the Jerusalem Bible version:

And indeed everything that was written long ago in the scriptures was meant to teach us something about hope from the examples scripture gives of how people who did not give up were helped by God. And may he who helps us when we refuse to give up, help you all to be tolerant with each other, following the example of Christ Jesus, so that united in mind and voice, you may give glory to the God and Father of our Lord Jesus Christ.

The second quotation is from Philip Brooks: 'To seek for the reproduction of Christ's mind in the mind of the community is the greatest aim that we can cherish.'

So it was with this appeal for denominational commitment to Christ and to each other in Christ he laid down his responsibilities to the assembly. He was convinced that the past taught us to be confident in the present and full of hope for the future.

The months after the assembly were spent in seeking to clear up the work. He had two other special publications in his honour, one in the *Baptist Quarterly* and the other in *The Fraternal*. These two taken together with the *Outlook of Christianity* give some idea of how his friends saw him. It is true that these publications conceal what he himself recognised: that there were those who were critical or suspicious of his ecumenical interests and activities, and others who wished that he had gifts and graces which were either denied him at birth or which he had failed to cultivate. He comforted himself with the famous comment made by Lord Salisbury, the Conservative Prime Minister, about William Gladstone and Joseph

Chamberlain. 'Mr Gladstone is much hated, but he is also much loved. Does anybody love Mr Chamberlain?'

On 11th July through the generosity of his friends, Mr and Mrs Vinson, a dinner was given in his honour at the Connaught Rooms. Several speakers paid tribute to him, most notably Kenneth Slack. He spoke of Ernest Payne's almost terrifying clarity and speed of mind, of his sound judgment and described him as 'a faithful Baptist, a profound ecumenist, a learned scholar and a very dear friend'.

On 27th July at the Baptist Church House, there was a staff farewell, when he was presented, with, of all things, a portable typewriter! The following day he handed over various keys to David Russell, cleared out most of his personal belongings and left the Church House. During the first week in August he and his wife moved out of 30 Prothero Gardens to Elm Cottage, Pitsford. So ended a notable period of service to the Baptist denomination.

So began an extremely active retirement.

5

Retirement Years

I: 1967-75

In an interview published in the *Baptist Times* on 21st April
1977, Ernest Payne commented, 'As I look back over my life,
one thing I am sure of, the Almighty does not leave any loose
ends, he ties things up.'

A divine tidiness

In retrospect, his retirement years do show what he would have
called a 'divine tidiness'. They lasted twelve and a half years.
For the first eight and a half until December 1975, he remained
deeply involved in World Council of Churches affairs and
played relatively little part in the life of the Baptist Union.
When his term as a vice-president of the World Council of
Churches concluded at Nairobi in December 1975, he became
immediately deeply involved once again in the Baptist Union
through his election of the vice-presidency in April 1976. Thus
it was with the affairs of his beloved Baptist denomination that
he was chiefly occupied until his term as an officer concluded
in the Spring of 1979. At that point he was re-elected to the
General Purposes Committee of the Baptist Union for what
would almost certainly have been a final year of service. Three
months before that year was completed he died. Who dare say
other than that it was divinely neat and tidy?

But in 1967, his first reaction to retirement was that he was
living in an atmosphere of unreality, mingled with considerable
relief. He resisted firmly attempts by various Christian bodies,

for example, the Churches Committee on Gambling, to make him accept office. He derived great pleasure from a notable occasion, a dinner, organised at the House of Commons in his honour by Sir Cyril Black, a distinguished Baptist and then Member for Wimbledon. Ernest Payne always respected Sir Cyril's ability and consistency though they did not always agree on matters of politics nor of ecclesiastical affairs. Nevertheless, there existed between them mutual respect and a relationship which sometimes eased the passage of difficult developments in the life of the denomination. The House of Commons dinner was a generous act and, for Ernest Payne, a memorable occasion. It was particularly so because Sir Cyril gave him the opportunity of naming some of the guests. This meant that a number of friends from earlier days could be present including Max Hancock and his wife, Dr and Mrs Raymond Holmes and W. R. Matthews who had just resigned as Dean of St Paul's at the age of 85. Also present were Lord Fisher of Lambeth, the Bishop of London, Nathaniel Micklem, Norman Goodall and many other friends from a variety of contexts. The Prime Minister sent his apologies, and a message. For Ernest Payne the whole evening was one to remember.

Within a few days of the House of Commons dinner he was on his way to Australia. He had accepted an invitation from Mervyn Himbury, Principal of the Baptist College in Victoria, and one of his Oxford students, to give the first Holdsworth-Grigg Memorial lecture in Melbourne. This generous invitation enabled him to plan a two month visit to Australia and New Zealand in the course of which he could be in Perth on 3rd October when his Aunt Flossie celebrated her 100th birthday. It was a happy coincidence – if coincidence it was – that Mervyn Himbury's invitation coincided with Aunt Flossie's birthday. Typically, Ernest Payne arrived in Perth with a copy of her birth certificate in his pocket! He was somewhat startled to discover that she admitted to being only 97! Apparently on arrival in Australia in 1897 she had deducted three years from her age!

At the end of November, Ernest Payne began the journey home which he interrupted to spend some weeks in Uganda with Gordon and Hilary Holmes. On 6th December they had been on a picnic expedition on the Nile. On their return there was a message that he should telephone the British High Commissioner in Kampala as soon as possible. His immediate reaction was that it was either an invitation to tea, or possibly some crisis connected with the World Council of Churches. After considerable difficulty he managed to contact the High Commissioner who told him that he had a message from Downing Street for a Dr Ernest Payne to the effect that the Prime Minister wished to recommend to the Queen that he should be made a Companion of Honour. He was somewhat bowled over at the news. Honours, of whatever sort, seemed – so far as he was concerned – quite undeserved. But he accepted them with dignified surprise.

The award was made public in the New Years Honours List on 1st January 1968. On 29th February he received the award from the Queen at a private audience. The Order of the Companion of Honour was established by King George V in 1919. It was at first limited to fifty members but later extended to a possible sixty five. The Insignia is presented, not at a public investiture, but at a private audience with the sovereign. This emphasises its distinction. In 1968 three other members of the order were linked with Church life – and Ernest Payne had had close contact with two of them. These were W. R. Matthews, Dean of St Paul's, and C. H. Dodd, the New Testament scholar. The third cleric was 'Tubby' Clayton, the founder of Toc H. What happened at the presentation is best described in Ernest Payne's own words:

At about 12.20 the Equerry ... announced me to the Queen who was standing waiting in her sitting room with a CH insignia in its open box in her hand. She greeted me, saying that she was very glad to give it to me and always admired the design and the words around the Medallion: 'In action faithful and in honour clear.' I thanked her and she invited me to sit down. She went to a chair beside the fire place. I mentioned I was in Uganda in December, when unexpectedly I heard of the honour and this led to a conversation about Africa which seemed to flow quite easily. We had a discussion of the Nigerian situation about which the Queen was obviously well informed ... Soon after 12.40 the Queen rose and touched the bell on the table ... and I took my leave.

Prior to his retirement from the secretaryship there had been a move to nominate him for the vice-presidency of the Baptist

158

Union. He was determined, however, not to spend his last year doubling the office of secretary with that of president. To have been president the year after his retirement would have been unwise, he believed, for a number of reasons. There was first the question of his uncertain health. But more important was his conviction, repeatedly expressed, that an ex-secretary could and should only stand for election if he was assured of the goodwill of his successor and if requested to stand by the Baptist Union Council. In any case he thought that to continue as an officer of the Union for a further three years immediately after laying down office as secretary was unfair to David Russell and bound to inhibit him.

In 1970 there was a further concerted effort to put forward his name. He consulted David Russell who said he would have no personal objection to the nomination. The General Purposes and Finance Committee was somewhat non-commital and indicated that it did not feel that there should be pressure put upon him to stand. He did not accept the nomination. Most of the friends he consulted privately were hesitant about the wisdom of returning to office so quickly. Not only was the health question raised but by this time there had been changes in the structure of Baptist Union organisation at the Church House about which it was known that he had considerable doubts. Whilst he rarely criticised these changes openly he never found them wholly acceptable. During the early years of retirement the only Baptist Union committees on which he served were the Continental and Commonwealth Committees which were soon united in the Overseas Committee.

During the year following his retirement his health continued to stabilise. He found plenty to occupy his time. He was still Chairman of the Executive Committee of the British Council of Churches; he was giving an increasing amount of time to the Dr Williams Trust of which he was a Trustee, as well as to the Dr Williams Library. As an ex-moderator of the Free Church Federal Council he remained a member of that council and continued to have particular responsibility in the field of education. More often than not he found himself coming up to London twice a week. But it was the World Council of Churches that claimed most of his attention during his early retirement years.

In August 1967 the World Council committees met in Crete. It was very hot and once or twice he feared he was going to faint, but recovered himself. Franklin Fry was not so fortunate. During the time in Crete he became ill and although he recovered quickly, this event may well have heralded a more serious illness. The committees were concerned largely with preparation for the Fourth Assembly of the World Council which was to be held in 1968 in Uppsala, Sweden, from 4th to 20th July.

The following year, at the beginning of June, a letter arrived in Pitsford written at Fry's bidding by his son, saying that his father was seriously ill and would not be able to come to Uppsala. Ever since Ernest Payne had been elected as Vice-Chairman of the Central Committee, he had always had an uneasy feeling at the back of his mind that one day he might have to face an emergency situation caused by an accident to Fry or illness. As the time went on and the Uppsala Assembly approached at which both of them would almost certainly come out of office, the feeling of apprehension had tended to fade. Now it all came flooding back. Fry would not be at Uppsala, and much of the extra responsibility would devolve on to him. But yet sadder news was to follow. On Thursday 6th June the telephone rang at Pitsford with Victor Hayward on the line from Geneva telling him that Fry had died in New York early that morning.

Whilst the news was not totally unexpected, Fry's death came as a great shock to Ernest Payne and he felt a very profound sense of loss. It was not simply, nor so much, the implication that now loomed for him at Uppsala; it was more personal and far deeper than that. For one thing, they were close in age, Fry having been born in August 1900, and therefore just eighteen months older than Ernest Payne. More importantly a strong bond of trust and affection had developed between them. When Fry told the Baptist Union Assembly in April 1967 that Ernest Payne was a man whom 'I love', he was speaking literally. Fry's son was later to write to Ernest Payne to express appreciation that his father 'was nourished by your friendship in a singular way'. Ernest Payne flew over to New York for the funeral and was given a place amongst the honorary pall bearers. He received from Fry's office the Report of the Central Committee for the Uppsala Assembly which

160

Fry was in the process of preparing when he became ill. Ernest Payne's first task was to complete that report.

Uppsala

He was now going to be faced with the responsibility of presiding over the Uppsala Assembly. It was the most substantial and exposed task that ever came his way. All through the three weeks from 29th June when he arrived at Stockholm, to 21st July, in spite of considerable physical strain, he felt 'upheld', basically confident, and never as apprehensive as he had been in Enugu in January 1965. Those who were present testified to the firmness of his hand. At the end of the assembly the Metropolitan Lakdasa De Mel on behalf of all the delegates paid tribute to 'the magnificent work of Dr Payne in his chairmanship'. Much later, Trevor Beeson writing in the *Christian Century* in June 1971 said 'those who saw him carry the burden of chairmanship of the Uppsala Assembly of the World Council of Churches are aware of a marked toughness in the shy, diminutive Englishman'.

It is perhaps significant that although Ernest Payne kept a careful record of all his travels abroad, the one exception was that of Uppsala. His record is very sketchy indeed, and he simply records that he had neither the time nor the energy to maintain his usual travel diary. He was required to preside over the Executive Committee and the final meeting of the Central Committee which had been appointed seven years earlier in New Delhi. He was comforted by a Latin inscription over the door opposite which he sat which spoke of a ship sailing on even though the captain was lost.

Early on in the proceedings of the assembly he had to take a firm line in rejecting a claim that the restless group of youth participants should share in voting with the delegates. This was not an easy issue to deal with because it was the days of student concern and unrest, and there was considerable sympathy with the desire that the voice of youth should be heard. But the rules were very clear and he held to them. After this initial challenge to his authority he received unwavering support from the assembly as a whole. There were a number of other difficult moments within the assembly. Both sides in the

161

Nigerian Civil War tried to gain support and all the efforts made to bring them together were unsuccessful. The American representatives at Uppsala were very much under the impact of the current Civil Rights agitation in the United States and the growing strength of the Black Power Movement. The main decisions of the assembly it is generally agreed showed more interest in Life and Work issues than in Faith and Order. It was left to Visser't Hooft to stress the importance of keeping the horizontal and vertical together.

One of the more difficult issues within any World Council Assembly is the work of the Nominations Committee set up to produce nominations for the Praesidium and for the new Central Committee. At Uppsala, Ernest Payne found that the members of the committee in their initial list for the Central Committee had overlooked the Salvation Army and he had to spend some anxious hours resolving this particular problem. Not surprisingly the list of nominations for the new Presidents of the World Council contained his own name. The new Central Committee comprised a majority of newcomers and a much stronger and more vocal representation from Asia and Africa than previously. This is illustrated in that the successor to Franklin Fry as Chairman of the Central Committee was M. M. Thomas, a distinguished Asian layman. The World Council of Churches was still more clearly becoming a council of churches representing the whole world.

It fell to Ernest Payne as chairman to give the closing address to the assembly. His opening words were undoubtedly autobiographical:

We have had some busy and exhausting days and it is perhaps that sense of exhaustion that predominates. These days have been exhilarating and significant days, for there has been constant evidence that the World Council of Churches, established twenty years ago, has now come of age and, it begins to face the problems and responsibilities which come when childhood and youth are over.

He concluded:

'There is a phrase which comes from some of the earliest Christian liturgies and is still used at the end of many eucharistic services today as it was in earlier times – *ite missa est*. The scholars argue how it should be exactly translated. We make it our own and may interpret it as 'Go, this is the sending forth'. As we come to this moment let us recognise that there are not a few in the assembly who are going back home to very uncertain situations, some of them very dangerous situations . . . We remember one another. We commend one another to God's guidance – to him who gives upholding grace for the days that lie ahead.'

Important as is the work of the World Council assemblies and committees, for Ernest Payne the richer rewards in his ecumenical experience came from the friendships made. These linked East and West – whether geographically or politically. Earlier in his closing address he had referred to Franklin Fry. In the closing sentences he certainly had in mind Joseph Hromadka of the Evangelical Church of Czech Brethren whom he had known since 1948. One particular moment at Uppsala remained always with Ernest Payne. It was when he stood with Hromadka on the steps of the Assembly Hall at Uppsala and spoke with him of the liberalising movement which had occured in the previous months under Alexander Dubcek. Hromadka welcomed the relaxations but feared lest they would provoke a reaction. He believed that the test would come in the Autumn when it would be seen how far the Czech people would accept what was happening. Only a few weeks later, on 21st August, the Russian Army entered Czechoslovakia. The last six months of Hromadka's life were months of deepening distress and disappointment shared – albeit at a distance – by Ernest Payne and many other ecumenical friends.

Racism and violence

One of the decisions at Uppsala which was referred to the Central Committee for further consideration and action was the development of a campaign against racism of whatever sort. Following on the Uppsala decision, a World Council of Churches consultation on racism was held in May 1969 at the Methodist Centre in London's Notting Hill district. This began a controversial chapter in World Council history in which Ernest Payne became involved. Notting Hill was a restless and depressed neighbourhood with a large coloured population. The consultation did not get off to the best of starts, for there was immediate criticism that it had been arranged without prior consultation with the British Council of Churches. There was a widely representative group of participants but one which Ernest Payne judged, at the time, to be weighted on the side of the militants. World Council of Churches representation was led by the Secretary, Carson Blake. The meetings of the consultation were interrupted from time to time by black demonstrators at the sessions in Notting Hill and by 'white militants' at a public meeting at Church House, Westminster at which Bishop Trevor Huddleston was amongst the speakers.

This 'happening' faced many people including Ernest Payne, for the first time with the kind of challenge which had become familiar in the United States. The consultation reached certain conclusions which were formulated – somewhat hastily some thought – into 'recommendations'. These were forwarded to the Geneva Secretariat and then passed to the Central Committee which was due to meet in August 1969 at the University of Kent. This did not prove a very easy occasion – certainly not for Ernest Payne.

Linked with the Notting Hill recommendations was the suggestion of an appeal for a large fund to develop the Programme against Racism, the greater part of which would be used for grants to organisations of oppressed peoples or those working to aid them, notably in Southern Africa. It was the Canterbury Central Committee which established the Programme to Combat Racism, set up the commission with a five year mandate and created the Special Fund. Ernest Payne, like a number of others, was somewhat concerned with the high emotional atmosphere which this whole matter generated. He had considerable sympathy with the basic objects of the programme but he was often less than happy with the way the programme was operated. This was particularly true of the proposals to initiate the Fund discussed at Canterbury. These included the use of money from the reserves of the World Council including its divisions of World Mission and Evangelism. This suggestion caused him deep concern. He believed that the reserves had been built up with great difficulty and that they were already somewhat low for so considerable an enterprise as the World Council. He judged, then, that if they were eroded too far it could make the Council vulnerable in any international monetary or economic crisis. He thought also that there needed to be specific authorisation for the use of the reserves for hitherto unthought of purposes. In the light of all this he opposed the suggestion in the Finance Committee. He was outvoted there but decided to challenge the decision when it came to the Plenary Session of the Central Committee. Once again he gained little support and the proposal carried easily.

There were two meetings of the World Council's Executive in 1970. The first, in February at Geneva, discussed further the Programme to Combat Racism and set up an International Advisory Committee to deal with the distribution of the Fund. The second, at Arnoldshain, near Frankfurt, was faced with growing indications that the financial situation of the Council was becoming difficult. Sadly the highly efficient new Chairman of the Finance Committee appointed after Uppsala, Bishop Reed of Ottawa, had died suddenly. The Earl of March, an Anglican layman, had agreed to take over the vacant chairmanship. Much time was also given to the progress of the Programme to Combat Racism. It appeared to Ernest Payne that the International Advisory Committee had – probably through lack of time – left the financial recommendations to a small sub-committee. Indeed the list of grants presented was still incomplete. When the recommendations came before the executive it was apparent that there was little money to distribute except that which had been withdrawn from the reserves. The list submitted included grants to ZANU and ZAPU, liberation movements in what was then Rhodesia. There was a further grant to organisations in Britain supporting the activities of the African National Congress. All these grants were made to organisations for humanitarian purposes only and were governed by laid-down criteria, the first of which ran 'the purpose of the organisation must not be inconsonant with the general purposes of the WCC and its units, and the grants are to be used for humanitarian activities (*i.e.* social, health and educational purposes, legal aid, *etc*)'.

At Arnoldshain, Ernest Payne pointed out to M. M. Thomas the chairman, and later to the other members of the executive that at Canterbury he had made his position about the use of reserves quite clear. He recognised, however, that his view was very much a minority opinion and therefore he would simply refrain from voting. He stated his disapproval of the proposed grant from the small amount of money available to organisations in Britain. The executive was assured that all the organisations involved accepted the condition that the money should be used only for humanitarian purposes and never for the purchase of arms. The list of 19 grants was then approved.

A press release was prepared by a small group to announce these decisions. This was issued from Geneva and when Ernest Payne saw a copy on the last morning of the executive meeting he realised that it could well cause controversy. He was not alone in that view. It seemed to him that the press release did not make clear enough the qualification with regard to the use of the money. His fears on this matter were soon to be confirmed. When he returned to London at the beginning of September he was challenged by a number of church leaders, both within the British Council of Churches and outside it – about the implications of the Programme to Combat Racism in the light of the press release. The question being asked was whether the World Council had now really committed itself to what many viewed as terrorist organisations. Complaints were received that there had been all too little information as to how the programme was developing and virtually no consultation with member churches. The reaction was, on the whole, one of strong disapproval.

The developing situation distressed Ernest Payne. Whilst firm in his opposition to racism, from the beginning he had had hesitations about certain aspects of the Programme to Combat Racism and certainly about the way in which the scheme was being funded and developed. Nevertheless he was a loyal member of the World Council of Churches and the only British president. He judged that some of the criticism reflected over-reaction and misunderstanding. Consequently he reflected upon what he could do to ease the situation. He was due to travel to Cromer and during the train journey he drafted on a scrap of paper a letter which he thought might be sent to *The Times*. He redrafted it at Cromer and sent a copy off to Hugh Wilcox of the British Council of Churches asking that he should contact Pauline Webb, the British Methodist, who was Vice-Chairman of the Central Committee, to suggest that her signature might also appear if it was decided to send the letter or something similar to the press. On 15th September he was interested to read the letter in *The Times* very much as he had drafted it! The letter read:

Sir, You will allow us, we hope, as two British members of the Executive Committee of the World Council of Churches present at its recent meeting in Arnoldshain, to comment on the decisions which have clearly aroused the greatest interest in this and other countries, namely, those connected with the Programme to Combat Racism.

This programme was agreed upon last summer by the Central Committee of 120, with only a handful of members expressing dissent to the use of the nucleus of the fund then set up, of reserves from the WCC itself and from its Divisions of Interchurch Aid and World Mission and Evangelism.

It was agreed that such funds as become available be granted to organisations of oppressed racial groups or organisations supporting victims of racial injustice, provided their purposes were not inconsonant with those of the WCC and its divisions. An International Advisory Committee has been appointed, and it was the recommendations of this body that were approved by the recent executive.

The situation in Southern Africa is recognised as deserving priority because of the strength of white racism throughout that area, but grants have also been made to groups in Australia, Japan and Colombia. The organisations have indicated for what purpose aid is sought and have given an assurance that they will not use any amounts received for military purposes, but for activities in harmony with purposes of the WCC and its divisions.

Clearly there may be differences of opinion as to whether this or that grant is wise. There are two kinds of violence in the world: violence exercised from above by those in power, and violence resorted to from below by those who see no other way of securing the redress of their grievances. Regis Debray distinguishes them as 'the violence that represses' and 'the violence that liberates'. It is unlikely that those exercising repression from above will favour any kind of help being given to their opponents.

The WCC, like mankind at large, has still not solved the issue of how much force is justifiable in any particular situation. Those who approved or shared in resistance movements in Europe thirty years ago must clearly be careful in their reactions to the present decisions.

Meantime for the churches of the world, piety is not enough; pity is not enough. The Programme to Combat Racism aims at helping

167

forward efforts to secure basic human rights and to do so within certain agreed and well defined guide lines. It is those who do nothing or are content with words only who can rightly be described as 'pessimistic'. (signed Pauline M Webb, Vice Chairman Central Committee of the WCC and Ernest A Payne, Member of the Praesidium).

In reading the letter, it should be recalled that Ernest Payne was himself one of the dissenters mentioned in the second paragraph. However, on the same day on which the letter was published he received a telegram of thanks from Geneva which read: 'We appreciate very highly your letter to *The Times* of 15th September. Kindly accept our profound thanks for such reassurance of your understanding and support. CCIA Geneva'. One can well imagine that he read it with a rueful smile!

He found himself involved in three other experiences related to the racism issue during the autumn. He attended a residential meeting at Haywards Heath of the International Affairs Department of the British Council of Churches. Members of that department had before it the report *Violence in South Africa* prepared by a special working party, on which a number of African missionary society secretaries served. The report was radical and recommended sympathetic attitudes towards Africans who felt that they could secure justice only by resorting to force. The reception of the report at Haywards Heath was mixed. It was likely that the public reaction to it, even in church circles would be as critical as that towards the World Council grants. It was finally decided not to present the report to the British Council of Churches at its autumn meeting but to allow it to appear solely under the names of those who had prepared it.

The report deeply impressed Ernest Payne. Its indictment of the policies of South Africa, of the Rhodesian Government, of Portugal seemed to him to be unanswerable. It confirmed the impression left on him by his visit – certainly of only a few days duration – to Johannesburg in 1967. At Haywards Heath, also, he met an African who told him of the lift of spirit which he felt when he heard of the proposed World Council grants, that money should be entrusted to Africans on their own recognisances without any constraining paternalistic controls.

The second experience came in the middle of October when President Kaunda of Zambia came to London with other representatives of the Organisation for African Unity to protest against the proposed resumption of arms sales to South Africa which had been announced by Sir Alec Douglas Home, then Foreign Secretary. Kenneth Kaunda had spoken at one of the evening sessions at Uppsala and agreed to meet a World Council deputation during his London visit. Ernest Payne led the delegation which met the President on 17th October in the Dorchester Hotel. President Kaunda made clear his strong Christian convictions, his belief that the churches in the West had very limited time in which to make their message credible to most Africans who hear the white leaders in Southern Africa claiming to be upholders of Christian civilisation, and his view that material and financial aid should be given by the World Council of Churches only in close collaboration with the Organisation for African Unity. He pointed out that if Africans appeared to be deserted or betrayed by western nations then they had few alternatives to seeking help from the communist world in the shape of technicians and materials from Russia and China.

In Britain, criticism of the Programme to Combat Racism gradually subsided – or at least became somewhat less sharp. But in Germany the situation remained much more difficult, particularly as the German churches were generous in their support of the World Council. Ernest Payne was asked by Carson Blake to join a group he was taking to Munich to meet with the Synod of the Evangelical Church. Though the Hesse-Nassau Church had made a grant to the special fund to combat racism, the action had been challenged on legal grounds and had been sharply criticised in a number of quarters in Germany. This third experience in only two months relating to the racism question was in some ways the most strenuous for Ernest Payne. The meeting with the German Christians proved strained and somewhat inconclusive. Late in the afternoon he was pressed into service to share with the German professor Ludwig Raiser in the drafting of a non-commital communiqué. Throughout the day reporters and television crews had been waiting outside to interview participants at the close of the meeting. Carson Blake had to leave for Geneva and it was Ernest Payne who became involved in the final stages of a large press conference. One lasting memory of the occasion for him was how the restraint and good humour of at least one African participant, Samuel Amissah (General

Secretary of the All Africa Conference of Churches) contrasted ·
with the stiff seriousness of many of the German participants.

There was further discussion of the programme at the Addis
Ababa meeting of the Central Committee in January 1971.
The initial aggression about the programme which Ernest
Payne attributed to defensiveness had been replaced by a more
reflective mood. It was evident that the comments – not to say
criticisms – had taken effect. There was no question of back-
peddling on the opposition to racism nor of withdrawing support from the programme. Rather was there an attempt to
clarify the bases of the programme. This change of mood was
extremely congenial to Ernest Payne. The resolution which
was passed, in his judgment, eased the situation considerably.

The churches must always stand for the liberation of the oppressed
and of victims of violent measures which deny basic human rights. It
calls attention to the fact that violence is in many cases inherent in
the maintenance of the status quo. Nevertheless, the WCC does not
and cannot identify itself completely with any political movement,
nor does it pass judgment on those victims of racism who are driven
to violence as the only way left to them to redress grievances and so
open the way for a new and more just order. (*Addis Ababa Central
Committee Minutes* p. 55)

The period of Carson Blake's service as Secretary of the
World Council was due to end in 1972. The Central Committee
decided to elect by ballot a nominating committee of 18 who
would have the responsibility of nominating a successor to
Blake. Much to his concern, Ernest Payne was amongst the
number elected. He had had sufficient experience of the difficulties and dangers of nominating committees to wish that he
could be spared this responsibility. In the event, however, the
work passed off very much more smoothly than on the previous
occasion.

The city of Addis Ababa is more than 7,000 feet above sea
level. A number of Ernest Payne's friends thought it was unwise for him to go. He consulted his doctor who told him that
there was no undue risk – provided he was cautious! As it
turned out he was convinced that he felt far better in the
Ethiopian sunshine than he would have done in the damp
coldness of an English January. What the trip did do was
to encourage him all the more that his health was now as

170

good as any man could expect approaching his seventieth birthday.

Soon after he returned to England, he gave an address at the Annual Meeting of the Protestant Dissenting Deputies, an organisation founded in 1737 to link London laymen of Baptist, Congregational and Presbyterian Churches in the interests of the civil rights of the nonconformists. He chose the subject 'Violence, Non-violence and Human Rights.' Although only about 60 people heard the address it was soon evident that he had awakened considerable interest by the way in which he had dealt with the subject. The issue was very much alive. He set it within the context of the grants made through the Programme to Combat Racism. He quoted the Addis Ababa Committee resolution given above and also the further agreement of that committee:

The Central Committee notes that the question of violence cannot be fully discussed or resolved in the context of racial issues and requests that a study be undertaken under WCC auspices on violent and non-violent methods of social change in view of the growing concern about this issue among Christians in every part of the world.

In a wide ranging address he went on to illustrate the complexity of the problem and the various possible solutions suggested over the centuries, starting with the Bible and travelling via Tertullian, Augustine, Aquinas, Thomas Müntzer and many another source to the present day. The lecture was a historical *tour de force* – apart from anything else. The final paragraph begins:

The Christian must try to minimise, not maximise violence, but in the actual situations today in South Africa and South America, the only hope of doing this would seem to be to stand beside the oppressed and the exploited and to encourage them in their efforts for greater justice; to restrain them from their excesses that would damage their cause; and at the same time to give no respite to those in power. Not a few of those who talk about charity and love of neighbour are supporters of social systems which are the opposite of love. By being complacent and doing nothing, one shares in 'the violence that represses'.

Not surprisingly this address achieved a considerable circulation in Britain and the United States. It was commended in the *Christian Century* and reprinted in the *Ecumenical Review.*

171

The result was that he found himself yet again, as in the previous September, hailed as the literary champion of the World Council's stand against racism, in the face of what was still a good deal of hesitation from many in church circles and a sharp negative reaction from not a few both in ecclesiastical and political life. What emerges is that whilst Ernest Payne was an astute reconciler of differing opinions in possible compromise, he was never, on crucial issues, one who sat for long on any fence. After his natural initial caution which tried to curb excesses, once he made up his mind upon the rightness of a cause he was a doughty fighter, skilfully using both the spoken and the written word.

In the Council Chamber of the Baptist Union there is a plaque recording the formation there of the British Council of Churches on 23rd September 1942. As the thirtieth anniversary was due the following year, Ernest Payne decided to put together a brief history. Earlier in 1971 he had finally retired from the chairmanship of the Executive Committee of the council, an office which he had held since 1962. He himself believed that this was too long a period but he had been pressed to remain to ensure continuity in a council where it seemed to some there were not very many people who had lengthy and wide experience of its life. His own intimate association had lasted for twenty years. He found the experience of writing the history salutary. It was more difficult to write of very recent events than of those long past. For one thing, there were still those alive to contradict; for another, so much detail is available that the process of selection becomes much more difficult. His hope in publishing *The British Council of Churches 1942–1972* was that it would remove some of the misconceptions of the work of the council, and show how much important and far seeing co-operative work had been undertaken during thirty years. He thought, too, that it might assist in the necessary task of determining the nature and function of the council for the next decade or so.

What manner of Jesus?

Meanwhile, within the Baptist Union, an extremely difficult and potentially dangerous situation was developing. It stemmed from an assembly address given by the Rev. Michael Taylor on the theme, 'How much of a man was Jesus Christ?' The address was given at the request of the President of the Baptist Union, Dr G. Henton Davies who took as the assembly theme, 'The Incarnate Presence'. Michael Taylor's address was the second of three on the theme, all framed as questions, the first being 'How dead is God?', and the third 'Is the Holy Spirit a Person?' Such subjects, however treated, would provoke discussion and probably difference of opinion in any context. Michael Taylor's subject was particularly difficult because as the question was framed there could be only one answer for Christians, namely that Jesus was fully and completely man. If he were not, then there is no salvation. Given the subject, if anyone has problems with the idea of paradox in the Incarnation, then the adequate answering of the question would be complex enough in any context, but in the setting of the Baptist Union Assembly, basically an inspirational occasion, much more so. In retrospect, a number of people, including Ernest Payne, wondered how the Baptist Union Council came to accept such a formulation of the theme for the assembly. But it did.

This is not the time nor the place to discuss either the course or the rights and wrongs of this particular episode. The present concern is to indicate Ernest Payne's attitude. Suffice it to say that Michael Taylor's address was extremely impressive in delivery and given with total intellectual honesty. In the outcome, some people expressed concern about the content. At the Baptist Union Council held during the week of the assembly, an attempt was made to call Michael Taylor to account and the council was invited to repudiate the address. When Ernest Payne realised that Michael Taylor was not present, he tried to move that the meeting proceed to the next item. This was not immediately taken up by the Chair but he persisted and his view was accepted almost unanimously.

The matter was raised again at the November council of 1971 when the General Purposes and Finance Executive produced a resolution reaffirming the Baptist Union's Declaration of Principle, and asserting the faith of the Union in the deity of Christ. Ernest Payne and Leonard Champion prepared what was, in effect, a substitute motion. They felt that it set the issue in a wider context than did the executive's motion by making

173

reference to doctrinal statements to which the Baptist Union had assented (*viz:* the Declaratory Statement of the Free Church Federal Council, the Baptist Union Reply to the Lambeth Appeal, and the Basis of the World Council of Churches) and by including a paragraph about the traditional stand for religious freedom and tolerance. After the rejection of two other amendments, Ernest Payne's substitute motion was taken up. Although in the end it was rejected, the paragraph of freedom of speech and tolerance was incorporated into the Statement of the General Purposes Executive which was then accepted.

After the November council, the controversy did not die down; rather did it increase. He was due to go to New Zealand in February 1972 and together with many others he was concerned lest there might be an extremely difficult and dangerous situation developing which could reach the floor of the 1972 assembly. Before and after his visit to New Zealand he had a number of personal contacts by letter and by telephone with some of those most deeply involved in and concerned about the controversy including Sir Cyril Black. Whether Ernest Payne did any good he was never sure, but he did not think he did any harm. In the event a long resolution which reasserted amongst other things, the Declaration of Principle of the Baptist Union and the requirement for all who belong to the ministerial accredited list to accept it, was moved by Sir Cyril Black and passed by an overwhelming majority at the assembly. Ernest Payne abstained from voting, for he viewed the resolution as too restrictive. More than once in the whole business he reflected that troubles of this kind stem from what Shorthouse describes in his novel *John Inglesant* as 'the greatest of all problems, that of granting religious freedom, and at the same time, maintaining religious truth'.

Throughout what he calls 'this sorry business' he had tried on the one hand to reconcile and on the other to hold to the right of freedom of individuals to speak the truth as they received it in their Christian experience. He was sure, too, that things might not have been quite so difficult if there had not been three unexpected deaths in 1970. First W. G. Channon, who had been a good friend to Ernest Payne and Chairman of the Ministerial Recognition Committee, then Leslie Larwood, a distinguished and faithful Baptist pastor, and finally Hugh

Butt, Superintendent of the West Midland Area; all died within two months of each other, all in their early sixties. These three, all conservative in theology, were all loyal in the service of the denomination and deeply concerned for its unity.

Soon after his seventieth birthday, Ernest Payne gave an interview to Brian Cooper which was eventually published in the *Baptist Times* on 15th June 1972. It is of particular interest because he was pressed to indicate what he judged to be the most satisfactory events of his secretaryship. He singled out three. The first was his part in the break through to renew contact in the 1950s with the Baptists of Eastern Europe, and the subsequent relationships which developed. The second was the Ter-Jubilee Campaign of 1959-63 which he believed strengthened the denomination. The third was the pleasure it gave to him to represent British Baptists within the ecumenical movement. So to represent was to be loyal to his heritage and to bring its truths and insights to enrich the growing ecumenical fellowship. The article gives further evidence of how deeply he felt that the growing theological and political polarisation amongst Baptists weakened the denominational witness and effectiveness. His last years were clouded by the concern that the denomination was in danger of losing its way in its mission, by overmuch introversion and theological sniping.

He remained involved in Free Church Federal Council affairs, most notably in the field of education. His chairmanship of the Education Committee had already been extended beyond the normal three years, but before his successor took office he became involved in a further series of discussions about grants to denominational schools. This meant a meeting with the Minister of Education and Science who was then Mrs Margaret Thatcher.

The financial difficulties experienced by the Anglicans and Roman Catholics because of the steep rise in building costs and high interest rates could not be denied. At the same time, Free Church circles, particularly, thought that the Roman Catholics had sometimes involved themselves in building schemes which, even in more favourable circumstances, would still have been difficult to finance. They had not heeded the views of some of their own leaders that they could no longer hope to provide schools for the growing number of Roman Catholic children. The Anglicans had reversed the policy –

begun after the 1944 Education Act – of reducing the number of their schools. The Free Church Federal Council was opposed to any further increase in the rate of grants for new buildings, although it was ready to concede some kind of emergency aid of a temporary kind. A letter had been sent, indicating this point of view, and had been received very unfavourably by the Roman Catholics and Anglicans. Ernest Payne had been equally emphatic in response!

It was against this difficult background that the representatives of the three ecclesiastical traditions met Mrs Thatcher on 17th July 1972. Ernest Payne records that Mrs Thatcher whom he found a charming and decisive woman, gave the deputation short shrift! She dismissed out of hand the idea of 'emergency aid' which Ernest Payne suggested. The group left the meeting somewhat discomforted and promised to reflect upon what had been said.

Nearly a year later there was a further meeting. By this time, the summer of 1973, Ernest Payne had been replaced by Douglas Hubery as Chairman of the Education Committee but it was suggested by the Free Church Council that, because of his previous involvement in the discussions, he should go. The meeting was held on 11th June in the new offices of the Department of Education and Science. Mrs Thatcher had with her Lord Sandford, Norman St John Stevas, and five of the permanent staff of the department. She conducted the proceedings herself with a characteristic blend of authority and charm, giving her companions little chance of independent contributions.

Mrs Thatcher showed herself unimpressed by the efforts of the Anglicans and Roman Catholics to avoid committing themselves to any promises that this would be their final request for additional financial help. After an hour's conversation, she said she thought that the permanent officials must examine whether there was some way of providing emergency temporary help to the denominational schools. This was a return to the idea which Ernest Payne himself had suggested the year before and which Mrs Thatcher and others had then declared impossible administratively. He came away from that interview feeling that the minister was playing for time, and that perhaps by the Autumn there might have been governmental changes which would involve her advancement to an-

176

other post. Her successor would then inherit the unsolved problem, and those responsible for the denominational schools might well find themselves back again at square one. In the event, before the matter was taken up again, there was a change of government.

Whilst all this was going on there had been further happenings on the ecumenical front. At the Central Committee of the World Council of Churches in Utrecht in the summer of 1972, Philip Potter had been cordially and unanimously elected to succeed Carson Blake. The whole proceedings were in striking contrast to the difficulties encountered six years before. A farewell dinner was held in honour of the retiring secretary. The day before the dinner, Ernest Payne was suddenly asked to draft the official resolution of thanks to Carson Blake and to read it to the assembled company at the completion of all the speeches. This he did. After all the tensions of the recent years, he felt that Carson Blake could feel a comforting recognition of his courage and sincerity and also of the importance of his championship of black Americans and those of the Third World. He judged that history would probably award Carson Blake an important place in the evolution of the World Council of Churches. It was significant in that evolution that his successor was a West Indian.

Human Rights

There was a debate in the Central Committee on the Programme to Combat Racism. The committee had a recommendation before it that funds should be withdrawn from South Africa. The Finance Committee, of which Ernest Payne was still a member, pointed out all the difficulties and disadvantages of disengagement. Some Central Committee members tried to modify the recommendation. But it was clear that the overwhelming majority favoured this gesture and the implications that lay behind it. When the vote came Ernest Payne abstained.

This decision deeply troubled a number of committee members, not least some of those from England. A somewhat hostile editorial appeared in the *Baptist Times* on 7th September which Ernest Payne felt did not put the situation in a satisfactory perspective. So he wrote a long letter to the paper which was published on 14th September. The editorial had stated 'At the recent meeting of the WCC Central Committee new tensions were present which were probably stronger than any ever felt before during its 25 years of meetings. For the first time delegates from African Churches appeared to be trying to make political issues the main programme of the WCC.' But the editorial's conclusions were firmly in favour of continued Baptist participation in the WCC.

Ernest Payne reacted somewhat sharply: 'I do not think that in your editorial of 7th September you have quite caught or understood the mood of the World Council of Churches.' He pointed out that the admittedly controversial decision about investment in Southern Africa was only one of the many matters under consideration by the council. A balanced perspective of the work of the council was the only fair perspective to consider. He went on to show that the World Council of Churches was now far more representative of the Christian Communion than it had been 15 or 20 years ago when the views of the United States and the United Kingdom tended to dominate.

Let us be careful before we get unduly excited or displeased, by properly arrived-at decisions which do not immediately commend themselves to us. Is the only politics to be our politics, the only economics our economics? You must be well aware, Mr Editor, that all decisions are in measure political, either the politics of the *status quo* or the politics of change ... In Utrecht I heard the Old Testament prophets come alive as they rarely have in this country for many a year. We who say we base ourselves on scripture, should read the prophets on exploitation. I believe that they have a more salutary word for us than the ecstatic singing that we heard in Utrecht from a 'Children of God' commune.

Ernest Payne tended to abstain on a number of the votes on matters relating to the Programme to Combat Racism. He was neither apathetic nor neutral. It reflected his tension. He could not bring himself to vote for all the recommendations but his conscience would not allow him to vote against. Within the letter there is this further paragraph relating to the financial question involved in the recommendation:

There are no simple answers, financial or moral, to these questions: The WCC Finance Committee produced some wise, cautionary words (in which, let me say, I had some share, lest you think I am now in the ranks of the anarchists), but they failed to convince the majority of the Central Committee, white, black and brown.

He was in a dilemma which he faced honestly. He was never one to escape from the reality of a situation nor to pretend that things were other than they were. He knew full well that the growing African presence in the World Council of Churches would not just go away. An attitude of stubborn dogmatism in the face of any challenge was quite foreign to his nature. He believed that it would be a betrayal of heritage and an act of cowardice to opt out of the ecumenical scene. His was the dilemma of a nonconformist radical, born in the West, nurtured in the early twentieth century Liberal political ethos, trying to understand and to interpret to others the vehement radicalism of those who were now struggling to free themselves from oppression, and to gain human rights not very different from those which the nonconformist radicals had won for themselves in England in earlier days. He came to suspect that there were too many Baptist ostriches burying their heads in the sands of narrow parochial denominationalism.

It was not only Baptists who continued uneasy about the racism programme and its various outworkings. Concern surfaced in Anglican circles both about grants made to the liberation movements and about financial withdrawal from South Africa. He received an invitation to speak at the Truro Diocesan Synod which had before it a resolution from one of its deaneries criticising the World Council of Churches. He was invited to visit the synod and to oppose the resolution. He did so on 1st May 1973. The outcome of the debate was that a motion 'that the Resolution be not put' won the day. The Ecumenical Officer of the Diocese thought that he had done a good days work! A letter subsequently thanked him for his 'masterly contribution' to the synod debate. It was apparently the first time that a Free Churchman had ever addressed the diocese of Truro in conference and the first time that a spokesman for the World Council of Churches had done so. That the two 'firsts' should be combined in the person of Ernest Payne is worthy of note!

Later in that summer of 1973 he attended the Baptist World Alliance meeting in Einsiedeln, a small town in the Swiss mountains and a centre of pilgrimage for Roman Catholics. One of the main purposes for going was to meet the new and younger generation of Russian Baptists now coming into prominence, most particularly Alexei Bischcov, the new Secretary of the Russian Baptist Council and Michael Zhidkov. He was concerned to discuss with them the mounting pressure for more public protest and agitation in Western Europe on behalf of the dissidents amongst the Russian Baptists. This pressure was coming from several very different sources. One was the campaign mounted by organisations such as Underground Evangelism; another was the list of publications emanating from the Centre for the Study of Religion and Communism at Keston; a third was a 'spin off' from the well-published campaign by world Jewry on behalf of Jews who wanted to leave Russia for Israel. The Russian Baptists at Einsiedeln emphasised strongly that agitation from outside at that time did not appear to make any difference and it certainly made their own task much more difficult. On the whole, Ernest Payne accepted their judgment on this matter and whilst he worked tirelessly to alleviate the position of imprisoned and suffering Christians in Eastern Europe he operated through diplomatic and ecumenical channels and did not become identified with public protest.

Whilst at Einsiedeln he was interested in the considerable number of Baptists present who went unhesitatingly into the great Roman Catholic Church of the Black Madonna – the place of Roman Catholic pilgrimage – to attend an organ recital. This seemed to him to be an interesting sign of change in the ecclesiastical climate since the alliance meeting in Oslo in 1962 when there had been such determined resistance to any possible Baptist representation at the Second Vatican Council. He was fascinated to be told by one of the senior priests at the church that he constantly used Bunyan's *Pilgrim's Progress* in teaching the young catechumens!

The possibility of a consultation on human rights was one which he pressed strongly in World Council circles. The subject was one very close to Ernest Payne's heart for it stemmed from his strong convictions about religious freedom. This conviction had been strengthened still further from his detailed study of

180

the Radical Reformation – particularly the so-called Anabaptists amongst whom was Balthasar Hubmaier whose plea for religious toleration *Concerning Heretics and those who burn them* in 1524 was the earliest of the Reformation era. Hubmaier's plea was echoed by the seventeenth century English Baptist pioneer Thomas Helwys in his address to James I in 1612.

In Einsiedeln, at the Baptist World Alliance meetings, Ernest Payne had been on the commission discussing human rights and as a result of the paper he had drafted for it, he was asked to share in introducing the subject at a main session of the Baptist Union Assembly in April 1974. It was his first appearance on the Baptist Union platform for seven years and he appreciated greatly the opportunity of speaking for half an hour on the subject of human rights. He was pressed to allow his address to be printed, so he re-wrote what he had said and collated it with his Baptist World Alliance paper. The result was published by the Baptist Union in the *Living Issues* series. When the Central Committee finally decided at the West Berlin meetings in the summer of 1974 to proceed with the human rights consultation he was able to give copies of his pamphlet to influential people in the council and notably to representatives of the Soviet Union.

There was now a Labour government in office – but only just. During the General Election campaign of February 1974, the Labour spokesman on educational affairs, Edward Short, had hinted strongly at further aid to church schools. Eventually, on 4th June the Joint Education Policy Group was invited to meet the new minister, Reginald Prentice. Douglas Hubery was unwell and Ernest Payne was again acting as chairman of the Free Church Council's Education Committee. Mr Prentice was definite that there could be no increase in the 80% building grant. He offered to the Anglicans and Roman Catholics, however, a reduction of interest on loans taken from government sources since 1967. This he estimated at coming out at about £450,000 per annum and £7,500,000 over a 20 year period. The Roman Catholics and certainly the Anglicans were obviously expecting a larger figure, probably because of Edward Short's remarks. But the Anglicans were clearly not disposed to look a gift horse in the mouth. After more than an hour's discussion it was agreed to adjourn matters so that the

Anglicans and Roman Catholics might work out in detail the effect of the proposals.

Seven weeks after meeting Reginald Prentice for the first time, the same group was hastily summoned to see him again. There had been a conference in the interim with representatives of the Joint Education group and officials of the department. It was now clear that some increase in the grants to the denominational schools would be easier administratively and probably fairer than the somewhat complicated scheme put forward on 4th June. There had been some lobbying on this matter due in part to the expectation of the Roman Catholics and the Anglicans of rather greater financial help and a more generous offer than had come at first from Mr Prentice. Ernest Payne had himself come to the conclusion that the Free Churches might have to agree to an increase in the grant of $2\frac{1}{2}\%$ or 3%. There was considerable difficulty as to what the attitude of the Free Churches should be. There were some who thought it should be of benevolent neutrality. Others felt it should be neutrality without the benevolence! Others agreed that the time had come to say firmly that the present grant was high enough already.

The meeting took place on 24th July. Mr Prentice said that he had consulted his colleagues again and they agreed that the scheme suggested earlier would give quite inadequate help to the churches in their difficulties. An increase in the grant was really the simplest way of giving aid. The new proposal was that it should be a 5% increase taking the grant to 85%. This would involve a sum of about £1,500,000 per annum. The Cabinet had considered an increase of $2\frac{1}{2}\%$ or 3% but felt that continued inflation would mean that almost certainly the question would be re-opened in a year or so. He hoped that the church leaders would be able to state that an increase of 5% was likely to be accepted as a 'durable' settlement.

The Anglicans and Roman Catholics naturally expressed gratitude to the minister for his understanding and the government for its generosity, though they were careful to say that they would still have difficulty in meeting their obligations, and whilst they felt an offer of this kind would be durable, they could not say that they or their successors might not have to re-open the matter one day. When Ernest Payne's turn came to speak, he expressed surprise and some concern. What they were now being told was so different from what had been said on 4th June. The Free Churches would have agreed to an increase in the grant to 82% or even 83% and for a limitation of the addition to say ten years. It would be difficult to convince all Free Church people that so large an increase was either necessary or desirable. Though opposition to the dual system had abated, it still had inherent dangers. Denominational schools might be demanded by other religious groups in the new developing multi-racial society.

In the circumstances, Ernest Payne's was a thankless and difficult task, though it was some consolation for him to learn later that it was rumoured that neither Mr Prentice nor his Secretary, Mr Ernest Armstrong, a Methodist layman, was entirely happy with the change in policy between June and July. It was very difficult for the Free Church people not to relate this to the fact that a general election in the early Autumn seemed certain! Ernest Payne went home that July afternoon feeling more cynical about politicians than ever before! When the proposals became known, however, there was not very much critical comment in the Free Church press. At the end of September the Free Church Federal Council did not show any disposition to protest though the executive later decided to send Mr Prentice a letter which Ernest Payne drafted, making clear that the executive was not happy at what had occurred. It seemed well to have this on record.

Called to office

The Baptist Church House library contains portraits of distinguished Baptists including former secretaries. Many people thought it was time that Ernest Payne's likeness was added, so Horace and Ronald Gale, two brothers from Bedford, who were good friends of Ernest Payne and his family, offered to provide the Church House with a portrait of him. The portrait was unveiled by his granddaughter, Elizabeth, on 10th September 1974. The *Baptist Times* of 19th September reported the occasion in full, notably the words spoken by David Russell who described his predecessor as 'A World Christian Statesman, who is surely the greatest British Baptist in our generation'. The editorial column commented on the event under the heading 'He belongs to us'.

The *Baptist Times* of 3rd October printed a letter from Eirwyn Morgan, Principal of the Baptist College in Bangor in which he wrote of the sad irony that one who had served the denomination and the World Council of Churches with such distinction had not been elected President of the Baptist Union. Within a few days of the appearance of that letter, Ernest Payne had been asked by three associations to allow himself to be nominated for the vice-presidency in 1975. However gratifying this reaction may have been to him, he knew already that other nominations had been made of worthy people and he did not think it right to stand against them. He clung to the view also that it would not be fitting for an ex-general secretary to stand for the vice-presidency unless encouraged by the General Purposes Committee or the council. He discussed the matter with David Russell who certainly thought that the question should be discussed by the General Purposes Committee. Ernest Payne indicated that he doubted whether he would feel it right to accept nomination for the vice-presidency in 1976, when he would be already 74 years of age. When he consulted friends he was surprised to find them united in their encouragement to him to accept nomination.

The Baptist Union Council in March 1975 therefore had before it a recommendation that he should be nominated for the 1976 ballot for the vice-presidency. This resolution was accepted unanimously by the council and this early action made it highly improbable that counter nominations would be forthcoming. His own fears were not completely allayed. Once again, however, he recognised that the decision was made for him. He found the number of those who expressed pleasure at the nomination gratifying, and this helped to confirm the rightness of his decision to risk accepting nomination. He spoke to his friends about his hope that, if elected, his health would not break down, that he might be given something worthwhile to say at the assembly of 1977 and that, as an officer of the Union for three years, he might prove a wise counsellor in the changed circumstances since his retirement.

The Fifth Assembly of the World Council of Churches had been planned originally for Indonesia. Circumstances in that country had brought about a change of venue to Nairobi, and a change of date to December 1975. At the beginning of October a 'briefing' was held at Swanwick for the British delegates. Ernest Payne had been asked to lead the early morning Communion service and, against his better judgment, agreed to do so. As he began his address he fainted. This was the result, he was sure, of having just got up and having had no breakfast. He had fainted four months earlier, at the reopening of the Loughborough Baptist Church, but that, he believed, was due to standing bareheaded in very hot sunshine. In both cases he recovered after only a minute or so. To his chagrin, but wisely, at Swanwick, an ambulance was summoned but on arrival he persuaded the ambulance crew that he really did not need their services! Later he was driven to see a doctor who duly confirmed his own diagnosis. But it taught him that he must learn to live within sensible limitations. He took the point and there were no further incidents.

The finances of the World Council of Churches were causing growing concern. The prospects for 1976 did not look good. During the Autumn the officers of the council met and they were faced with the necessity of immediate cuts in expenditure under the general budget amounting probably to as much as 40%. The situation would have to be put clearly and frankly to the Nairobi assembly and decisions taken. Ernest Payne heard this with some concern, particularly because the Earl of March, the Chairman of the Finance Committee had indicated that he would not be attending the assembly.

At the beginning of November Ernest Payne received two letters from Geneva. The first asked him to preside over the session of the assembly to be addressed by Mr Manley, Prime Minister of Jamaica. The second confirmed that the Earl of March would not be at Nairobi and indicated that the general feeling was that, in all the circumstances, he should be the one to present the difficult finance report. He found both these requests daunting. He had hoped that at Nairobi he could enjoy the assembly without much responsibility and then bow quietly out of World Council affairs. He was 73 years old, increasingly aware of his limitations, and he knew that he was reacting less well to the strain of such public duties. But he recalled George Bell's admonition at Lucknow some twenty years earlier and felt duty bound to accept both tasks.

When he undertook the latter task he asked the Earl of March for a message supporting the financial retrenchment proposals. By the time he left for Nairobi that message had not arrived and his concern grew. Fortunately the message arrived by telex just a few hours before the presentation and he was able to read it to the assembly. The report that he presented was marked by the skill of its analysis and the clarity of its proposals. The Nairobi report records that it was 'a detailed and technical report, presented with great skill'. Only afterwards did he reveal to one or two friends that during the presentation he became afraid that he was about to faint again.

In addition to presiding at the session addressed by the Prime Minister of Jamaica, he was asked to take the chair on several other occasions. Undoubtedly the most difficult moment came at the business session on 6th December at which the election took place of the presidents and of the Central Committee. At this session, Ernest Payne found himself in conflict with William Thompson, an American Presbyterian lawyer. Thompson wanted to move that the vote on nominees for president should be taken by a written ballot permitting a separate vote for or against each nominee. Ernest Payne ruled that the motion was out of order because a decision had been taken on 2nd December that the vote be taken in a single action on a complete list by a show of hands. The mover challenged this ruling. Ernest Payne then asked if the assembly would sustain his ruling. It did so by an overwhelming majority.

The Nairobi assembly went much more smoothly than many had anticipated. The Kenyan hospitality was warm and the fears of some that there would be strident African voices raised proved unfounded. For Ernest Payne the occasion proved a pleasing and exciting end to his formal contact with the World Council of Churches. After 21 years on the Central Committee, 14 of them as Vice Chairman and seven as a member of the Praesidium he felt it was time for him to go. Being there at all over the years had remained a surprise to him. The demands of time and energy had been colossal, but he did not begrudge a moment of the time nor an ounce of the energy. He revelled in the giving and the receiving within the ecumenical fellowship which excited and enriched him. Typically, he commented that the only word truly to describe it was a Russian word *Sobornost* which he explained as 'the fellowship in Christ created by the Holy Spirit'.

The assembly closed with a service which reached its end as

186

all those present shared in a litany, 'Break down the walls that separate us and unite us in a single body' set to music and interpreted in dance. Indeed, still singing and, as best they could, still dancing, the members of the assembly streamed out from the Kenyatta Conference Centre into the transparent darkness of the Nairobi night. The delegates caught their last glimpse of Ernest Payne as an officer of the World Council of Churches as he moved to the music down the aisle in an improvised dance routine arm in arm with Mrs Cho, his fellow President from Japan. It symbolised the joy and the fellowship which his ecumenical years had brought to him.

II: 1976–80

Reconciliation and unity

Soon after his return from Nairobi he became involved in trying to resolve difficulties which had arisen within the context of Christian Aid. There had been criticism of what had and had not gone on during the drought in the Sahel and in certain other African situations. The criticisms had been firmly refuted. The process which developed out of this initial disagreement became long and drawn out and was settled finally some two years after Ernest Payne's death. Hopefully it is now a closed chapter and will remain so. It is relevant only to record that for the last few years of his life Ernest Payne spent many long hours seeking to reconcile the parties involved. The position of reconciler in the dispute was not one he sought but one he undertook on the initiative of others, who believed he could be of help. It cost him much effort. On more than one occasion he was afraid it was going to cost him some friends. In the end it did not, but the strain of the continuing episode told on him.

He found the Baptist Union Council faced with questions relating to church relations in England. Towards the end of 1975 the Churches' Unity Commission in which the Baptist Union had been largely involved, had produced ten propositions about church relations and asked the participating churches to indicate by the summer of 1977 whether the propositions were acceptable. The approach of the propositions showed a change from earlier attempts to produce a scheme for union. Instead, mutual recognition of each other's members and ministries was proposed to be accompanied by a covenant to move forward on that basis towards still closer relationships. Certainly the approach was different from more recent attempts at relationships as for example in the Anglican-Methodist scheme of the 1960s; but Ernest Payne did not think it was particularly novel. Indeed his own view was that the approach was a return to attempts of much earlier decades of the twentieth century to the days of Bishop Headlam and probably P. T. Forsyth. Nevertheless he was firmly of the opinion that Baptists should take the propositions seriously.

The Advisory Committee for Church Relations of the Baptist Union recommended that the propositions must be submitted to all churches and associations in membership with the Union before any reply could be given to the commission. Explanatory documents were prepared and sent to the churches in the Spring of 1976. Views were asked from the churches about the fundamental issues raised. The documents sent to the churches safeguarded the right of the Baptist Union Council to give advice to the churches. This right Ernest Payne judged to be basic to the existence of the Union. Whilst the decision making body of the denomination was the annual assembly, that assembly delegated to the council responsibility to act for it within defined limits in decision making. However the Assembly itself was to give leadership through advice on every issue. Ernest Payne was always concerned when people spoke of the Baptist Union or the Baptist Union Council as if they existed apart from the assembly which was representative of all the churches. The Baptist Church House was the administrative manifestation of the whole denomination and carried through the assembly's decisions. The Baptist Union Council acted on behalf of that assembly.

No other nominations were received for the vice-presidential election of 1976. This gave him considerable personal satisfaction. His family were present on 26th April when his election was approved. He was warmly welcomed by the assembly and by the incoming President, Frank Goodwin of Hinckley. In his response Ernest Payne expressed his appreciation and commented that he could personally remember four presidents who had served in the 19th century and all but three of those who had held office since 1900!

He was now, once again, an officer of the Baptist Union with new responsibilities reaching out into the next three years. He was in his 75th year. From time to time he turned for inspiration to literature. Although no expert in the subject he was widely read and had catholic tastes. He turned to the writings of Rabindranath Tagore and in the *Gitanjali* he found words that expressed his feelings as he contemplated the immediate future:

I thought that my voyage had come to its end at the last limit of my power – that the path before me was closed, that provisions were exhausted and the time come to take shelter in a silent obscurity.

But I find that thy will knows no end in me. And when old words die out on the tongue, new melodies break forth from the heart; and where the old tracks are lost, new country is revealed with its wonder.

Back to Oxford

During the early months of 1976 what occupied his thoughts as much, if not more than, the prospective vice-presidency was the possibility of a move from Elm Cottage, Pitsford. The cottage had a garden which required attention; petrol prices were on the increase; with renewed responsibility in the Baptist Union he would need more transport; pleasant though Pitsford was, its position was rather isolated. These all combined to suggest the possibility of a change. Various factors pointed to Oxford. It was a place of happy memories for the Paynes; the medical advisers who had cared for Freda Payne in her recent illnesses were there; they had good friends living there; the train connections were good; the chance of renewing informal contact with Regent's Park students was attractive.

A block of flats was being erected on the Banbury Road on a site adjacent to where Sir James Murray, the editor of the Oxford Dictionary, had lived and worked at the turn of the century. The development was to be called Murray Court and a suitable first floor flat was available. They moved on 24th August and settled quickly back into life in Oxford. He found he could walk gently down to St Giles and to Regent's Park

College in 20 minutes with little or no discomfort. He discovered that he was privileged to travel on the buses anywhere within the city limits for two pence! There were still several people in the neighbourhood whom they knew in the 1940s. When term began they invited students to Sunday tea and found it as mutually agreeable as it had been 30 years earlier.

He had one further experience of the World Council Committees. He was asked to represent the Baptist World Alliance at the Central Committee meetings in Geneva during August 1976. This gave him an unexpected opportunity of seeing the new committee in session at its first meeting since Nairobi. He found the meetings full of interest. The new chairman (now called Moderator), Edward Scott, Anglican Primate of Canada, he felt brought a pastoral touch to the proceedings, and his style seemed to be in marked contrast to any of his predecessors, George Bell, Franklin Fry and M.M. Thomas. But there was obvious strength and efficiency beneath his somewhat simple and friendly approach. It was also clear to Ernest Payne that new figures were appearing on the World Council horizon. He felt that Archbishop Sarkissian, who had been Moderator of the Programme Guidelines Committee at Nairobi was likely to play a considerable part in the years ahead. This Central Committee meeting was the last he attended. Even then he felt himself apart from it as if he had already made his exit from the stage and was standing in the wings watching the new cast at work.

The assembly in Nottingham on April 1977 at which he took office as President was residential and held at the university. During January 1977, David Russell had been seriously ill but with characteristic vigour and determination returned rather more quickly than anyone had expected, having succeeded in getting a discharge from the doctor in mid-April. This enabled him to put in an appearance at the Assembly. J.B. Morris, the Head of the Department of Administration had also been taken ill. All this had meant some extra responsibility for the officers of the Union. It had not made preparations for the assembly easy. In the event it proved an enjoyable occasion – if not memorable.

Amongst the significant events was the election of the first woman Vice President of the Union in the person of Mrs Nell Alexander. In welcoming her, Ernest Payne recalled that 46 years earlier, in 1931, as Secretary of the Northamptonshire Association, he had transmitted to the Church House first the nomination of Mrs Hetty Rowntree-Clifford of West Ham and then when that had been rejected as not in order, the joint nomination of the Reverend and Mrs Rowntree-Clifford which was also refused! Times had changed – and for the better in this respect at least! The assembly was also notable for the presence of five Baptist visitors from the Soviet Union led by Alexei Bischcov. Bischcov publicly thanked David Russell and Ernest Payne for the way in which they had taken up the cause of the dissident Baptists with the authorities.

During the presentation of the Annual Report determined efforts were made to initiate general discussion. Ernest Payne felt this was a healthy development but that it was difficult to manage in so large a gathering and without some prior notice and previously agreed procedure. He did not find it easy to handle the situation, but in the outcome the Union was faced with a request from the assembly for an 'inter-departmental commission to examine the causes of the numerical and spiritual decline of our denomination'.

His presidential address came at the end of a very lengthy session. Before he began he commented to the delegates in assembly that he did not know whether to be more sorry for them or for himself! The title was 'Ways known and to be known'. It was delivered in his own quiet way and recalled, amongst other things, the special significance of Nottingham in denominational history. The theme was how the known ways of the past may help the unknown future without limiting the full acceptance of newly revealed paths. His own judgment was that the address was rather better in the reading than in the hearing. His self-criticism was usually right! For most of the delegates the high point of the assembly was the communion service which he had introduced into the programme.

Immediately after the assembly, the *Baptist Times* published yet another interview with him which contains a piece of public self-revelation – a somewhat rare event. He said:

I am a shy person and don't really find public speaking very easy. I prefer doing things more quietly and privately. I think it is much better, on the whole, to feel a little nervous. The speaker or preacher who has no nerves is often in danger. On the other hand, if you are

191

somewhat nervous and shy, as I am, you sometimes spend more time and use up more nervous anxiety than you really should do. One ought to be able to get over it and trust to the inspiration of the moment a little more.

If this is true – and there is no reason to doubt it – it makes all the more remarkable the achievement of this so essentially private man to live his life so constantly in the public eye.

His presidential year was full of the usual nationwide travelling. In the first two months after the assembly he visited no fewer than ten association assemblies. Each of them asked him to do something different and although he found the occasions somewhat tiring, they were full of interest to him and on the whole encouraging. As he travelled, he recalled that 27th June 1977 marked the 60th anniversary of his baptism, and he was still an active Christian pilgrim. In his visits to local churches he was not content simply to conduct the Sunday worship. When he went to Exeter for the weekend, for example, he led the Sunday morning service in the South Street Church, preached in the evening at a united service in Exeter Cathedral, attended the local Baptist Fraternal, called on the Deputy Mayor and visited O. D. Wiles who was in Exeter hospital.

There were particular events during 1977 in which he was involved. It was the year of the Silver Jubilee of the Queen's accession to the throne. Whilst public interest mounted rather slowly, it reached remarkable proportion in June and there could be no doubting the genuineness and warmth of the reception given to the Queen in all parts of the United Kingdom. On 7th June there was a thanksgiving service in St Paul's Cathedral. When this was first mentioned in 1976 Ernest Payne had asked the British Council of Churches Executive whether it was to be a 'national' and 'ecumenical' occasion. No-one was clear as to whether the Dean and Chapter of St Paul's intended to involve all the churches in Britain. It was agreed that there should be an initiative taken from the side of the British Council of Churches to alert the Dean to the hope and expectation that there would be generous recognition of changed ecclesiastical relationships.

In the event, the result was disappointing. The Secretary of the Free Church Federal Council handled the matter of tickets for Free Church people and met with little encouragement.

The Free Church Moderator was given a seat in the chancel with the Moderator of the Church of Scotland and the Cardinal Archbishop of Westminster. And Ernest Payne, as President of the Baptist Union, and his opposite numbers in the Methodist and United Reformed Churches, together with their wives, received tickets. They were for seats well back on the north side of the nave. The service was led by six Anglicans. The occasion was a great one, nevertheless, a fine spectacle, with magnificent music and good hymn singing!

That the pattern of the service worked out as it did caused considerable regret within Free Church circles, particularly to Ernest Payne who had worked so hard with Anglicans. The failure to make the service evidently ecumenical provoked many protests. A deputation from the Free Church Federal Council was received, early in July, by the Archbishop of Canterbury, but obtained no satisfactory explanation of an awkward and disappointing episode. Ernest Payne could not help reflecting how different was the situation when, very soon after the St Paul's service, as President of the Baptist Union, he attended the opening of the Ecumenical Centre at Grove Hill, Hemel Hempstead. At the dedication service there, he gave the address flanked on one side by Bishop Butler, the Roman Catholic, and on the other by the Anglican Bishop of Hertford. He found this contrast yet another illustration of how far in advance is the ecumenical situation at grass roots compared with the attitude of the Establishment.

During the summer of his presidential year, he spent just over two weeks in the Soviet Union. During the Central Committee Meetings at Geneva in 1976, Alexei Bischcov had hinted that an invitation could well be forthcoming to Ernest Payne, David Russell and Morris West, together with their wives. David Russell thought it unwise to attempt the trip during the months after his illness and in his place, Peter Clark, a Baptist layman, with his wife Audrey, were invited. As Ernest Payne's granddaughter, Elizabeth, was soon to be 21, the family suggested as a present that she should go instead of Freda Payne. The presence of a member of the younger generation was warmly welcomed by the Russian hosts.

The itinerary took the party to Moscow, Tbilisi in Georgia, Kiev and Leningrad. The presence of Ernest Payne ensured that there was contact with the Orthodox as well as with the

Baptists. Metropolitan Nikodim received the party to tea and greeted Ernest Payne with evident warmth and affection. The impression Ernest Payne gained was that the general atmosphere was more relaxed than on any of his four previous visits and the party brought back encouraging news of the churches in the Soviet Union.

Throughout the early months of 1977 the replies to the questionnaire about the Ten Propositions had arrived in large numbers. Nearly 1,000 churches in total responded. Five people, including Ernest Payne, were asked to read and collate the returns. By a majority of almost two to one the churches welcomed what seemed to be a new approach, but the response to the suggestion of mutual recognition of members and ministers involving as it would agreed rites of initiation and ordination was very much more hesitant. The Advisory Committee on Church Relations was asked to draft a Baptist response. This response, 'Visible Unity in Life and Mission' was ready for presentation to the Baptist Union Council in November 1977.

One of the changes in Baptist Union procedures which occurred during Ernest Payne's secretaryship was the appointment of a chairman of Baptist Union Council who would serve for three years. Previously the chair had been taken by the president for the year. Ernest Payne never really approved the change, for it was something of a denial of history. For the office of president itself had evolved out of the chairmanship of the Union and its meetings. It so happened, however, that there was a delay in electing a new chairman in 1977 and standing orders required that in the absence of the elected chairman, the president should preside. So it was that Ernest Payne found himself in the chair of the council for the debate on the document 'Visible Unity in Life and Mission'. Many anticipated that the debate might be difficult. In the event, it was not. The reply was skilful and gave little away, whilst posing some important questions to other churches notably the Anglicans on episcopacy. At the same time it asked the Baptists to think through the theology of their practice: for example, of the existence of area superintendents. The document was not wholly negative. With the help of the chairman, the debate was friendly and valuable. Unexpectedly, but to the pleasure of Ernest Payne and others, it was given unanimous approval by the Council.

194

The *Baptist Times* printed its report under the headline 'We Can't Say Yes'. Ernest Payne thought it should have added 'But We daren't say No' to give a proper balance to report its conclusions.

One of the greatest pleasures of a most pleasurable year came to Ernest Payne through the British Council of Churches. A fortnight before the assembly at Swanwick, he learned, at an Executive Committee, of a proposal by the nominations committee that he should be appointed honorary president of the British Council of Churches. To him this was a totally unexpected development and he wondered whether he should agree to the nomination. Harry Morton, then secretary of the council, pressed him to do so. He was duly made honorary president at Swanwick on 1st November after some generous words by Derek Pattinson, Chairman of the Nominations Committee, supported by the Archbishop of Canterbury. His surprise was further increased when he discovered that (unlike the World Council of Churches) the office of honorary president was to be written with the Constitution as 'for life'.

His service to the British Council of Churches spanned thirty years. It was less obvious than his work for the World Council of Churches but nonetheless of great value. His was a service to enable others to be effective in the work of the council. He was always there or thereabouts, available for consultation and advice, suggesting, commenting but not attempting to lead. He was very much at home in the council for he found being an 'enabler' of others much more natural to him than being a leader. The honour that the council bestowed on him at Swanwick recognised how much the British Council of Churches as a whole and many people within it owed to him for just being there – and for being just himself.

Constant changes

There were changes within his circle of contacts. On 11th November J. B. Middlebrook died. He was 83 and had had a stroke a few weeks earlier. They had not always related easily to each other but had maintained contact in their retirement years. Ernest Payne was glad when he received a friendly response to a letter he had written to J. B. Middlebrook in September. They parted on good terms.

During the same period there was a further deterioration in the condition of John Barrett. He died on 24th January 1978. Ernest Payne had visited him on 19th January and had come away deeply distressed although they had been able to talk together. They had been friends for more than 50 years. Their correspondence had been maintained through the whole period. John Barrett's comments, thoughtful, honest and balanced, had been of the greatest help to him. In many ways they had been like brothers. A few weeks later Leonard Brockington died. He had been a colleague in the early days of Regent's Park College at Oxford, a man of quiet disposition, of considerable scholarship, and learning. Ernest Payne always believed that the Old Testament translation of the New English Bible owed far more to the assistance which Brockington gave to Sir Godfrey Driver than perhaps was ever acknowledged.

So it was in the midst of these events, a reminder of the passing of the years, that he completed his presidential year. The incoming President, Mrs Alexander, had asked him to preside over the Monday afternoon business session at the 1978 assembly in London. He claimed that this gave him particular joy and satisfaction as he completed his year by welcoming to the vice presidency the first of his former pupils to be elected to that office. Reflecting upon the year he discovered that he was at the Church House for meetings on more than 75 occasions. More importantly he warned, 'our greatest danger comes from those who sit lightly to denominational obligations and emphasise, rather than hold, in creative tension, the diversity there is among us about theological and other matters'.

The reactions to the Programme to Combat Racism became more noisily critical when in July 1978 it was announced that a grant of £45,000 had been made to the Patriotic Front, the Liberation forces in Rhodesia. This particular grant from the special fund had been held up for nearly a year and its release left in the hands of the officers of the World Council of Churches. Not long before the announcement of the grant was made, missionaries of both the Salvation Army and the Elim Mission had been murdered and a civilian plane had been shot down and then the survivors killed. At once there was a storm

196

of criticism and protest from England and elsewhere concerning the grant. The flood of letters reached every church headquarters in Western Europe as well as Geneva. The Salvation Army and, later, the Presbyterian Church of Northern Ireland, suspended their membership of the World Council. This understandable reaction deeply concerned all those in England devoted to the cause of the World Council.

Gradually the reaction became more balanced but no less questioning both of the grant and its timing. The British Council of Churches had a meeting with Archbishop Scott but the outcome and the explanations offered were not generally thought particularly satisfactory. The problem remained and much damage had been done to the image of the World Council of Churches.

An attempt was made by Geneva to enlist the aid of Ernest Payne. Replies had to be drafted to some, at least, of the shoal of letters that had descended upon the World Council headquarters. It was suggested that he might go to Geneva for ten days to draft some of the replies. This was just not possible, but he did offer to draft replies from Oxford if copies of the letters could be sent to him. In the end he drafted replies to 18 different protests and denunciations. Amongst those who were in communication with Geneva was David Russell, writing on the instruction of the Baptist Union. This letter turned out to be included, whether intentionally or accidentally, as one of the 18 to which Ernest Payne was to draft a reply. Subsequently he sat in the Baptist Union General Purposes and Finance Committee listening with wry amusement as his reply, virtually unaltered and signed by Philip Potter, was solemnly read to the committee at its meeting. The committee was well satisfied with the reply! Perhaps it was a pity that only Ernest Payne and one other at the committee knew who had drafted the letter – or perhaps not!

The new Pope John Paul I, was installed in Rome in September. Metropolitan Nikodim who was representing the Moscow Patriarchate at the ceremony collapsed and died in the Pope's Audience Chamber. It was almost exactly a year since Ernest Payne and the other travellers had taken tea with him in Leningrad. Ernest Payne felt his death as something of a personal bereavement. He had always been impressed by Nikodim's ability and believed in his sincerity. In their seven-

197

teen years' friendship, Ernest Payne had often sided with him and once or twice had publicly defended him. He would have liked to have attended the funeral in Leningrad but this was not possible and he had to content himself with cabling his sympathy to Patriarch Pimen whom he had also met on the visit to Russia the previous year.

Five weeks later the new Pope died in his sleep after being Pontiff for only 33 days. The cardinals came together once again and this time chose the first non-Italian Pope for 400 years, one indeed from Eastern Europe, in the person of the Polish born Archbishop of Kracow who took the name of Pope John Paul II. A whole new dimension was thus added to the remarkable changes within the Roman Catholic Church which had followed the election of Pope John XXIII in 1958. Ernest Payne was sure that this new pope would soon begin to make a quite original contribution to the papacy. Just how original this was going to turn out to be even he could not have foreseen!

At the end of 1978 the Churches' Unity Commission brought its work to a close. The responses to the Ten Propositions had been received from the churches and a Committee for Covenanting was set up by Anglicans, Methodists, United Reformed Church and the Moravians with the Roman Catholics and Baptists as observers. Ernest Payne wished the enterprise well but was dubious of its success because of the difficulty of obtaining a concept of episcopacy and its functions satisfactory to all the covenanting churches and also to all parties within the Church of England. The Chairman of the Committee for Covenanting was Bishop Kenneth Woollcombe who had been succeeded as Bishop of Oxford by Patrick Rodger. Ernest Payne felt that the divine compensation for previous disappointments is not always as clearly seen as it was in that appointment. He was delighted to find himself being able to refer to Pat Rodger as 'my Bishop'!

One matter which surfaced within the denomination during his period as an officer was a proposal to change the name of the Baptist Union of Great Britain and Ireland. Concern had been expressed, particularly from Scotland, about the anomalous nature of this title which it was felt was quite inaccurate. A suggestion was made that the phrase 'Great Britain and Ireland' should be removed. Ernest Payne made it crystal clear that he thought such a suggestion both unnecessary and untimely. He believed that such an alteration would be highly dangerous to the denominational image. The present title arose in history and reflected the relation of the other union to what he judged to be the mother union. In the discussions, however, he was in a minority. His opposition to the proposal continued absolute and he indicated that he would oppose any suggested change both in the Baptist Union Council and, if necessary, in the assembly. However, agreement upon an alternative title proved so difficult that the matter was eventually dropped.

The winter of 1978–79 was long and more severe than for a number of years. There was much more snow in Oxford than usual. During that winter he felt the cold more than ever before and during the early months of 1979 he replied to enquiries about his health by saying that he had never been so cold nor felt so old.

In those early months he was growingly concerned to discover that, at the Baptist Union Assembly, there was to be a resolution moved by a local Baptist Church known as Lighthouse, Bow, calling for the Baptist Union to withdraw from the World Council of Churches because of the grants made by the Programme to Combat Racism. An amendment had been tabled suggesting six months suspension to show disapproval. The Baptist Union Council had tabled a further resolution in favour of retaining membership but affirming concern about the grants and commending Dr Russell for his representations to Geneva on the matter, and urging him to maintain his position. The assembly allocated most of a morning for the discussion which was restrained in tone allowing the matter to be sensibly debated. The Baptist Union's resolution which, it was agreed, could be taken as an amendment, was overwhelmingly carried after a lengthy debate. Ernest Payne did not find it necessary to intervene in the debate, although ready to do so. He was very well satisfied with the outcome which confirmed yet again his view that the collective attitude of the churches, as reflected in assembly votes, was rarely extreme and usually well balanced.

The brink of the river

The last year of his life was as busy as ever, full of activities and experiences, most of them pleasurable. In the early part of the year his wife's health gave some cause for concern, but after skilful treatment in Oxford, the prognosis was very favourable. His grandson, James, at Cambridge, not only rowed in a successful Sidney Sussex boat, but also passed his final engineering examinations gaining a good class in his degree. His granddaughter Elizabeth, now a trained teacher, obtained her first job in a distinguished Bath school. The progress of James and Elizabeth brought him immense joy.

A considerable honour came his way when he was invited, as guest of honour, to the annual dinner of the Nikaean Club at Lambeth Palace. This was an unusual honour, as the club was intended primarily for the entertaining of distinguished foreign ecclesiastics. The Archbishop of Canterbury, Dr Coggan, presided over a company of about 80 guests including such distinguished clerics as the Apostolic Delegate, Archbishop Athenagoras and Metropolitan Anthony Bloom. The guest of honour is required to speak for his dinner! Ernest Payne had been asked to talk on 'Ecumenical Trends in this Century'. So far as is known, his own handwritten manuscript is the only surviving record of what was said. He was clearly in good heart, in good form, and spoke with considerable humour and conviction.

He began by speaking of the remarkable change in the ecclesiastical climate which could bring a Baptist, as guest of honour, to such a gathering. To illustrate how things used to be he quoted from Parson Kilvert's diary: 'Some barbarian – a dissenter no doubt, probably a Baptist – has cut down the beautiful silver birches.' He quoted also a story of the formidable Bishop Headlam who once asked a clergyman whom he was interviewing whether he knew any Hebrew. The reply was, 'Golgotha, the place of a skull, is the limit of my knowledge.' 'I am very glad,' said Headlam, 'only Baptist ministers and regius professors know Hebrew and both are slightly mad.' More seriously, he traced his own development through the changing years paying tribute to J. H. Shakespeare, W. R. Matthews, and King's College, Wheeler Robinson and C. F. Andrews. He went on:

200

We can surely see an enlarging purpose through the years. We know one another better. We respect one another more. All of us are less self-confidant. We have now to remind ourselves, when we disapprove of how some people in other lands act, that in the past, and even more recently, our own behaviour towards one another was not very creditable.

His concluding words were these:

I wish I were going to see what new surprises the Lord has for his people in the 21st century. The sciences and technology as well as economics and politics are presenting mankind with many new and teasing problems; Christians clearly need help from one another if they are to find the right way to react. Meantime we must follow such light as we have, with such faith and courage and compassion as we can muster. In the end, as George Bell emphasised in his last sermon, 'We are all unprofitable servants'. But by the grace of God things don't turn out as badly as they might!

It was his last address in an ecumenical setting and his words form a fitting finale. During the autumn and winter of 1979 he found that his lot was indeed cast in pleasant places. Freda Payne's health improved, the grandchildren continued to do well, and he was able to maintain his interest in Baptist life. He preached at Bloomsbury, spoke at association autumn assemblies, shared in inductions, celebrated the 300th anniversary of Bristol Baptist College, lectured to the Friends of Dr William's Library and attended the committee reflecting on reactions to the Baptist Union report, 'Signs of Hope'. He visited his friends the Vinsons at Faversham and went to the Baptist Church where he had preached as a student 50 years earlier.

He accompanied the President of the Baptist Union and two or three others to Claridges on 11th December to wait upon the President of Liberia, who was a prominent Baptist and in London as President of the Organisation for African Unity to try to assist in the Lancaster House Conference on the future of Rhodesia.

In the New Year he attended the Regent's Park College Council in Oxford on 5th January and was invited to preside in the absence of the chairman, Sir Godfray Le Quesne. He enjoyed himself greatly, and the council meeting gave him much cause for encouragement. There was an increasing number of ministerial candidates and courageous plans for further development at the college, both of staff and buildings, were in preparation. It was all in keeping with the attitude he had always adopted from 1938 onwards: 'When we have built we have been right, when we have postponed building, we have been wrong.' When this meeting was over he was full of excitement and hope for the future of the college which he loved so dearly. If he had known it was to be his last meeting in Regent's, he would have been well content.

The end came totally without warning and with merciful suddenness. Tuesday, 15th January was fixed for a meeting of the Baptist Union General Purposes and Finance Committee. He travelled to London on the Monday and planned to stay at the Bonnington Hotel in Southampton Row. One of his cousins was in need of his counsel and advice. Like so many people, she turned to him for help and he never refused. As he entered the Bonnington Hotel his heart which had soldiered on for so long simply stopped. Thus God tied the final end. That it should happen in the midst of the sights and sounds of the city which bore him was fitting enough: that it should happen so close to the Baptist Church House which had been for him – perhaps almost too literally – a home from home might have been expected; that it should happen whilst he was travelling on an errand of compassion was as he would have wished. He had always been a traveller, he remained a pilgrim to the end, and he died whilst still on the journey.

His family bade him a simple and private farewell on the morning of Monday, 21st January. On the afternoon of that day a representative company of friends from all churches and contexts gathered in the Helwys Hall of Regent's Park College. They met on the very spot where he had stood one summer's afternoon more than 50 years earlier and became the first Baptist to cast his eyes over the future site of Regent's Park College. The address was given by the Principal of the College, Dr Barrie White who spoke with moving simplicity and great discernment of the man who had given so much to so many and asked so little in return.[17]

Although the hall was full, the occasion was intimate for all had come with a common purpose: to thank God for one who was indeed 'a faithful Baptist, a profound ecumenist, a learned scholar and a very dear friend'.

Epilogue

... And so that is why they came, too, in their hundreds to Westminster Abbey on the evening of 27th February. Each member of the congregation had his or her memory, whether it was of the incisive comment, the twinkling eyes, the balanced judgment, the encouraging word, the compassionate letter, the generous gesture – or just of EAP himself. All recognised that with his passing the whole Christian church had lost a leader of outstanding quality. All knew that he was a man whose roots were firmly embedded in the soil of the scriptures and nurtured by the nonconformist tradition, yet whose fruitful life was the result of responding to the impulse of God's future purpose for the unity of Christ's church. His was a life of Christian integrity. He accepted that he had to live in the creative tension of his denominational loyalty, which was unswerving, and his ecumenical commitment, which was total. True, some who understood only half the tension thought that he was trapped in a Baptist yesterday, whilst to others he seemed to live overmuch in an ecumenical tomorrow. But he lived and acted as he did because he believed that a proper understanding of yesterday was the surest way both of living faithfully today and of ensuring the fulfilment of tomorrow's hopes.

In the author's note prefixed to his book *The Fellowship of Believers*, Ernest Payne quotes the words of Kierkegaard, 'Life can only be understood backwards but it must be lived forwards.' He claimed those words as the motto for his book. They could well do as the motto for his life. As the preacher at the Thanksgiving Service in Westminster Abbey said, 'The heritage that he received, he has handed on to us, enhanced and enriched. The mission of the Christian church and the unity of the Christian church, the tasks to which he put his hand, are still tasks that are unfinished. We can do no better in honouring him than to set our hands the more firmly to these same tasks.'

But it is the voice of John Bunyan's Valiant-for-Truth who should have the final word in the confident hymn of the Christian traveller:

> He knows he at the end
> Shall life inherit.
> Then fancies fly away
> He'll fear not what men say
> He'll labour night and day
> To be a pilgrim.

Notes

1 D. L. Edwards *Leaders of the Church of England 1828-1944* Oxford University Press 1971 (pp 303-4)

2 *Report of Baptist World Alliance Fifth Conference, Berlin 1934* ed. J. H. Rushbrooke, London 1934 (pp 160-5)

3 E. A. Payne *The Baptist Union: A Short History* Carey Kingsgate Press, London 1959 (p 210)

4 *Report of the Baptist World Alliance Sixth Congress, Atlanta 1939* ed. J. H. Rushbrooke, Atlanta, Georgia 1939 (pp 244-6)

5 E. A. Payne *Free Church Tradition in the Life of England* SCM Press, London 1944 (p 8)

6 Article by E. A. Payne on P. W. Evans April 1974

7 Ibid

8 *Baptist Times* 3rd May 1951

9 *Baptist Times* 28th April 1955

10 W. A. Visser't Hooft *Memoirs* SCM Press, London 1973 (p 250)

11 *Baptist Times* 2nd September 1954

12 *Report of Baptist World Alliance Golden Jubilee Congress, London 1955* ed. A. T. Ohrn Carey Kingsgate Press, London 1955 (p 373)

13 A. Muir *John White C. H., DD, LL.D.* Hodder and Stoughton, London 1958 (p 117)

14 Ibid (p 102)

15 *The Pattern of the Church* ed. Alec Gilmore Lutterworth Press, London 1958 (p 117)

16 Agatha Christie *Cat Amongst the Pigeons* Collins 1962 (p 54)

17 See *Baptist Quarterly* July 1980 for the addresses given at Regent's Park College on 21st January 1980 and at Westminster Abbey on 27th February 1980

Index

207

211